University of Cambridge Department of Applied Economics

OCCASIONAL PAPER 56

GROWTH, ACQUISITION AND INVESTMENT

An analysis of the growth of industrial firms and their overseas activities

DAE OCCASIONAL PAPERS

DAE PAPERS IN INDUSTRIAL RELATIONS AND LABOUR

Other titles in both series may be obtained from:
The Publications Secretary, Department of Applied Economics,
Sidgwick Avenue, Cambridge, CB3 9DE

Growth, acquisition and investment

An analysis of the growth of industrial firms and their overseas activities

MANMOHAN S. KUMAR

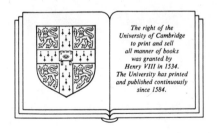

The right of the
University of Cambridge
to print and sell
all manner of books
was granted by
Henry VIII in 1534.
The University has printed
and published continuously
since 1584.

CAMBRIDGE UNIVERSITY PRESS

CAMBRIDGE
LONDON   NEW YORK   NEW ROCHELLE
MELBOURNE   SYDNEY

82691

Published by the Press Syndicate of the University of Cambridge
The Pitt Building, Trumpington Street, Cambridge CB2 1RP
32 East 57th Street, New York, NY 10022, USA
296 Beaconsfield Parade, Middle Park, Melbourne 3206, Australia

© Department of Applied Economics, University of Cambridge 1984

First published 1984

Printed in Great Britain at the
University Press Cambridge

Library of Congress catalogue card number: 84–12128

British Library Cataloguing in Publication Data

Kumar, Manmohan S.
Growth, acquisition and investment. –
(Occasional papers/University of Cambridge.
Department of Applied Economics; 56)
1. Corporations – Great Britain – Growth
I. Title   II. Series
338.7'4   HD2746

ISBN 0 521 26794 3

AN

Contents

Tables and figures

Figure

Preface

During the last two decades, economic analysis has focused increasingly on the nature and determinants of the forces governing the growth and performance of firms in capitalist economies. A number of important theoretical problems have been explored, and a wide range of empirical investigations have been carried out. This book presents the results of an investigation into some aspects of firm growth which have either been relatively neglected hitherto, or on which there is no recent evidence. Four aspects are examined in some detail: (i) the relationship between size, growth and profitability of firms; (ii) the degree of trade-off between growth by acquisition and growth by new investment; (iii) the role of different forms of financing; (iv) the implications of external markets and overseas production for firms' performance. These issues are important both for understanding firm growth and as they bear on the industrial and competition policies which have been pursued in industrialised countries in recent years.

The investigation is based on a population of UK quoted companies for the period 1960–1976. In all, the records of over two thousand companies were investigated. Thus, to the best of the author's knowledge, the results are based on the most comprehensive recent data on industrial companies in the UK or, indeed, in any other advanced country.

Acknowledgements

I am most grateful to Dr Ajit Singh, who gave me constant and always helpful advice and encouragement whilst I was working on this study. I am also grateful to Mr A. Hughes who made a number of important suggestions. Of the many other individuals who offered advice or commented on the book, I should like to thank especially Professor K. George, whose thorough reading of the penultimate draft resulted in many improvements, and also Dr G. Meeks, Professor P. Grinyer, Professor W. B. Reddaway and Professor Sir A. E. G. Robinson. Extremely helpful advice was also received from Dr A. Cosh, Ms G. Campanelli, Ms S. Fairfield, Dr M. L. S. Sørensen, Mr M. Landesmann, Mr M. Presser and Mr D. Sharpe. Ann Newton's help in revising the final draft and in bringing the book to its completion has been invaluable. I should also like to thank Mrs B. Coe, Ms S. Seal, Ms S. Sibson-Turnbull and all the other DAE staff for their help in the preparation of the manuscript.

My deepest gratitude is to my parents, and to my sister, Sukhpal, for their invaluable encouragement and support throughout the several years I was engaged on this study. This book is dedicated to them.

Cambridge
April 1984

MANMOHAN SINGH KUMAR

1

Some issues in firm growth

Introduction

The objective of this study is to analyse some issues relating to the growth
of firms in the UK economy, mainly in the period 1960–1976. It reexamines certain issues which have already been extensively studied in the literature, such as the
relationship between the size, overall growth and profitability of firms. But the
central part of the study examines issues which have been relatively neglected
before now. The most important of these relates to the magnitude of, and the
relationship between, the two main components of firm growth, *viz.* growth by
acquisition and growth by new investment. The study undertakes a detailed investigation of these components and also of the associated financing behaviour of firms.
Another important set of issues which is examined is that relating to the relationship between firms' overseas activities such as exports and foreign production, and
firms' overall growth and performance.

The main motivation of the study was provided by two major developments in
the UK in the two decades since 1960. The first was the unprecedented wave of
merger activity in UK industries, which has drastically altered their entire structure.
This intense activity also occurred in a number of other advanced countries, but
nowhere was it equal in magnitude to that in the UK. The second was the dramatic
increase in the integration of the UK economy with the rest of the world. This has
taken two forms: (a) a sharp increase in the import penetration of the economy as
well as its export activity; (b) direct foreign investment from the UK and investment from foreign countries into the UK.

These developments, whilst having important implications for the performance
of individual firms, also have macroeconomic implications. For instance, although
for the individual firm acquisitions and new investment are two alternative forms
of growth, for the economy as a whole this is not so. When individual firms grow by
merger or acquisition this does not necessarily mean growth for the economy as a
whole. The immediate effect of the merger is simply to combine the sales of two
previously independent companies. There may, however, be longer-term effects
which do affect the overall performance of the economy and these may be positive
or negative. A merger may lead to higher profits, more investment and innovation,
and thus have a positive impact on growth. On the other hand, expenditure on
acquisitions may be a substitute for investment in new plant and equipment; net
investment would then be lower than would otherwise have been the case, with an
adverse effect on the overall growth rate.

The issues examined below, although covering a range of firms' activities, are

1

strongly interrelated. An examination of them is important for an understanding of the behaviour and performance of these firms. In addition, since these firms account for a high proportion of net output and employment in UK industries, the study has an important bearing on developments in the economy as a whole. Although there is a considerable amount of empirical literature on the growth of firms, there have been no recent studies which have examined these issues in detail for UK firms, or indeed for firms in any other advanced country, over the period under consideration. Furthermore, as will be discussed presently, in a number of areas the existing evidence is far from conclusive, and some others have not been investigated at all.

In this chapter we begin by discussing briefly the interrelationships between the various activities of the firm which are examined later. We then turn to the different frameworks within which some of these activities have been examined previously. The emphasis is on analysing three factors: the motivations and the opportunities for firm growth, and the constraints on it. Section 1.2 considers firm growth in the neoclassical analysis, whilst Section 1.3 examines the stochastic framework, incorporating various recent extensions. Section 1.4 considers the non-stochastic models of Downie, Penrose and Marris. The next three sections examine respectively the role of acquisitions, the effect of different forms of financing, and the behaviour of firms in an open economy. The last section provides a plan for the rest of the study and gives details of the data used in the empirical analysis.

1.1 Growth and the interrelationships between firms' activities

At the firm level, activities such as acquisitions and investment, as well as exports and foreign investment, are interrelated. Whilst these links are well recognised in the literature on corporate strategy, they are less emphasised in the theory of firm growth. This is particularly so for the firm's domestic and overseas operations. The models of firm growth which were developed in the late 1950s and 1960s often had an implicit assumption of a closed economy: the focus was on studying the growth and product diversification of firms in the domestic economy. While these models may have been quite appropriate for the earlier period, they are much less so for the period under consideration.

There may be a number of possible strategies to follow to achieve a particular growth rate. Consider, for example, growth *via* new products: these products may be supplied to markets in the domestic economy, or to overseas markets. For the domestic market, production may be undertaken by one of the following: (i) acquisition of existing firms – this would provide not only productive capacity but also managerial and labour resources; (ii) commissioning of new investment – this may be a more gradual process than acquisition, but in many cases it may be the preferred, or the only, alternative. For the overseas market, supply may be *via* exports from domestic production, or it may be undertaken by production overseas. The latter may itself be undertaken by new investment overseas, or by acquisition of existing firms operating abroad.

The presence of alternative strategies does not, of course, mean that a firm would be free to choose amongst them. At any given time, there may be a number of constraints which would circumscribe its behaviour: e.g., the availability of information on the alternatives themselves, organisational structure, existing resources

2

and the competitive environment. We discuss some of these constraints in detail below but here we should note two important considerations regarding the alternatives themselves. First, most of them are regarded as open mainly to the largest firms in the economy. For example, acquisition, or significant reliance on growth by exports or overseas production, tends to be associated with large size. The reasons for this and the empirical evidence on it are considered later in the study. Second, whichever combination of alternatives is chosen, the availability of finance is crucial. There are two main sources of finance: retentions, that is, internally generated funds, and external funds. The two sources may differ in availability as well as cost between firms. A particular source may be appropriate for some activity and not for others. These considerations, which can exercise an important bearing on firm growth, need to be examined in detail, and are investigated below.

It hardly needs emphasising that, in the existing theoretical literature, the role of different activites in firm growth is not often considered explicitly. The focus is on studying the growth of the total operations of the firm – without distinguishing the methods by which it is attained. Whilst our main purpose is to examine the different activities themselves, it is nevertheless instructive to consider briefly the existing theories. An examination of these yields a number of important insights into the growth process of firms, which are of direct relevance to this study. Therefore in the next three sections we examine the neoclassical model of firm growth, the stochastic model, and the models of Downie, Penrose and Marris.

1.2 The neoclassical approach

In the orthodox perfect competition approach, growth is an incidental factor in an analysis of the firm: the focus being on the static concept of the optimal size. As Eatwell put it, 'economic analysis concerning the size of the firm has centered traditionally around the concept of optimum size, with growth part of a loosely defined adjustment mechanism which operates in a yet more loosely defined time dimension' (1971, p. 399). In this approach, the objective of the entrepreneur, who is the sole decision-maker (possessing full information), is to maximise profits, defined as the difference between the firm's revenue and the opportunity costs of all the employed factors, including those supplied by the entrepreneur. The main constraint on the firm is provided *via* the production function – which gives the technically efficient region – a set of points where output is maximised for given inputs.[1] In such an approach, the concept of optimum size had to be introduced to solve the so-called 'Marshall's Dilemma'. In the perfectly competitive environment, the demand curve facing the individual firm is horizontal. To maximise profits each entrepreneur goes on expanding output so long as marginal cost is less than price. But if long-run average costs fall as output expands, because of economies of scale, marginal cost is less than average cost. There is no position of long-run equilibrium until one firm has established a monopoly.[2] Pigou's introduction of the optimum size was based on the premise that there are diminishing returns to 'management' (see Pigou, 1924). After a certain point, diseconomies of large-scale management are supposed to set in: the long-run average cost curve for the firm is assumed to have a 'U' shape. This approach portrays the technology in terms of a family of short-run cost curves representing costs associated with firms of different size. Once the size of the firm is determined – that is, the short-run cost curve is chosen – it will operate at the point on that curve where marginal cost equals the output price. Prior to determining its size, however, the opportunity set for the firm consists of the envelope of the family of short-run curves: this envelope is the long-run cost curve. The minimum of the envelope defines the optimal size of firm.

In the extension to imperfect competition, a further constraint is added in the form of market opportunities for selling outputs and buying inputs. The elasticity of demand for outputs becomes a critical factor, and output price is replaced by the notion of marginal revenue. Although the possibility of constant returns is admitted, the firm's reaction to its environment is still based on the assumption that this environment is beyond its control. In such circumstances the firm is again highly constrained in its decisions, the theory being based not on real decisions but on the conditions which would maintain industry equilibrium (see Loasby, 1971).

In this framework, a firm grows for essentially 'exogenous' reasons. It expands if there is a shift in either the cost or demand curves which it faces. The shift in costs arises from technical change or changes in factor prices, the shift in demand from changes in income and tastes. It is interesting to note that there is no expectation of any relationship between growth and profitability when firms are in long-run equilibrium. Such a relationship can arise in the short run. Resources are expected to move towards areas of high profitability, which would yield a positive association between profits and growth, but one which would not, however, be sustained as soon as equilibrium is restored.

Recently, time has been introduced explicitly into this analysis and the theory has been adapted to a dynamic equilibrium determined not just by the environment in the present period but by the environment of all future periods within the firm's time-horizon (see e.g. Solow, 1971). The firm is assumed to solve a multi-period constrained maximisation problem and determine the optimal values of all decision variables over the given horizon. The objective now becomes the maximisation of the present value of the future stream of profits.[3] It is assumed that the relevant environment at the horizon is such that the firm's 'optimum' size is larger than its present size and that it wishes to adjust to the larger size but will not do so instantaneously because of adjustment costs.[4] Growth however is still incidental to the main analysis, which focuses on the response of the firm to change in exogenous environment.

In any case these 'long-run profit maximisation' models still have elements of the traditional 'black box' type of approach. The firm's objectives are still dictated by external interests. Even though it is accepted that there is likely to be greater uncertainty in maximising over time, this uncertainty relates to objective expectations of the future – in the sense of being common to all agents in the market in which the firm is operating. This presents at best a partial picture of the firm's environment (see Wood, 1975). Associated with this, the capital market is assumed, unrealistically, to be competitive in the sense that lenders and borrowers have the same opinion as to the particular risk-adjusted interest rate that is appropriate to any specific investment project.

The point to note is that the dynamic version of the orthodox theory has come to be differentiated from the newer theories of the growth of the firm (considered in Section 1.4) simply by the differences in the firm's objectives assumed by the two types of theories. Whilst these differences are in themselves not trivial, there are other fundamental conceptual differences in the frameworks within which the two approaches are constructed.

1.3 The stochastic framework

One motive for the development of this framework arose from the observation that the size distribution of firms, whether within a single industry or in a whole economy, is almost always highly skewed, and that its upper tail resembles the Pareto distribution. (See the seminal article by Simon (1955), and Kalečki (1945) for an earlier discussion.) The stochastic framework considers the economic explanation of this observation based on the shape of the long-run average cost curve to be inadequate. The characteristic cost curve for the firm is regarded not as U-shaped, but as exhibiting virtually constant returns to scale about some critical minimum. Under these circumstances, the traditional analysis may 'predict the minimum size of firm in an industry with a known value of critical minimum, but it will not predict the skewed size distribution of firms' (Ijiri and Simon, 1977).

Within the simplest stochastic model, it is postulated that size has no effect upon the expected percentage growth of a firm. This postulate, known as the Law of Proportionate Effect (LPE), assumes in fact that the distribution of percentage changes in size, over a given time period, of the firms in a given size class, is the same for all size classes. Thus a firm randomly selected from those with a given value of assets has the same probability of growing at any given rate as a firm randomly selected from those with a hundred times the assets.

To see how a particular skew distribution, say the log-normal, corresponding to the size distribution of firms can be generated, consider the following example (cf. Ijiri and Simon, 1977, p. 142. The example assumes a constant population). Assume that there is a minimum size of firm in an industry and that for firms above this size, constant returns prevail. Individual firms in the industry will grow at varying rates, depending on such factors as profitability, new investment, acquisitions and retention policy. These factors, in turn, may depend on the technical and managerial efficiency of the firm, the degree of monopoly power, consumer tastes and many other factors. The operation of all these will generate a probability distribution for the changes in size of firms of a given size. (Note that there is a strong assumption that the factors are small, are independent of each other and do not act in a systematic manner. It rules out, for example, serial correlation in growth rates.) The strictest stochastic models make the strong assumption that this probability distribution is the same for all size classes of firms that are above the minimum size. Actual growth rates will differ over any particular period simply because some firms will have more luck than others. In other words growth of firms is a random process (see Curry and George, 1983). Following this assumption of the LPE, the steady-state distribution of the process will be log-normal.

The question which naturally arises is, how adequate is this theoretical explanation? This can be judged on two grounds: the plausibility of its assumptions and the goodness of fit of the derived distributions. The latter criterion corresponds to the position adopted by Friedman (1953). The former bears a close resemblance to Simon's (1963) views. Evaluating the goodness of fit of these mathematical models involves considerable theoretical difficulties, with no formal criteria being available for accurate discrimination between extreme hypotheses. In the case of the size distribution of firms, the observed distributions do resemble the log-normal or the related Pareto or Yule distributions. Since the observed distributions are very different from those expected from explanations based on static cost curves, stochastic models appear worthy of consideration on that basis alone.

However, the plausibility of the assumptions under these circumstances is also important. It has been shown that the assumptions can be made weaker and more consistent with empirical data whilst retaining the essentials of the stochastic process. For example, new firms can be allowed to enter the population albeit in restricted form by assuming that they are 'born' in the smallest size class at a relatively constant rate. This results not in the log-normal form but in the related Yule distribution. Equally importantly, the assumption of the serial correlation in firm growth has been admitted. This leads to very complex stochastic models in which the probability that a firm will increase in size during a given time period is assumed to be proportional to a weighted sum of the increases in the past. Using numerical simulation, it has been established that this process also generates equilibrium distributions resembling the Yule distribution. We shall test some of the assumptions in Chapter 3. It should be emphasised, however, that this framework does not preclude a causal theory of firm growth and, indeed, the stochastic and causal theories of firm growth are not mutually exclusive. Stochastic influences may, for instance, be reinforced by systematic ones, and it is to a review of some recent theories that emphasise systematic influences that we now turn.

1.4 The newer theories of firm growth

1.4.1 Efficiency and the means of growth
The process of firm growth was first analysed in detail in a relatively neglected study by Downie.[5] There are three aspects of Downie's analysis which should be noted: (a) the motive for growth; (b) the relationship between growth and profitability; and (c) the nature of oligopolistic rivalry.

(a) A firm is assumed to want to grow for three main reasons: from a desire to maintain its relative position in a particular market; to gain the security and stability associated with bigger size; and because the business standing and social prestige of a firm's management are associated positively with the size and growth of the firm.

(b) Assuming a given demand curve, it is argued that new customers can be attracted from rivals only by price reduction. (Expenditure on sales promotion is not considered but it makes little difference to the analysis if this method is used. This restriction on a given demand curve is a shortcoming in the analysis which was removed in Penrose's framework, discussed below.) Beyond a certain point, the further attraction of customers will be at the expense of profitability and thereafter a conflict arises between the growth of capacity and the growth of markets to be supplied from available capacity. The more efficient the firm, the faster will be its maximum sustainable rate of growth and the more rapidly will it add to its share of the market. The maximum rate of growth is set by the interaction of capacity and demand constraints.

(c) Downie placed the analysis of firm growth in the context of a competitive process. Oligopolistic interdependence, a continuing process of active rivalry, underlies his basic approach. This aspect of Downie's study has generally been neglected, subsequent formal analysis having focused on the individual firm, largely isolated from its rivals, with interdependence effectively assumed away.

One main drawback of Downie's approach is that it does not regard diversification as a general phenomenon. Profitability falls as growth increases, because of the increasing costs of obtaining an increased share of the set of markets corresponding to the firm's industry. It is in Penrose's work that this restraint is removed by incorporating diversification as an option open to all firms in all industries. In its place, she postulates 'managerial' restraint as the reason why there may be a trade-off between profitability and growth.

1.4.2 Management and diversification

In Penrose's framework, the objective of the firm is assumed to be the maximisation of total long-run profits and so any marginal investment with positive net return is assumed to be undertaken. (Penrose considers maximisation of the size of annual gross profits equivalent to growth maximisation; the problem of definition of profit in a dynamic context is not, however, considered.) The impetus to growth comes from two sources: externally, where changes in demand preferences, technological innovations and alterations in market conditions offer scope for the firm to improve its competitive position; and internally, from the unused pool of productive services which can be employed by the firm only in the course of expansion. These services exist because of indivisibilities in the resources at the firm's disposal.

A major aspect of her framework is that there is an upper limit on growth in any given period because of managerial restraint. The existing management of the firm can undertake only limited growth – if the firm expands too fast, the efficiency of the firm declines. (Penrose divides managerial functions into two kinds: 'entrepreneurial', which involve undertaking new projects; and 'managerial', which involve management of these.) This does not, however, rule out the possibility of continuous growth over time. This is because, as growth proceeds, the managerial limit continually recedes: managerial services specific to the planning and execution of expansion are released as particular growth projects are realised and become part of the firm's routine operations. Further, the managerial services available to the firm alter over time owing to the experience acquired by both the original members of the managerial team and the newcomers who have been absorbed into it. Once the firm has achieved the maximum rate of growth by internal expansion and has come up against the managerial restraint, this restraint may be eased by recourse to external expansion *via* acquisition. There is no presumption, however, that the eventual size of the firm would be limited.

The analysis of diversification is based on the concept of areas of specialisation which it has been profitable in the past for the firm to develop. These areas may be in technological bases or marketing activities in which the firm has acquired experience. Since opportunities to add new products arise from changes in the productive services available to the firm as experience accumulates, and from changes in the environment as perceived by the firm, the type of diversification undertaken by the firm will be closely related to the nature of its technological bases and market areas. In addition, the exigencies of competition and changes in consumer preferences may provide further reasons for profit-seeking firms to diversify. The key significance of this process is that it frees the firm from the restrictions on its expansion imposed by the demand for its existing products, although not from the restrictions imposed by its existing resources.

1.4.3 Growth and valuation

Marris's theory of firm growth (see Marris, 1964) builds on the contributions of both Downie and Penrose. It is a theory of internal growth in which it is assumed (for simplification) that finance is obtained from retained profits and that management maximises growth subject to certain constraints. The analysis is undertaken in a 'steady state' framework in which variables grow at a constant rate for the duration of the firm's planning horizon. Variables in ratio form (for example, the valuation ratio) remain constant. The values of these variables are initially chosen by the firm so as to obtain supply–demand growth equilibrium in each period within the time horizon under consideration.

In order to increase the growth of demand faster than the rate of growth of markets in which it is established, the firm has to increase its market share and/or carry out diversification. This would, however, involve expenditure in one or all of the following ways: higher expenditure on advertising and other promotional and marketing activities; higher expenditure on product or process research and development; the adoption of a price lower than that of competitors, to attract more customers. If the expenditures are regarded as capital costs, they would result in an increased capital-output ratio. If they are regarded as current costs, they result in a lower profit margin, as does a lower level of prices. In addition, a firm's efficiency declines as the rate of diversification increases, owing to the managerial constraint, as noted by Penrose. For these reasons there is likely to be an inverse relationship between growth of demand and the profit rate. In Marris's original contribution there is in fact a non-linear relationship: the taking up of an opportunity of diversification into a buoyant market may permit faster demand growth and profitability. But, with any new opportunity for a given profitability, there is a maximum to the demand growth that can be generated; growth any faster than this would be at the expense of profitability. In his later work however this was simplified and the demand growth–profitability function was postulated to exhibit negative first and negative second derivatives over the whole domain (see Marris, 1979).

The commissioning of capacity to match the growth of demand depends critically on the finance available for new investment. In the absence of recourse to external funds, new investment equals retained earnings, and so the growth of supply can be related (linearly) to the return on capital. When external finance is available, the total funds for new investments will exceed retained earnings but, over the long run, they will still be proportional to total earnings. This is because, *ceteris paribus*, the higher the profits of the firm the more funds it will be able to raise externally.

Marris's general model can be summarised using the following symbols: G_d denotes demand growth, d denotes rate of diversification and p denotes rate of profit. G_s denotes growth of supply and s the maximum growth that can be financed for a given profit rate. G denotes the equilibrium growth rate; h_1, h_2 and h_3 are functional forms.

Demand–growth curve

$$G_d = h_1(d) \qquad h_1 > 0 \tag{1.1}$$

Diversification–profitability curve

$$d = h_2(1/p) \qquad h_2 > 0 \tag{1.2}$$

Supply–growth curve

$$G_s = sp \tag{1.3}$$

Equilibrium condition

$$G_d = G_s = G \tag{1.4}$$

To obtain the solution for the model, substitute for d in equation (1.1) giving

$$G_d = h_3(1/p) \tag{1.5}$$

That is, the growth of demand is an inverse function of the rate of profit. Equations (1.3), (1.4) and (1.5) then determine both the profit rate and growth rate.

A novel feature of Marris's model is the constraint on a firm's management *via* the capital market. It is argued that management would be constrained because of its unwillingness to increase the retention ratio (r) beyond a certain point to avoid the threat of takeover. Too high an r would lower current dividends resulting in a reduced demand for the firm's shares (assuming that the shareholders, and the stock market generally, have a preference for current dividends). This would lead to a lower share price, making the firm open to possible takeover by other companies. There is thus an explicit relationship between the valuation ratio (V) and the firm's equilibrium growth. (The valuation ratio is defined as the ratio of the market value of equity capital to the book value of assets.) The firm maximises $G = f(V)$ subject to $V > \bar{V}$, where $\bar{V}$ is the minimum below which the risk of takeover becomes unacceptable. In his later work, Marris generalises the firm's objectives, postulating that in its growth plan management may aim to maximise the welfare of shareholders, in which case the maximand would be the valuation ratio. Alternatively it may aim to maximise growth, or some objective lying between these extremes (Marris, 1979, pp. 122–125).

Marris's development of a formal growth model extends the Downie–Penrose framework by incorporating the influence of the stock market through the market valuation of a firm's shares and the influence of takeovers on a firm's growth, and by formulating a general managerial utility function. However, there are two well-recognised shortcoming. First, unlike Penrose's theory in which growth occurs at an uneven pace, or in spurts, in Marris's theory a steady state is assumed. In an uncertain environment this is unrealistic. Further, in the cost-of-growth function it is implicitly assumed that a constant rate of expenditure will produce a constant rate of demand growth. This is an essential characteristic of the steady-state approach and it requires the assumption that the exogenous environment determining the cost-of-growth function remains constant. This, however, produces a paradox, since the firm is supposed to attempt actively to change its environment. The paradox is supposedly resolved by distinguishing between the 'static' environment and the 'super' environment (see Marris and Wood (eds), 1971, ch. 1). The former can be changed by the firm, but not the latter. But over time it is unlikely that 'super' environment will remain constant. Second, there is the problem of the asymmetrical treatment of takeovers. The takeover mechanism is based essentially on the long-run profit maximisation assumption. This may appear incongruous in a framework based on growth maximisation. Further, firms pursuing growth objectives do not themselves regard acquisition as a feasible option. In this regard Penrose's theory is particularly illuminating on takeovers, which can be an extremely important source of growth for the firm. In the next section we note the way that takeovers may affect the various constraints on growth, and their relationship with new investment.

1.5 Internal and external growth

'External growth' excludes all growth except that which is achieved by acquiring firms (or their subsidiaries) which previously had independent existence. Internal growth is total growth *minus* external growth (see Chapter 2). External growth may be due to consolidation or acquisition. In consolidation, normally all the participating firms lose their legal identity and a new firm is created. In acquisition, the acquiring firm retains its identity, and it is in this sense that external growth is studied below. (We use the term acquisition or merger to denote only the purchase of one or more firms by another.) External growth through acquisition and internal growth through new investment are the two methods of growth for the firm and it is imperative that the decisions regarding these, and the relationships between them, should be analysed to understand the process of firm growth. This issue is also important from the point of view of the economy. This is so since in general, whilst internal growth entails an increase in output, employment and productivity, acquisitions have no similar direct effects.[6]

There has been an extensive study of the motivation of acquisitions (see Steiner, 1975, and Hughes and Singh in Mueller (ed), 1980). But relatively little attention has been paid to the relationship between the two forms of growth. Acquisition growth is quicker and safer compared to internal growth for the following two reasons. First, new investment involves not just the commissioning of new productive capacity, but also the allocation of resources for creating markets. This is a much more gradual process than acquisition, and it may involve considerably more uncertainty, especially in an oligopolistic environment, about the final outcome. If uncertainty is the hallmark of the investment process, then for an individual firm acquisition is more than just another investment opportunity. Associated with this is the relative importance of the two methods of growth in diversification. Alchian (1957) argued that diversification may be a logical response to the uncertainty inherent in specialisation in production. The cost associated with diversification, however, is itself one of the reasons for expecting an inverse relationship between profitability and diversification. For this reason it seems likely that diversification through acquisition may entail lower costs than internal growth (Channon, 1973).

Second, within the firm itself, acquisition may, in the long run, alleviate the managerial constraint. The assimilation of significant newcomers to a firm's existing management team may create problems in the short run but, compared to managerial requirements in undertaking new investment, it is likely to have a favourable impact (Penrose, 1959). Even in the short run, there need not be assimilation problems if the acquired firm's operations are not fully integrated with those of the acquiring firm. Several commentators have bemoaned the fact that acquisitions do not always entail significant reorganisation (Newbould, 1970, and Monopolies and Mergers Commission Report, 1978). However, if the acquiring firm has a multi-divisional form structure ('M' form) in the way discussed by Williamson (1975), it may still obtain the financial and other benefits associated with risk reduction, without fully integrating the operations of the acquired firm into its own (cf. Lynch, 1971).[7]

It seems that partly because there is less uncertainty involved in growth by acquisition, the capital market may be more willing to supply funds on favourable terms than it will for growth by new investment (Meeks and Whittington, 1975b). It is possible that the discount factor applied for new investment may in some cases be lower as, for example, for the exploitation of a product or process innovation. It may also be that acquisition activity is correlated with some other firm characteristic (for example, size), and that it is this which brings a favourable response from the capital market. Nevertheless, in general, because of the lengthy gestation period involved in internal growth, and the associated risk, it is not unlikely that funds may be more readily available for acquisition.

For these reasons, acquisition growth may be a more attractive route from the firm's point of view. The central question with which we are concerned in this study is, how likely is it that acquisition will displace new investment? There may be a potential conflict between them, for three main reasons. First, the availability of managerial resources at any given time is limited, and so an acquiring firm may not be in a position to exploit as many new investment opportunities (see for example Kaldor, 1981). (This doesn't invalidate the earlier argument which was in terms of the relative managerial requirement in internal and external growth.) Similarly, the availability of finance may be limited. Second, if acquisition satisfies those components of managerial utility which are derived from the size and rate of growth of the operations of the firm, it may displace investment. Third, acquisitions may bring about a major change in the structure of an industry and so affect investment indirectly in so far as there is a relationship between market structure and investment. One possibility is that if acquisitions lead to a much higher degree of monopoly this may reduce investment. On the other hand, acquisitions may be necessary to reduce what businessmen see as an intolerably intensive degree of competition before they are prepared to invest. As the discussion in Chapter 4 shows, the effect could be either way depending upon the circumstances of individual firms (see George, 1971).

There are in fact two issues here. First, in a cross section of firms, what is the relationship between internal and external growth? Since the objectives and constraints are not invariant across firms, this need not tell us much about the second issue which is, how does acquisition affect subsequent investment performance? Both these issues are elaborated and examined empirically in Chapters 4 and 5.

1.6 Capital market constraints

The financing of firms has received considerable attention in recent years (see Wilson, 1980). Finance is a crucial factor in the development of firms, affecting both their acquisition and investment activities. Factors affecting the availability of finance, and the efficiency with which it is utilised, can and do play a dominant role in firms' growth. Financial sources may be divided into retained earnings (internal finance) and all other sources (external finance). Both internal and external growth in the sense used above may be financed from either internal or external sources. (Internal financing includes retained profits and depreciation provisions, and external financing includes borrowing as well as equity funding.) Two issues which have received increasing attention in recent years are the following: the availability and preference of firms for a particular source of funds; and the implications of organisational changes for the efficiency with which funds are utilised. According to Marris's 'supply-growth' curve, the availability of finance to the firm is largely dependent on current profitability. This is because of higher internal funds, and also because of the imperfections present in the capital market. The latter may mean that it is current profitability rather than expected future profitability which is most closely related to the provision of external finance. The return on existing assets thereby becomes important in shifting the capacity constraints.

It has been generally accepted that management would prefer to rely on internal funds. Writers as diverse in their analysis of the capitalist economy as Galbraith (1972), and Baran and Sweezy (1966), have suggested that firms would like to minimise their reliance on the capital market for the financing of any given project. This is because equity financing is considered to entail considerable transaction costs; there is uncertainty as to the state of the stock market when the issue is placed, and there may be a high opportunity cost in convincing the market of the worthwhileness of the project. In the case of borrowing, if there is uncertainty about future income, management, presumed to be risk averse, may feel reluctant to commit an increasing proportion of income to regular fixed interest payments.

More importantly, internal funds are regarded as less subject to the discipline of the capital market (Mueller, 1969). It has been suggested that these funds may be used in a less efficient manner than is the case for external funds. The basic assumption is that the firm operates in imperfect product markets which allow managerial discretion but that the capital market is relatively more competitive. However, this view seems to overlook the constraint which may operate on a firm's actions, *via* the takeover mechanism, and by competition in product markets in an open economy. (For a discussion of the discipline imposed by the capital market, see Baumol *et al.*, 1970; Whittington, 1972; and McFetridge, 1978).

The notion of minimum reliance on the capital market may also require some reconsideration in the case of firms which have relied heavily on growth by acquisition. There has been a tendency for such firms to rely considerably on external funds (see Prais, 1976). Retentions may be insufficient to finance both investment and acquisition. This gives an important role to the availability of external finance. For the firm relying on the stock market for funds the price of its common shares assumes an added significance.

In Marris's model the share price plays a negative role in the sense that, through its direct influence on the firm's valuation ratio, it constrains management from pursuing its own goals at the expense of the firm's shareholders. If firms rely on the capital market, especially in the case of share-for-share exchange in acquisition activity, it plays a positive role. Rather than impose a constraint, it is in the interest of the management to attain a high share price. The important variable in the share-for-share exchange is the exchange rate between the acquiring and acquired firm's shares. In such a situation, the factors governing the share price obviously become important. There is, however, a complex of factors involved in the influence on growth. A high payout ratio may be a prerequisite for a favourable share price, which would facilitate growth through acquisition. But such a strategy would result in a diminution of internal funds.

Some writers have emphasised the 'feedback effect' operating on the market valuation of firms who use their shares for acquisition of other firms which have lower price-earnings ratios. Each time such an acquisition is made, it leads to an increase in the earnings per share of the acquiring firm.[8] If this process is continued, it creates a pattern of growth in earnings per share which may cause the market to place a high price–earnings ratio on the share of the acquiring firm. A high price–earnings ratio is what enables the process to continue, which it can only do as long as the capital market continues to hold favourable expectations of the firm's future profitability.

Even if the management does shun the capital market, the efficiency with which internal funds are utilised may have to be viewed differently following the changes in the internal structure of firms. Multidivisional, or 'M-form', firms now account for a majority of the largest companies in developed market economies (see Dyas and Thanheiser, 1976). According to Williamson (1975), M-form behaviour may be more conducive to profit maximisation than any other form. This is because each division of the firm can be a profit centre whose performance can be closely monitored. But this does assume that the head office itself wants to pursue profit-maximising objectives.

More importantly, M-form firms are assumed to act as miniature internal capital markets which are more efficient than external markets in the capital allocation process. As well as reinforcing the curtailment of managerial discretion, this is supposed to lead to a speedier and more certain transfer of funds according to yield than would occur by relying only on the external market. This superiority of internal markets is thought to derive from certain advantages held by the general head office *vis à vis* the shareholders. These centre on access to internal information, and the scope to influence divisional policy in a continuous, selective fashion rather than in a delayed and drastic way which is the only means normally available to shareholders (for example, by the replacing of directors). So the mechanism through which the M-form operates may make for the efficient utilisation of internal funds even when the scrutiny of external markets is lacking.

1.7 The firm and the international economy

In the models of Downie, Penrose and Marris, by postulating product diversification, the constraint on growth emanating from the demand side is relaxed. Their framework does not, however, include the role which foreign markets, and overseas production, can play. Consider first exports: a geographical diversification need involve little or no change in a firm's existing production activities. The Ricardian theory of comparative advantage indicates the general pattern of trade which may occur across national boundaries. But there is little indication of specific advantages which may vary across firms within any economy; the homogeneity of production functions across firms is implicit in the notion of the economy possessing a comparative advantage. Still less does the theory identify the different objectives of the firms engaging in export activity. In practice, of course, there are likely to be considerable differences in objectives. Firms may regard exports as an expedient to be resorted to when the domestic market is depressed (Hague *et al.*, 1974). When the domestic demand is buoyant, the incentive to export may be reduced. Indeed, since they are not investing in extra capacity to produce exports, they may be unable to meet foreign orders when domestic demand is high. Alternatively, firms may engage in export partly in the belief that only thus will total production be large enough to keep costs down to a competitive level. So exporting would be a means of creating comparative advantage. A regular reliance on exports would then require marketing and selling organisations to deal with the export business. Because of indivisibilities in these activities it is generally reckoned that larger firms have an advantage over smaller ones when selling abroad, and that it is firms in the large size classes which, most frequently, will rely regularly on exports.

The largest firms are also the ones which undertake most direct investment abroad. Here the production itself is located outside the domestic economy. In so far as constraints on capacity are concerned – arising, for example, from uncertainty about domestic rivals' responses to an increase – investment overseas would tend to ease these constraints, though not necessarily remove them altogether, since large firms operate in an international oligopolistic environment (cf. Hymer, 1970). There has been a considerable literature analysing the motivation of firms undertaking direct investment (Dunning, 1981; Caves, 1982). These investment activities are thought to be due to imperfections in the international product and capital markets, to transaction costs, and to oligopolistic rivalry.

An important issue in this context, and one which is investigated below, is whether, regardless of the precise motivation, the characteristics of firms engaged in foreign direct investment are very different from those relying on production in the domestic economy. There is little existing evidence on this, or indeed on another aspect of business behaviour which may affect trade and overseas investment: the choice between internal and external growth. The part played by the acquisition of overseas firms by domestic firms is clear enough. For the acquiring firms, it is similar to domestic acquisition – both productive capacity and markets are made available, and this action may be a prelude to the growth and development of newly-acquired subsidiaries. More interestingly, it has been argued that acquisitions in the domestic market may also exert considerable effect on trade and overseas investment. Singh (1975) has suggested that acquisitions, by increasing the size of the firm quickly, allow it to undertake investment abroad. This is so since it seems likely that there is a threshold size for foreign investment and that firms below this threshold may exceed it after merger. Even if a firm's total new investment does not decrease following acquisition, it may be the case that new domestic investment is reduced. There may also be some indirect adverse effect on exports if acquisitions lead to foreign investment.

Some writers have suggested that there are also likely to be direct adverse effects. Thus Newbould and Luffman (1978) note that acquisition activity may distract managerial resources during the course of assimilation, to the extent that the firm does not have the ability (or the willingness, if acquisition satisfies the urge for growth) to plan and undertake exports. We have already noted that the converse may also be true: managerial resources may be increased by acquisition. It may, however, be argued that if acquisitions occur at the expense of new investment, this may be deleterious for exports. This may be because, as several recent theories of international trade have emphasised, the role of product quality and other non-price factors is crucial in competing in world markets (see, for example, Barker, 1977). In so far as new investment is likely to utilise production technology of the latest vintage, embodying process innovations, it will lead to better quality products which would compete better internationally. High productivity in the latest vintage plants would, of course, be advantageous for price competition as well. In such circumstances, acquisition of existing capacity would be less useful.

1.8 Summary of contents, and data sources

This chapter has touched on a number of the key issues involving acquisitions, investment and firm growth. These are further discussed, and examined empirically, in the following chapters. Detailed contents are given in the introduction to each chapter. This section provides an outline of the specific themes pursued in each. Chapter 2 examines briefly the relationship between size, total growth, external and internal growth, profitability and the other variables noted above. Chapter 3 studies in some depth the relationship between size and growth, and growth and profitability. It also examines the birth and death process of firms.

Chapter 4 examines the relative importance of internal and external growth in different industries, and analyses whether there is any systematic relationship with firm size. It also investigates the cross-sectional relationship between the two forms of growth, taking into account the differential impact of profitability. It then reexamines the magnitude of external growth, taking into account the growth of acquired assets.

In Chapter 5 the direct *impact* of acquisitions on new investment is investigated. A methodology which takes into account the changes in firms' external environment is employed for this purpose. Both single and multiple acquirers are included in the large sample of mergers studied. An analysis is also undertaken into the effect of acquisitions on new investment at the industry level. Further, the impact of acquisitions on profitability is investigated.

Chapter 6 examines the contribution of different sources of funds to firms growing at different rates, and in different size classes. It also examines the role of external funds in influencing firms' growth and profitability. Chapter 7 undertakes a further analysis of investment, acquisition and financing activities. It examines them within the context of a simultaneous equation model which traces the direct and indirect relationships between the variables. Specialised models are also used to study acquisition and finance behaviour where, in any given year, the value of some of the variables would be zero for a high proportion of firms.

Chapter 8 examines the role of exports in firm growth. It analyses two main issues: the relationship between size and growth on the one hand and the proportion of goods exported and the rate of growth of exports on the other, and the relationship between growth by acquisition and growth of exports. Chapter 9 examines the relationship between exports and overseas production activity, as well as the comparative characteristics and performance of firms with and without overseas production. The last chapter presents a summary of the main results and discusses their implications for economic theory and policy.

This study is based on the standardised accounting records, assembled by the Department of Industry and Trade (DI), of over two thousand quoted industrial companies. These companies accounted for nearly 60 per cent of the net output of UK industry, and about 70 per cent of its exports. For the period 1948–1964 it is mainly the published accounts of companies which are included in the Databank, but for the later period a considerable amount of supplementary information is also included.[9] These data are extremely carefully prepared and provide one of the best sources of information for investigating the issues raised in this study. In addition to these data, for Chapter 9 some further data were also obtained from company reports and from a survey carried out by the author.

The empirical analysis focuses on the period 1960–1976. In four of the chapters (Chapters 2, 3, 4 and 6), rather than study the seventeen-year period as a whole, we examine three sub-periods: 1960–1965, 1966–1971 and 1972–1976. (For other chapters, the time period was chosen according to the issues being investigated. The details of these are given in the individual chapters.) The first reason for this was that only in this way was it possible to obtain a sufficiently large numbers of firms for which analysis could be done by individual industrial sectors. The second, more important, reason was that if we considered only the firms surviving the whole of the seventeen-year period, the sample of firms would have been biased. In the merger wave of the 1960s proportionately a very large number of small and medium-sized firms were taken over. By focusing on shorter time periods we obtain greater variety in terms of the characteristics and performance of firms, and the results are unlikely to suffer from any sample bias.

The actual sub-periods were chosen in the first place to provide roughly equal numbers of years for comparing the average performance over a medium-run time period. But they also differ considerably: for example, the first sub-period had relatively low acquisition activity, the second sub-period saw a very sharp increase, whilst the third had a combination of high and low activity. The decision to consider companies continuing in independent existence in each of the sub-periods suffers from the drawback that the population of companies varies between time periods. Therefore comparisons between the time periods may be affected by changes in population as well as by other factors. Of course, to the extent that the study considers the entire population of companies available in the Databank, the results give a description of the behaviour of companies in that period which would be of interest in its own right. Nevertheless, in order to highlight any major changes which may be due to population changes, in a number of cases we also note results for the population of firms continuing for the entire seventeen-year period.

2

Firm characteristics and performance

The first purpose of this chapter is to discuss the variables used to measure growth, acquisition activity, export performance and other characteristics of firms. Frequency distributions of the firms classified by some of these measures are presented. Second, a preliminary analysis of the interrelationship between the various characteristics is carried out using matrices of correlation coefficients between each pair of variables used in the investigation. It thus gives a descriptive profile of a major part of the quoted company sector of the UK for the period 1960–1976.

2.1 The distribution of variables

To obtain a broad picture of the data, 7 indicators were calculated for each firm. A separate set of indicators was computed for each of the three sub-periods (1960–1965, 1966–1971, 1972–1976). Each indicator was calculated for each individual firm over the relevant sub-period. Thus a firm which survived over the whole period (1960–1976) will have three sets of the following seven indicators, one for each of the three sub-periods: measure of size, total growth, growth by acquisition, growth by investment, rate of return, growth by retentions and growth by external finance. In addition, it will have a set of 10 indicators for the last period, since indicators 8 to 10 (sales margin, export rate and export growth) could not be calculated with reference to the two earlier sub-periods. (This is because disclosure of this information only became compulsory after the 1976 Companies Act.) Apart from opening size, the indicators are averaged over the periods for which they are calculated. They are thus medium-run indicators in which annual fluctuations would be expected to cancel out, highlighting the more permanent aspects of the behaviour and performance for firms.

The basic method of calculating some of the indicators is similar to that of Singh and Whittington (1968). However, because the objective of this study is different, many new indicators have been introduced. Because of the large amount of information generated by the data, we present below only the aggregate results for firms in manufacturing industries, and for firms in all industries.

Measure of size. The balance sheet or the book value of 'net assets' is used as one main measure of the 'opening size' of the firm. Table 2.1 shows the opening size distribution of firms for each of the three sub-periods. In the first sub-period 7 per cent of all the firms had assets greater than £16m; this increased, mainly as a result of real growth and inflation, to 14 per cent in the second sub-period and to 22 per cent in the third sub-period. The sharp decline in the proportion of firms with

Table 2.1 *Percentage frequency distribution of firms classified by opening size*

Range %	1960–1965 Manufacturing	1960–1965 All industries	1966–1971 Manufacturing	1966–1971 All industries	1972–1976 Manufacturing	1972–1976 All industries
≤ 1m	41.0	41.8	13.0	14.1	2.2	2.2
≤ 2m	20.7	21.5	22.0	23.1	14.0	15.2
≤ 4m	15.7	15.3	24.9	23.7	25.2	24.6
≤ 8m	9.4	9.4	16.2	16.1	20.8	21.4
≤16m	5.3	4.8	8.8	8.7	13.1	14.3
>16m	8.0	7.2	15.1	14.3	24.5	22.3
Total	100.0	100.0	100.0	100.0	100.0	100.0
No. of firms	1308	1747	740	1021	587	824
Mean	6.6m	5.9m	14.7m	12.9m	28.7m	26.7m
Standard deviation	27.1m	24.0m	53.1m	46.4m	95.4m	92.5m

Sources: This table and all subsequent ones are based on the author's calculations.

assets less than £1m in the second and third sub-periods, however, is partly due to the exclusion of the smallest firms from the Department of Industry's population on the basis of minimum size criteria (see Meeks, 1977).

Growth. This indicator measures the rate of growth of net assets. It is measured as an arithmetic average of the annual rates (increase in size/opening size, for the individual year, for the individual company) rather than as a geometric rate, over each of the periods. This measure is suggested by Meeks and Whittington (1975b), and is preferred to geometric growth rates for two reasons. First, it has the convenient property of corresponding to the sum of individual sources or uses of funds. This allows us to break down total growth into various components. On the uses side, total growth is composed of growth by acquisition, growth by new fixed investment, growth by current assets, and growth by taking on minority interests. That is $TG = GA + GI + GC + GM$ where TG refers to total growth and the other four variables refer to the above components respectively. On the sources side, total growth is composed of growth by retentions and growth by external finance. Second, it has advantages in offsetting the effects of inflation in eroding the weight of growth achieved early in any period. For example, as between two otherwise similar companies which grew in real terms by equal proportions over say the sub-period 1972–1976, the one which grew relatively rapidly in the earlier part of the sub-period would have the older assets in 1976, and would tend to exhibit a greater gap between historic cost and current replacement cost. The use of an arithmetic average increases the relative weight given to growth achieved earlier in the sub-

18

Table 2.2 *Percentage frequency distribution of firms classified by total growth*

Range %	1960–1965		1966–1971		1972–1976	
	Manufac-turing	All industries	Manufac-turing	All industries	Manufac-turing	All industries
≤ 0	8.2	7.2	8.0	7.9	2.7	2.9
≤ 2.5	12.7	12.9	12.3	13.0	1.4	1.2
≤ 5.0	17.6	18.3	18.1	16.3	1.9	2.2
≤ 10.0	29.8	29.5	27.6	28.3	12.6	11.7
≤ 20.0	22.9	22.3	21.8	21.5	45.3	42.8
> 20.0	8.9	9.8	12.3	12.9	36.1	39.2
Total	100.0	100.0	100.0	100.0	100.0	100.0
No. of firms	1308	1747	740	1021	587	824
Mean	8.8	9.2	10.1	10.4	17.9	19.0
Standard deviation	9.9	11.1	15.6	15.7	11.4	13.2

period, partly offsetting the effects of inflation (see Meeks and Whittington, 1975b, Appendix A).

Table 2.2 shows that, relative to the size distribution of firms, the distribution of growth rates is more symmetrical for the first two sub-periods. For the third sub-period the distribution is narrower and skewed to the right. This is owing mainly to the rapid inflation experienced at this time.

Growth by acquisition. This indicator measures the expenditure on acquisition of new subsidiaries as a proportion of opening net assets. As can be seen from Table 2.3, the distribution by acquisition growth is skewed in all three time-periods – for all firms in manufacturing industries, as well as in all industries. During the second sub-period, the proportion of all firms growing by acquisition by at least a moderate amount (over 2.5 per cent) is greater than in the other two sub-periods, reflecting the very high acquisition activity. Another noticeable characteristic is that quite a large proportion of companies (of the order of a third) made no acquisition at all during any of the three sub-periods.

Growth by new fixed investment. This indicator measures the expenditure on new fixed investment as a proportion of opening net assets. As Table 2.4 shows, in contrast to acquisitions, relatively few companies undertook no expenditure on investment. Not surprisingly, in view of the constraints on growth by new investment, in all three time-periods fewer achieved extremely high rates of growth by new investment than did by acquisition. This is reflected in the standard deviation around the mean for investment growth being considerably lower than that for acquisitions.

19

Table 2.3 *Percentage frequency distribution of firms classified by growth by acquisition*

Range %	1960–1965		1966–1971		1972–1976	
	Manufac-turing	All industries	Manufac-turing	All industries	Manufac-turing	All industries
≤ 0	32.9	33.2	30.8	31.0	29.8	29.0
≤ 2.5	37.7	36.9	32.3	31.6	40.5	39.3
≤ 5.0	10.4	10.9	11.5	12.5	11.4	11.9
≤ 10.0	9.3	8.9	11.9	11.1	8.3	8.9
≤ 20.0	6.0	6.4	7.4	7.1	6.5	6.7
> 20.0	3.7	3.7	6.1	6.7	3.4	4.2
Total	100.0	100.0	100.0	100.0	100.0	100.0
No. of firms	1308	1747	740	1021	587	824
Mean	3.3	3.4	4.7	4.9	3.4	3.8
Standard deviation	7.5	8.7	13.5	13.9	8.0	9.1

Table 2.4 *Percentage frequency distribution of firms classified by growth by new fixed investment*

Range %	1960–1965		1966–1971		1972–1976	
	Manufac-turing	All industries	Manufac-turing	All industries	Manufac-turing	All industries
≤ 0	11.5	12.2	13.6	13.7	11.6	12.4
≤ 2.5	29.5	28.0	30.3	29.7	26.9	23.3
≤ 5.0	26.8	25.8	26.8	25.0	24.2	22.2
≤ 10.0	22.6	22.7	23.1	22.3	25.0	25.2
≤ 20.0	7.9	8.8	5.1	7.6	10.4	13.8
> 20	1.7	2.3	1.1	1.7	1.9	3.0
Total	100.0	100.0	100.0	100.0	100.0	100.0
No. of firms	1308	1747	740	1021	587	824
Mean	4.2	4.5	3.5	4.0	4.5	5.2
Standard deviation	5.1	6.0	4.6	5.5	5.5	7.1

Table 2.5 *Percentage frequency distribution of firms classified by the return on net assets*

Range %	1960–1965 Manufac-turing	1960–1965 All industries	1966–1971 Manufac-turing	1966–1971 All industries	1972–1976 Manufac-turing	1972–1976 All industries
≤ 0.0	2.0	1.8	2.2	2.1	2.4	2.3
≤ 2.5	2.4	2.1	1.4	1.1	0.9	0.7
≤ 5.0	3.9	3.5	3.1	3.1	0.7	1.3
≤ 10.0	15.0	15.3	15.1	14.8	6.3	6.2
≤ 20.0	46.9	48.3	49.1	47.9	47.5	44.5
> 20.0	29.8	29.0	29.2	31.0	42.2	44.9
Total	100.0	100.0	100.0	100.0	100.0	100.0
No. of firms	1308	1747	740	1021	587	824
Mean	16.3	16.3	16.1	16.6	19.3	20.1
Standard deviation	8.9	8.8	9.7	9.7	10.4	11.0

Rate of return on net assets. This indicator gives the average pre-tax rate of return on net assets, expressed as a percentage per annum.[1] It has two drawbacks: (i) owing to undervaluation of assets in company accounts (this understates the denominator of the rate of return, and overstates the numerator because depreciation charges are too low) actual profitability may be overstated; (ii) a similar effect would occur as a result of the inclusion of stock appreciation in profits. The justification for using it, despite the drawbacks, is twofold. First, in cross-sectional analysis it is likely to be a useful indicator of a firm's performance and ability to undertake growth – especially since it is an average over at least five years. Second, it is an indicator which is used by the firm itself, and the capital market, in taking decisions on financing etc.[2] Table 2.5 shows that for firms in all industries the distribution was quite similar in the first two sub-periods, with average profitability and variation around it also similar. In the third sub-period, mainly owing to stock appreciation, there was a considerable increase in the proportion of firms in the greater than 20 per cent per annum category.

Growth by retentions. This is one of the two long-term financial indicators. It is defined as the sum of retained profits, other receipts and future tax reserves, divided by opening net assets. It is worth noting that from the financing side, total growth of net assets is identically equal to growth by retentions and growth by external finance. That is, $TG = GR + GE$ where TG refers to total growth, and the other two variables refer to the above components respectively. As shown in Table 2.6, the first two sub-periods exhibit a similar pattern, with a majority of firms financing growth rates of up to ten per cent by retentions. In the last sub-

Table 2.6 *Percentage frequency distribution of firms classified by growth by retentions*

Range %	1960–1965		1966–1971		1972–1976	
	Manufac- turing	All industries	Manufac- turing	All industries	Manufac- turing	All industries
≤ 0.0	8.3	7.4	11.2	10.7	2.4	2.9
≤ 2.5	17.3	18.7	23.1	23.9	1.9	1.7
≤ 5.0	30.9	31.7	30.5	28.3	3.4	4.4
≤ 10.0	32.8	31.6	25.5	26.4	17.0	16.6
≤ 20.0	9.9	9.8	9.1	9.9	52.0	47.3
> 20.0	0.8	0.8	0.5	0.8	23.0	27.1
Total	100.0	100.0	100.0	100.0	100.0	100.0
No. of firms	1308	1747	740	1021	587	824
Mean	5.0	5.0	4.2	4.4	14.7	15.3
Standard deviation	4.5	4.4	6.7	6.3	8.4	9.3

period a much higher proportion of firms financed even higher growth rates by internal funds.

Growth by external finance. This indicator includes both growth by issues of equity and by gearing issue. It is defined as the sum of the issue of ordinary and preference shares, the change in the interest of minority shareholders, and the change in long-term liabilities as a proportion of opening net assets. As Table 2.7 indicates, a very high proportion of the firms did not use external finance at all in all three sub-periods. Interestingly, this proportion is the lowest for the second sub-period, which saw the most intense takeover activity. As we shall examine in Chapter 6, a high proportion of the takeovers were financed by reliance on external funds. Another notable feature of this table is the decline in the reliance on external funds in the upper ends of the distribution in the last sub-period.[3]

2.2 Correlation analysis

The detailed investigation of the causal relationship between the indicators is deferred to later chapters. In this section we examine the extent of association between each pair of indicators. A preliminary estimate of this is provided by computing zero order correlation coefficients between each pair. Despite the well-known limitations of the coefficients (capturing only linear relationship, not implying causality and with the possibility of spurious association), some useful indications can be obtained from such an analysis, and the changes in association over time.

Table 2.7 *Percentage frequency distribution of firms classified by growth by external finance*

Range %	1960–1965		1966–1971		1972–1976	
	Manufac-turing	All industries	Manufac-turing	All industries	Manufac-turing	All industries
$\leq$ 0.0	43.1	41.4	32.0	32.0	35.1	35.4
$\leq$ 2.5	20.0	20.7	22.2	22.7	29.0	27.5
$\leq$ 5.0	11.7	11.4	13.5	13.6	13.8	14.0
$\leq$ 10.0	13.2	12.9	15.1	14.5	13.6	12.7
$\leq$ 20.0	8.0	9.2	9.6	9.4	6.0	6.9
> 20.0	3.9	4.4	7.6	7.7	2.6	3.8
Total	100.0	100.0	100.0	100.0	100.0	100.0
No. of firms	1308	1747	740	1021	587	824
Mean	3.8	4.2	5.9	6.0	3.2	3.7
Standard deviation	8.1	9.3	13.3	13.6	7.3	9.1

The matrices of the correlation coefficients for firms in all industries together are presented in Tables 2.8 to 2.10 for each of the three sub-periods.[4] Each row and each column gives the correlation coefficient between the indicator named at the head of the row and the indicator named at the end of each successive column. Each table is symmetrical about the diagonal, with the number of firms given below each table.

These tables give a large amount of interesting information about the activities of quoted companies during the period. Consider first the correlation between opening size and the other indicators (Row 1 Tables 2.8 to 2.10). There is a mild negative relationship between size and the other indicators (except growth by external finance and export rate in Table 2.10). This is particularly surprising in the case of size and growth, and size and growth by acquisition, in view of the prevalent opinion that larger firms had grown faster than smaller ones in this period (see Prais, 1976, ch. 2).

The correlation between growth, and investment and acquisition is positive and consistently high, with acquisition in all three time periods exhibiting a somewhat stronger association with growth. The positive correlation between growth and rate of return is also quite high in the first and third sub-periods. It should be noted, however, that the highest value of the correlation coefficient is 0.56 in the third sub-period, indicating that profitability is associated with only about 30 per cent of the variance in growth rates ($R^2 = (0.56)^2 = 0.31$). It is considerably smaller for the second sub-period, with a value of only 0.32. (As noted in Chapter 1, the profitability of a firm depends as much on its growth as its growth depends on profitability. This issue is discussed in detail in the next chapter.) It is also noticeable that

23

Table 2.8 *Matrix of correlation coefficients, 1960–1965*

Indicator	Opening size (log)	Growth	Growth by acquisition	Growth by new fixed investment	Rate of return	Growth by retentions	Growth by external finance
Opening size (log)	1.00	–0.11	–0.06	–0.12	–0.21	–0.18	–0.05
Growth	–0.11	1.00	0.79	0.61	0.40	0.56	0.92
Growth by acquisition	–0.06	0.79	1.00	0.32	0.11	0.20	0.85
Growth by new fixed investment	–0.12	0.61	0.32	1.00	0.33	0.47	0.50
Rate of return	–0.21	0.40	0.11	0.33	1.00	0.85	0.07
Growth by retentions	–0.18	0.56	0.20	0.47	0.85	1.00	0.20
Growth by external finance	–0.05	0.92	0.85	0.50	0.07	0.20	1.00
Mean	7.40	9.20	3.41	4.51	16.28	4.95	4.25
Standard deviation	1.32	11.07	8.66	6.04	8.76	4.40	9.33

Notes: Number of firms 1747.

Coefficients above an absolute value of 0.07 are statistically significant at the 5 per cent level.

The mean refers to the average over the period, in per cent, apart from opening size which is in terms of natural logs (net assets, measured in £'000).

there is a much greater association between growth and external finance than between growth and retentions in the first two periods. For the last period there is a significant shift towards retentions.

Growth by acquisition is generally positively associated with that by new investment, although the relationship is not a strong one. Similarly, there is only a weak relationship between it and the rate of return. It is quite striking that there is no association at all between the rate of return and growth by acquisition in the third sub-period. As with total growth, there is likely to be a two-way relationship – acquisition would be expected to influence profitability, but would also in turn be influenced by it. Growth by external finance is much more highly correlated with acquisition than with internal finance. Indeed there is a negative correlation with internal finance in the last period.

Fixed investment has a consistently higher correlation coefficient with profitability than with acquisition. Further, the association between investment and retentions is considerably greater than that between acquisition and retentions, whilst the association between investment and external finance is consistently lower

Table 2.9 *Matrix of correlation coefficients, 1966–1971*

Indicator	Opening size (log)	Growth	Growth by acquisition	Growth by new fixed investment	Rate of return	Growth by retentions	Growth by external finance
Opening size (log)	1.00	−0.08	−0.04	−0.15	−0.31	−0.16	−0.02
Growth	−0.08	1.00	0.88	0.40	0.32	0.52	0.92
Growth by acquisition	−0.04	0.88	1.00	0.17	0.19	0.23	0.92
Growth by new fixed investment	−0.15	0.40	0.17	1.00	0.37	0.46	0.25
Rate of return	−0.31	0.32	0.19	0.37	1.00	0.63	0.08
Growth by retentions	−0.16	0.52	0.23	0.46	0.63	1.00	0.14
Growth by external finance	−0.02	0.92	0.92	0.25	0.08	0.14	1.00
Mean	8.21	10.36	4.91	3.95	16.63	4.41	5.95
Standard deviation	1.32	15.71	13.89	5.50	9.70	6.31	13.55

Notes: Number of firms 1021. For other notes, see Table 2.8.

than that between acquisition and external finance. The general picture which emerges is that of firms relying more on retentions for new investment, and more on external funds for acquisitions (cf. Meeks and Whittington, 1976). There are, however, differences between firms in different industries (not shown here) which are examined in detail in Chapter 6.

Growth by retentions has generally a low correlation with growth by external finance, indicating that, in a cross section, firms on average relied predominantly on either one source or the other. This suggests that an *a priori* expectation that fastest growing firms rely heavily on all sources of finance is not necessarily borne out (the reasons for this are explored in Chapter 6).

In Table 2.10, for the period 1972–76, we have provided correlation coefficients for three other indicators for which data were not available for the earlier periods. The profit margin, which is defined as operating profit as a proportion of sales, is an annual average over five years. It has a slight negative relationship with opening size and growth by acquisition. But its positive correlation with the rate of return (0.45) is not as high as might be expected, suggesting that the sales/assets ratio varies in a less systematic manner than profitability. This can be seen from the following identity

$$\text{Profitability} \equiv \text{Profit/Sales} \times \text{Sales/Assets}$$

(see Whittington, 1980, p. 343). If both profit margin and the sales/assets ratio

Table 2.10 *Matrix of correlation coefficients, 1972–1976*

Indicator	Opening size (log)	Growth	Growth by acquisition	Growth by new fixed investment	Rate of return	Growth by retentions	Growth by external finance	Profit margin	Export rate	Export growth
Opening size (log)	1.00	-0.20	-0.06	-0.12	-0.28	-0.30	0.02	-0.04	0.05	-0.03
Growth	-0.20	1.00	0.53	0.46	0.56	0.72	0.70	0.13	0.01	0.19
Growth by acquisition	-0.06	0.53	1.00	0.10	-0.02	-0.04	0.81	-0.10	-0.08	0.12
Growth by new fixed investment	-0.12	0.46	0.10	1.00	0.28	0.50	0.15	0.11	-0.11	0.08
Rate of return	-0.28	0.56	-0.02	0.28	1.00	0.76	0.03	0.45	-0.01	0.11
Growth by retentions	-0.30	0.72	-0.04	0.50	0.76	1.00	0.02	0.28	0.06	0.03
Growth by external finance	0.02	0.70	0.81	0.15	0.03	0.02	1.00	-0.10	-0.05	0.13
Profit margin	-0.04	0.13	-0.10	0.11	0.45	0.28	-0.10	1.00	0.03	0.02
Export rate	0.05	0.01	-0.08	-0.11	-0.01	0.06	-0.05	0.03	1.00	0.04
Export growth	-0.03	0.19	0.12	0.08	0.11	0.03	0.13	0.02	0.04	1.00
Mean	8.81	19.02	3.81	5.22	20.07	15.33	3.69	10.20	10.66	12.70
Standard deviation	1.40	13.16	9.11	7.07	10.95	9.35	9.12	5.70	12.66	13.27

Notes: Number of firms 824. For other notes, see Table 2.8.

Table 2.11 *Matrix of inter-period correlations*

Time period	Sector(a)	Opening size	Growth by acquisition	Growth by new fixed investment	Rate of return	Growth by retentions	Growth by external finance
1960–1965 correlated with 1966–1971(b)	I	0.95	0.25	0.19	0.20	0.58	0.19	0.29
	II	0.94	0.20	0.13	0.34	0.59	0.22	0.22
1966–1971 correlated with 1972–1976(b)	I	0.91	0.09	0.03	0.16	0.62	0.22	0.07
	II	0.91	0.11	0.09	0.25	0.64	0.27	0.08

Notes: (a) Sector I includes manufacturing firms.
        Sector II includes all firms.
     (b) First two sub-periods: no. of firms in Sector I 635
                                  no. of firms in Sector II 832
          Second two sub-periods: no. of firms in Sector I 510
                                  no. of firms in Sector II 694

     Correlation coefficients above a value of 0.08 are statistically significant at the 5 per cent level.

changed identically across firms, the correlation between profit margins and profitability would be higher than if the two components moved separately.

There is a slight positive relationship between the export rate, defined as the ratio of firms' exports to sales (averaged over five years) and opening size, and a slight negative relationship between growth by acquisition and export rate. There is a mild positive relationship between export growth and total growth.[5] (Note that firms which undertake no exports at all are excluded.) This result is very sensitive to the composition of the sample. As Chapter 8 shows, the relationship is stronger for a slightly different sample.

Finally, Table 2.11 measures the correlation between the value for each company of an indicator in the first sub-period and its corresponding value in the second sub-period (or the value in the second sub-period correlated with its value in the third sub-period). It shows to what extent an above-average value of a particular indicator for a given firm in one sub-period could be used to predict the deviation from the average of the same indicator for the same company in the next sub-period.

The results indicate that size in particular, and to a smaller extent profitability, exhibit a highly stable pattern of inter-temporal variation across firms. For the first two sub-periods, total growth and growth by external finance show stability but there are some noticeable differences between firms in manufacturing alone and firms in all industries combined. (Note that whilst the coefficients are low, they are generally statistically significant.) New fixed investment has a more stable pattern for non-manufacturing firms for both sets of time periods than for manufacturing firms. This pattern is the same for acquisitions in the last two sub-periods, but it is the reverse of that for the two earlier sub-periods.

This section has provided a preliminary description of the behaviour of some of the variables important in studying firm growth. A useful picture of the association between variables has been obtained thereby. In the rest of the study a more detailed analysis is undertaken, testing a number of formal hypotheses which were discussed in Chapter 1. We start by considering the relationship between firm size and growth.

3

Size, growth and profitability

The purpose of this chapter is to examine the relationship between the size and growth, and the growth and profitability of firms, using comprehensive data for the period 1960–1976. A number of issues relating to the sample of firms and the statistical techniques used in estimating these relationships are also explored and their implications for previous work in this area are examined.

The relationship between size and growth is of major importance in economic theory and in industrial organisation and a number of studies have attempted to assess the form of this relationship.[1] Relatively few of these studies have used a range of variables. As some writers have argued, results obtained from investigating the growth rates of firms of different size are not independent of the choice of variable to measure size (see, e.g., Smyth *et al.*, 1975). Also, only a few of these studies have used individual industry data. Industry is, however, an important variable, because the characteristics of the average firm vary significantly and systematically between industries (see Singh and Whittington, 1968). Furthermore, none of the previous studies is based on as comprehensive a set of *recent* data as is the analysis below. The results seem to indicate revision of some important generally accepted conclusions in this field.

One of the important systematic influences on growth is profitability. Since the relationship between growth and profitability has received considerable attention from both a theoretical and an empirical point of view, it is of interest to examine this relationship, particularly as at a disaggregate level the industry environment of firms is likely to be an important influence on this relationship. The theoretical expectations regarding this, and other relevant hypotheses, are discussed in detail later in this chapter, which is arranged as follows. Section 3.1 summarises the theoretical issues concerning the relationship between size and growth discussed in Chapter 1. Section 3.2 presents the detailed results of regression analysis, and discusses some of the econometric problems involved in testing this relationship, whilst Section 3.3 considers variation and persistency in firm growth. Section 3.4 summarises the issues relating to the cross-sectional relationship between growth and profitability, whilst Section 3.5 presents the empirical results on this relationship. Section 3.6 presents some evidence on the birth and death process, and the last section provides a conclusion.

3.1 Size and growth: theoretical considerations
It was noted in Chapter 1 that within the stochastic framework firm growth is envisaged as resulting from the cumulative effect of the chance operation

of a large number of forces acting independently of each other. The basic proposition is the following: there are a number of factors influencing a firm's growth, such as the quality of the firm's management, the firm's economic environment, the response of management to changes in the environment, and the supply of raw materials, intermediate goods and factor inputs. During any given time period some of these factors would tend to increase the firm's size, others would tend to cause a decline, and their combined effect would yield a probability distribution of the rates of growth for firms of each given size. One of the stochastic models which has received a great deal of attention, the law of proportionate effect (LPE), asserts that this probability distribution is the same for all size classes of firms; that is, the probability of a firm growing at a given proportionate rate during any particular time period is independent of the initial size of the firm. Thus, if size of the ith firm at time t is denoted by $S_{i,t}$, the LPE asserts that

$$S_{i,t}/S_{i,t-1} = E_{i,t} \qquad (3.1)$$

where $E_{i,t}$ is a random variable distributed independently of $S_{i,t-1}$.

The LPE yields three testable hypotheses concerning the cross-section relationship between the size and growth of firms:

(i) that firms of different size classes have the same average proportionate growth rate;

(ii) that the dispersion of growth rates about the common mean is the same for all size classes; and

(iii) that the rate of growth of firms in one period is independent of its growth rate in subsequent periods – that is, there should be no serial correlation in firm growth rate.[2] If this were not so, it might be expected that, other things being equal, opening size and subsequent growth would be related because both are related to past growth (see Hart, 1962).

The operation or otherwise of the LPE has a bearing on growth in industry and aggregate concentration. If the LPE is in operation, concentration rises over time. If the law is not in operation, concentration rises even faster if size and growth are positively related, but increases more slowly if they are negatively related. It is therefore also interesting from the point of view of the sharp concentration increase in the UK to enquire whether this occurred in the presence of the operation of LPE or not.

The LPE is contrary to the proposition that there is some optimum firm size. In this it resembles the managerial approach, which states that there is no limit to the absolute size of the firm. The latter approach postulates rather that there exists a limit to firm's growth at any given time. Penrose (1959, p. 212) has, however, argued that amongst firms facing the most favourable environment for growth, the rate of 'growth of the medium-sized and moderately large firms' may be expected to be higher than that of the new and very small firms and higher also than that of the very large firms. This is mainly because, for the latter two categories, prospects for acquisition (which is necessary to ease the managerial constraint) may be limited. (The rationale for this is elaborated in Chapter 4.)

In the neoclassical approach, the proposition of an optimum size occupies a central place, but there is no guidance in the theory as to the precise relationship between size and growth which one would expect to observe among a cross section of firms. If, however, it is assumed that all firms within an industry face the same U-shaped, long-run average cost curve, one would expect to observe a negative relationship between firm size and growth. This is because the large firms may be considered to have grown beyond the optimum, and so would be growing less fast (or even shrinking) compared to the small firms which are moving towards the optimum (see Singh and Whittington, 1975).

3.2 Size and growth: empirical results

One method of testing the growth-size relationship empirically is to study the association between the logarithms of firm size at the beginning and at the end of a period. If the LPE holds, then there will be a systematic relationship between the two variables, which would be reflected by the parameters of the following equation:

$$\log S_{i,t} = \alpha + \beta \log S_{i,t-1} + \log \epsilon_{i,t} \tag{3.2}$$

where $\log \epsilon_{i,t}$ is a homoscedastic random variable with zero mean.[3] If $b = 1$ (b denotes regression estimate of β), and the variance of $\log \epsilon_{i,t}$ is constant, it will indicate that the average and the variance of the logarithms of proportionate growth satisfy the requirements of LPE. If $b > 1$, the large firms will grow proportionately faster and if $b < 1$, the smaller firms will tend to do so (cf. Singh and Whittington, 1975). The dispersion in the size of firms will however also depend on $\epsilon_{i,t}$ – if it is strong enough it may outweigh the effect of $b > 1$.

The detailed results obtained by fitting equation (3.2) by ordinary least squares (OLS) to the cross section of firms in each industry for the three sub-periods are given in Tables 3.1–3.3. (Note that the disaggregate analysis throughout the study is at the 2-digit industry level – approximating to the 1968 SIC industrial orders.) The most noticeable feature of the results is that the coefficient b is less than unity in most industries and for 'all manufacturing' as well as 'all industries'. For all industries for the first period, using net assets, the regression analysis based on records of 1747 firms yielded a b value of 0.96 (Table 3.1), the same value being obtained for the second period, whilst for the third period it was even lower at 0.93. When growth is measured using fixed assets or equity assets, a similar conclusion is reached.

Although b is significantly below 1 in only a handful of industries, in view of the fact that it is almost always less than unity, and significantly so for the aggregate of industries, the data tend to reject the first requirement of the LPE. Equally importantly, the results suggest that, superficially at least, the view that during the last two decades large firms in the UK have been growing faster than small firms may need revision for the population of *quoted* companies (see Prais, 1976, p. 40; we discuss the conclusion of others at the end of this section).

There are, however, two important econometric qualifications to the above methodology. First, it is unlikely that the error term in equation 3.2 is homoscedastic. This is because, contrary to the expectation generated by the LPE (and which we examine presently), on *a priori* grounds it seems likely that the variance of growth rates would decline with increase in firm size. In this case, although the estimates using equation 3.2 would still be unbiased, their efficiency would be reduced (the standard errors would be larger and so the usual significance tests

Table 3.1 *Regression results for the LPE model, 1960–1965*

Industry	No. of firms	Net assets				Fixed assets				Equity assets			
		a	b	SE(b)	$\bar{R}^2$	a	b	SE(b)	R^2	a	b	SE(b)	$\bar{R}^2$
21 Food	53	0.58	0.99	0.04	0.93	1.02	0.95	0.04	0.93	2.10	0.80*	0.04	0.86
23 Drink	67	0.06	1.06	0.04	0.93	0.09	1.06	0.04	0.93	1.20	1.06	0.05	0.89
26 Chemicals	77	0.73	0.97	0.02	0.95	1.10	0.93	0.03	0.94	0.82	0.96	0.03	0.94
31 Metal manf.	88	0.84	0.95*	0.02	0.95	1.09	0.93*	0.02	0.95	0.93	0.94*	0.03	0.94
33 Non-elec. eng.	194	1.23	0.90*	0.03	0.83	1.46	0.89*	0.03	0.82	1.40	0.88*	0.03	0.83
36 Elec. eng.	89	0.87	0.96	0.03	0.91	1.31	0.92*	0.03	0.89	1.14	0.93*	0.03	0.91
38 Vehicles	51	1.06	0.93	0.05	0.88	1.09	0.95	0.05	0.89	1.05	0.93	0.05	0.89
39 Metal goods	135	0.78	0.96	0.03	0.89	1.03	0.95	0.03	0.87	0.90	0.95	0.03	0.89
41 Textiles	177	0.38	0.99*	0.03	0.84	0.69	0.97	0.04	0.80	0.80	0.94*	0.03	0.82
44 Clothing etc.	60	0.25	1.04	0.07	0.81	0.94	0.95	0.06	0.80	0.84	0.96	0.07	0.77
46 Bricks etc.	85	0.67	1.00	0.05	0.84	1.23	0.95	0.05	0.84	0.97	1.00	0.04	0.85
47 Timber etc.	50	1.27	0.89	0.07	0.76	0.68	0.99	0.08	0.76	2.12	0.76*	0.08	0.65
48 Paper etc.	91	0.31	1.02	0.03	0.93	0.57	1.01	0.03	0.93	0.62	0.99	0.03	0.92
49 Other manf.	50	0.89	0.94	0.05	0.88	1.22	0.90	0.05	0.86	1.22	0.90*	0.05	0.86
All manufacturing	1308	0.72	0.97*	0.01	0.89	1.06	0.96	0.03	0.85	1.03	0.94	0.04	0.87
50 Construction	56	0.75	0.98	0.05	0.85	1.26	0.93	0.05	0.86	0.75	0.98	0.06	0.83
70 Transport	39	1.45	0.88	0.06	0.84	1.92	0.83	0.08	0.75	1.30	0.90	0.06	0.85
81 Wholesale	155	0.83	0.95	0.04	0.82	1.00	0.94	0.03	0.84	0.96	0.94	0.04	0.82
82 Retail	123	1.13	0.93	0.04	0.83	1.58	0.88*	0.04	0.82	1.15	0.94	0.04	0.83
88 Misc.	66	0.59	1.02	0.07	0.79	0.64	1.02	0.06	0.81	0.74	1.01	0.07	0.78
All non-manufacturing	439	1.14	0.97	0.02	0.88	1.17	0.93*	0.02	0.82	0.99	0.95*	0.02	0.82
All industries	1747	0.77	0.96*	0.01	0.88	1.08	0.94*	0.01	0.86	1.13	0.92*	0.01	0.85

Notes: The disaggregate analysis is at the 2-digit industry level, approximating to 1968 SIC industrial orders. The industry numbers are those of the DI Databank. SE(b) denotes the standard error of b.
* denotes significantly different from unity at the 5 per cent level.

Table 3.2 *Regression results for the LPE model, 1966–1971*

Industry	No. of firms	Net assets				Fixed assets				Equity assets			
		a	b	SE(b)	$\bar{R}^2$	a	b	SE(b)	$\bar{R}^2$	a	b	SE(b)	$\bar{R}^2$
21 Food	30	0.62	0.99	0.07	0.88	0.91	0.97	0.06	0.88	1.03	0.94	0.08	0.84
23 Drink	49	-0.02	1.04	0.04	0.95	0.22	1.03	0.04	0.94	0.29	1.02	0.04	0.93
26 Chemicals	49	0.18	1.02	0.10	0.69	1.22	0.93	0.04	0.92	0.85	0.95	0.06	0.84
31 Metal manf.	46	1.55	0.87	0.06	0.82	2.02	0.83	0.07	0.77	1.63	0.85*	0.05	0.84
33 Non-elec. eng.	105	0.79	0.95	0.04	0.85	1.41	0.90*	0.04	0.82	0.94	0.93*	0.04	0.86
36 Elec. eng.	55	-0.37	1.10*	0.04	0.93	-0.08	1.08	0.04	0.94	0.08	1.05	0.04	0.92
38 Vehicles	32	0.41	0.98	0.20	0.93	2.46	0.79*	0.06	0.84	2.11	0.80*	0.05	0.89
39 Metal goods	81	0.52	0.98	0.05	0.80	1.27	0.91	0.05	0.81	0.45	0.98	0.07	0.70
41 Textiles	72	0.48	0.97	0.11	0.52	1.50	0.99	0.04	0.92	0.50	0.98	0.03	0.93
44 Clothing etc.	34	1.66	0.83	0.07	0.79	1.55	0.86	0.07	0.82	1.46	0.85	0.09	0.74
46 Bricks etc.	42	1.38	0.90	0.06	0.87	1.51	0.90	0.06	0.82	1.31	0.91	0.05	0.89
47 Timber etc.	31	1.60	0.84	0.09	0.74	1.84	0.81	0.11	0.64	1.26	0.90	0.07	0.84
48 Paper etc.	58	0.90	0.93	0.04	0.89	1.58	0.86*	0.04	0.87	1.08	0.91	0.05	0.85
49 Other manf.	24	1.14	0.92	0.07	0.84	1.22	0.93	0.08	0.82	0.89	0.94*	0.02	0.85
All manufacturing	740	0.85	0.96*	0.02	0.86	1.03	0.94	0.07	0.89	0.91	0.97	0.03	0.86
50 Construction	53	1.20	0.92	0.08	0.71	1.70	0.87	0.08	0.70	0.90	0.96	0.08	0.82
70 Transport	20	0.16	1.05	0.08	0.91	0.19	1.06	0.08	0.90	0.47	1.02	0.09	0.88
81 Wholesale	81	0.36	1.01	0.05	0.84	1.20	0.93	0.05	0.80	0.55	0.99	0.05	0.81
82 Retail	87	1.09	0.92	0.03	0.92	0.78	0.97	0.04	0.89	0.90	0.95	0.03	0.92
88 Misc.	40	0.92	0.96	0.07	0.83	1.23	0.94	0.06	0.85	1.50	0.90	0.08	0.76
All non-manufacturing	281	0.94	0.97	0.03	0.82	1.06	0.95*	0.02	0.84	0.86	0.96*	0.02	0.84
All industries	1021	0.70	0.96*	0.02	0.79	1.10	0.93*	0.01	0.86	0.86	0.94*	0.02	0.76

For notes see Table 3.1

Table 3.3 Regression results for the LPE model, 1972–1976

Industry	No. of firms	Net assets				Fixed assets				Equity assets			
		a	b	SE(b)	$\bar{R}^2$	a	b	SE(b)	$\bar{R}^2$	a	b	SE(b)	$\bar{R}^2$
21 Food	20	1.39	0.89*	0.04	0.96	1.03	0.97	0.06	0.93	0.83	0.99	0.07	0.92
23 Drink	39	0.92	0.96*	0.02	0.98	0.78	0.99	0.03	0.96	1.00	0.97	0.03	0.96
26 Chemicals	40	1.15	0.96	0.04	0.95	1.52	0.93	0.04	0.92	1.29	0.96	0.04	0.95
31 Metal manf.	33	1.36	0.93	0.04	0.95	1.59	0.92	0.04	0.93	1.23	0.95	0.05	0.91
33 Non-elec. eng.	77	1.43	0.92	0.04	0.86	1.46	0.92	0.05	0.84	1.41	0.93	0.04	0.86
36 Elec. eng.	44	0.42	1.01	0.14	0.56	0.91	0.98	0.04	0.94	0.90	0.99	0.03	0.96
38 Vehicles	26	1.25	0.92	0.06	0.89	1.24	0.94	0.04	0.96	1.59	0.90	0.07	0.87
39 Metal goods	59	0.93	0.98	0.03	0.94	1.39	0.97	0.04	0.93	1.11	0.97	0.03	0.95
41 Textiles	60	1.17	0.93*	0.03	0.95	0.87	0.98	0.02	0.97	1.38	0.92*	0.03	0.93
44 Clothing etc.	27	2.28	0.82*	0.06	0.88	1.72	0.89	0.06	0.89	1.69	0.91	0.06	0.90
46 Bricks etc.	44	1.04	0.96	0.04	0.95	0.92	0.97	0.05	0.89	1.28	0.95	0.04	0.91
47 Timber etc.	22	1.06	0.96	0.13	0.73	0.80	1.01	0.08	0.87	0.60	1.04	0.09	0.88
48 Paper etc.	52	0.63	0.99	0.03	0.95	0.81	0.99	0.04	0.94	0.97	0.97	0.04	0.91
49 Other manf.	26	1.99	0.85*	0.06	0.88	1.87	0.88	0.07	0.87	2.36	0.82*	0.07	0.85
All manufacturing	587	1.13	0.95*	0.02	0.86	1.19	0.97	0.08	0.95	1.10	0.94	0.08	0.87
50 Construction	50	1.84	0.83	0.07	0.76	1.25	0.96	0.07	0.80	1.96	0.88	0.07	0.75
70 Transport	13	2.31	0.82	0.10	0.85	1.18	0.96	0.05	0.97	2.11	0.84*	0.07	0.92
81 Wholesale	62	2.22	0.85*	0.05	0.82	2.10	0.87*	0.05	0.82	2.23	0.86*	0.05	0.80
82 Retail	63	1.43	0.92	0.05	0.82	1.06	0.98	0.04	0.91	1.66	0.92	0.05	0.87
88 Misc.	49	0.63	1.00	0.06	0.85	0.52	1.03	0.08	0.87	0.71	0.99	0.05	0.41
All non-manufacturing	237	0.79	0.97	0.08	0.87	1.31	0.95*	0.02	0.87	1.78	0.90*	0.04	0.66
All industries	824	1.29	0.93*	0.01	0.85	1.24	0.95*	0.01	0.91	1.71	0.90*	0.02	0.78

For notes see Table 3.1

would be inappropriate). By an appropriate transformation of equation 3.2, we obtained an equation with homoscedastic error terms. The results obtained using this exercise showed that the main conclusions reached above continue to hold (see Kumar, 1984c).

A second qualification concerns the use of OLS in testing the relationship. The procedure adopted has been widely used in the literature (see, for example, Smyth *et al.*, 1975, and Singh and Whittington, 1975). In a recent paper, Chesher (1979, pp. 404–408) has argued however that OLS estimation of equation 3.2 may be inappropriate. This is because serial correlation in the error term in equation 3.2 induces dependence between $S_{i,t-1}$ and $\epsilon_{i,t}$ which may render OLS estimators of β inconsistent. This may happen even when, as in the above case, estimation is done using cross-sectional data. The results are, however, only affected significantly if the period over which the analysis is undertaken is short. This is demonstrated in Kumar (1984c) where it is also shown that the general conclusions reached above about the negative (albeit weak) relationship between size and growth of firms, continue to be valid even when serial correlation is taken into account.

Three earlier studies support the above result. Smyth *et al.* (1975), in an investigation for 1971–1973 of five hundred of the largest firms, found a mild negative relationship between size and firm growth. Meeks and Whittington (1976), in a study of the financing of quoted companies, also examined their growth. They considered three groups of companies defined by ranking the population for each of the two periods, 1948–1964 and 1964–1971, and dividing it into thirds on the basis of opening size: high, middle and low. For the period 1964–1971, which corresponds roughly with our second period (1966–1971), they found that the average annual growth rates (using net assets) of the low, middle and high thirds were 14.7 per cent, 9.9 per cent and 10.9 per cent respectively (p. 14). These results can be consistent with a slight negative relationship between size and growth over the *full* range of company sizes for the period 1964–1971. Finally, Aaronovitch and Sawyer (1975b) examined the relationship for the largest, mainly quoted companies for the period 1958–1965. They also found a mild negative relationship between firm size and growth.

Two other studies reach different conclusions. Samuels and Chesher (1972, p. 46) considered a sample of 183 companies which survived over the period 1960–1969. In a regression analysis, they found that for 1960–1965, there was a negative relationship (significantly different from unity) between size and growth, but that there was a positive relationship for 1965–1969, although this was not significantly different from unity. Two factors may be responsible for the difference between these results and ours, for the second period. First, the population of firms used above is different from that used by Samuels and Chesher to select their sample, since they considered firms surviving over a longer time period. Second, the period for which the analysis is done is also different. It is not clear, however, why these factors should exert a systematic influence one way or the other.

Another factor, that due to using the DI Databank, may however provide a more plausible explanation. This is discussed in relation to the second of these two studies, which reached a conclusion different from the first conclusion above. Meeks and Whittington (hereafter MW), in a study in 1975 on the financing of 'giant' companies, had examined the growth of the largest firms against the rest of

Table 3.4 *Size and growth: alternative populations*

	a	b	SE(b)	$\overline{R}^2$	No. of firms
Population surviving 1966–1969					
Manufacturing firms	0.02	1.02*	0.006	0.96	1215
All firms	0.03	1.02*	0.005	0.95	1693
Population surviving 1966–1971					
Manufacturing firms	0.39	0.98*	0.009	0.94	740
All firms	0.43	0.98*	0.008	0.94	1021

Note: * denotes significantly different from unity at the 5 per cent level.

firms surviving over the period 1964–1969. Growth was measured by change in net assets as a percentage of opening net assets. Using the DI Databank they found that the average growth rate of the largest firms considerably exceeded that for the rest of the population. In their 1976 study MW reconcile the results of their two studies in the following way:

> the present [1976] study does not reverse this [the 1975b] result; rather, the results reported here supplement those of the 'giant' companies study. What these results can add to the earlier picture is that the mass of non-giant firms, formerly treated as a homogeneous group, is in fact very heterogeneous. Within this group, the smallest firms performed the best in terms of growth: the medium-sized performed less well in these respects. (Meeks and Whittington, 1976).

Whilst our results support this explanation in part, it is likely that there is another factor responsible for the difference in part between MW's 1976 study and our results for the period 1966–1971 on the one hand, and MW's 1975b study on the other. This factor is the inclusion in the latter study of a large number of firms which were not in the other two. Since MW's 1976 study considered the period 1964–1971, and we studied the period 1966–1971, firms which were taken over in the years 1970 and 1971 were automatically excluded from these. In addition, at the end of 1969 the DI excluded some 350 firms from its population on criteria based on size and gross income – these firms are thus not included in our study, or in MW's 1976 study, but *would* be included in MW's 1975b study.

To isolate the influence of these firms and possibly to reconcile the results of various studies a further exercise was carried out: we compared growth in the period 1966–1969 of all quoted firms which survived from 1966 to 1969 (the first half of our second sub-period) to growth in the period 1966–1969 for firms which survived the whole of the period 1966–1971. A regression equation similar to that used above (equation 3.2) was reestimated. The results given in Table 3.4 are very interesting and seem to confirm the explanation based on the difference in the two populations.

The first half of Table 3.4 reports estimates using the population of *all* firms which survived the period 1966–1969. The estimate of the coefficient *b* is significantly greater than unity for all firms, as well as for firms in the manufacturing sector. If one were to consider just these results one would conclude that in this period there was a mild tendency for larger firms to grow faster than small ones. This would thus tend to support MW's 1975b study. However, as the second half of the table shows, if one considered only the population of firms which survive the period 1966–1971, then for these firms over the same period (1966–1969) the larger firms grew more slowly than the smaller ones. These results thus support those obtained here for the period 1966–1971, as well as those obtained by MW in their 1976 study. This exercise demonstrates that the apparent conflict between our results and those obtained in other studies for the period 1966–1971, as also the conflict between these other studies themselves, is due mainly to using different populations of firms. The earlier conclusion, therefore, has to be qualified in the following sense: the negative size-growth relationship in the second period is for the population of companies *continuing* in the DI Databank for the period 1966–1971.

3.3 Variation and persistency in firm growth

3.3.1 Variation in firm growth

Next consider the relationship between the dispersion of growth rates and firms size. This is of considerable interest in its own right, as well as forming a part of the LPE as noted above, and as an indicator of the degree of heteroscedasticity affecting the estimate of the relationship between growth and size. One might expect large firms to have more uniform growth rates than small firms, for the following reasons:

(i) Large firms are likely to be more diversified and this would allow them to offset an adverse growth rate in one market against a good performance in another. As noted in Chapter 1, a large firm may also find it easier to diversify to maintain its growth (if its main industry was not growing fast enough) (see Utton, 1979). On the other hand, to the extent that diversification may lead to growth occurring in a variety of activities which persistently expanded at different rates, this might actually lead to greater inter-firm dispersion amongst large firms which were classified as belonging to the same *industry*, such a classification being less relevant for a diversified firm.[4] One would, therefore, expect to find a less systematic reationship between the dispersion of growth and size at the industry level, than when firms are pooled across all industries.

(ii) There may be other reasons for large firms exhibiting lower dispersion of growth between firms (or indeed through time), in so far as they may have similar managerial motivations and internal organisational structures, with possibly greater risk aversion.

The evidence on the dispersion in growth rates was examined by computing the standard deviation of growth rates for firms in each of a number of discrete size classes. The results are shown in Table 3.5. The standard deviation generally declines with an increase in firm size in all three periods, although the decline is

Table 3.5 *Mean and variation in growth by opening size class*

Opening size class	1960–1965			1966–1971			1972–1976		
	n	m	s	n	m	s	n	m	s
≤0.5m	291	13.3	14.7	144	15.0	20.4	17	32.6	13.9
≤ 1m	439	9.0	13.8						
≤ 2m	375	7.7	7.8	236	9.3	13.6	126	23.6	13.9
≤ 4m	268	8.2	8.4	242	9.4	14.8	203	20.6	14.2
≤ 8m	164	8.7	8.3	164	10.5	20.4	176	17.1	13.5
≤ 16m	84	8.4	7.0	89	10.0	10.3	118	17.4	11.5
> 16m	126	8.3	6.6	146	9.2	10.0	184	15.8	10.0
All firms	1747	9.2	11.1	1021	10.4	15.7	824	19.0	13.2

Notes: n = number of firms.
   m = mean growth rate (% per annum).
   s = standard deviation of the growth rate.

not monotonic. The Welch–Aspin test (see Chapter 4, n. 5) was used to examine the hypothesis of homogeneity – it was rejected at the 1 per cent level for the first two periods, and at the 5 per cent level for the third period.

To check the possibility of aggregation bias, the relationship was also examined in several of the individual industries. In most, the variation in growth rates in the largest size classes was less than that in the smaller ones, but the results were not statistically significant.

The second prediction of the LPE, that the dispersion of growth rates in different size classes is the same, is thus also rejected. In view of the earlier arguments, this was an expected result. An interesting extension, however, relates to the following. If a large firm was merely a group of smaller subsidiary companies operating independently of each other, then the mean-value theorem shows that the standard deviation of the holding company's growth would be inversely proportional to the square root of its size (cf. Prais, 1976). In fact, in none of the individual industry groups nor in 'all industries' together, does the standard deviation decline with an increase in firm size as fast as suggested by the theorem. This result is similar to that obtained by Singh and Whittington (1975) in their study of firms in the 1950s. However, in so far as diversification has increased substantially since then, and in so far as changes in the internal organisation of firms have in general given the operating divisions of diversified companies greater autonomy (Channon, 1973), this is a somewhat surprising result. It suggests that despite these recent developments the notion of firm as an integrated unit remains useful. That is, an analysis focusing on the behaviour and performance of firms is likely to be more appropriate than one focusing on their separate divisions or subsidiaries.

Table 3.5 also shows a comparison of the mean growth rates for different size classes. This yields additional information concerning the earlier conclusion about the relationship between growth and size and shows that the mild negative relationship found earlier is not continuous. For 1960–1965 and 1966–1971, it is only the first two size classes that have much higher growth rates from the rest. For size classes 3–7 there is no systematic relationship. The last period is different. There is a much stronger systematic relationship here across the 7 size classes.

3.3.2 Serial correlation in firm growth

Do firms which have high (or low) growth in one period also tend to have high (or low) growth in subsequent periods? The LPE in its strongest form implies no such serial correlation. However, several of the managerial models of firm growth incorporate assumptions of 'steady state' equilibria in which firms 'choose' long-run stable growth paths, the precise magnitude depending on managerial utility functions and on the constraints present (see Marris, 1979). These models suggest a high degree of serial correlation. It may also be argued that firms may have some assets, such as a particularly capable managerial team or access to technological or marketing information, which enable them to attain high growth in one period and which might well also enable them to attain high growth in subsequent periods.

The hypothesis that the growth of a company reflects its past growth is not satisfactory as an explanation because it does not indicate *why* the growth rate is as it is. But although it cannot tell us which factors determine the rate of growth, it can tell us how persistent those factors are. It may be that persistency of growth includes both factors causing it to increase and others causing it to decrease. However, a knowledge of the degree of persistency of growth does provide some information about the nature of these factors, since some might be expected to be more persistent than others.[5]

To test the hypothesis of serial correlation, we need to specify the period over which growth is measured. We have taken growth over a medium-run period – future growth is measured over the period 1966–1971 (or 1972–1976), and past growth is measured over the period 1960–1965 (or 1966–1971). These periods have the advantage of averaging out short-term fluctuations in growth rates. The disadvantage is that any systematic trend in growth within the 6-year periods 1960–1965 or 1966–1971 is ignored. In other words, there could be an alternative hypothesis that growth say from 1972 to 1976 is explained by growth from 1966 to 1971, plus an indicator of the direction of the trend in growth during 1966 to 1971. This hypothesis could be tested by introducing growth for shorter periods into the analysis. It should be noted that in the present cross-sectional framework, the analysis is undertaken across firms within individual industries and, therefore, it considers the growth of each individual firm relative to the average for the industry in the given time period. The attempt is, therefore, to explain the deviation of the firm's growth from the industry average in the later period.

The following equation was fitted by OLS to the data:

$$g_{i,t} = \alpha + \beta g_{i,t-1} + \epsilon_{i,t} \qquad (3.3)$$

where $g_{i,t}$ denotes the average annual growth of the ith firm over the period 1972–1976 (or 1966–1971) and $g_{i,t-1}$ denotes growth over the period 1966–1971 (or 1960–1965).[6] The results, given in Table 3.6, show that there is some relationship between relative growth rates of firms over succeeding time periods. Consider first the periods 1960–1965 and 1966–1971. Growth in the first period provides merely a 3 per cent explanation of the variance of growth in the second period ($\bar{R}^2 = 0.03$) for all manufacturing firms together, and 2 per cent ($\bar{R}^2 = 0.02$) for all firms. But within manufacturing, there is a considerable heterogeneity; for example, in the case of Vehicles and Textiles past growth has notable explanatory power. For non-manufacturing as a whole, and for individual industries within it, the variance explained by past growth is negligible.

The parameter β, relating growth in one period to growth in the next period, is significant for a number of industries and for all industries together. The significant value of β, 0.27, in Textiles indicates, for example, that a growth rate of 1 percentage point above average in the first period was associated with a growth rate 0.27 percentage points above average in the second period. There is a non-significant negative value of β for Chemicals, Clothing and footwear, Bricks etc., and Paper in manufacturing, and for Construction, Wholesale, and Miscellaneous Services in non-manufacturing.

The pattern for the periods 1966–1971 and 1972–1976 is somewhat similar to that for the first two periods. The variance in growth in the third period explained by growth in the second period is again small (2 per cent) for the population of all firms. Interestingly, however, there are some notable difference in both the value of $\bar{R}^2$ and β coefficients across industries between the two sets of time periods. For example, in contrast to the first two periods, in Chemicals the β coefficient is positive and statistically significant, with $\bar{R}^2$ a value of 0.16.

So whilst there is some tendency for above average growth of individual firms to persist throughout either of the two sets of periods in certain industries, there is no systematic strong relationship. Even where the regression coefficient is positive and significant, its value is never greater than unity, indicating that there was a tendency for growth to regress towards the mean.

3.4 Growth and profitability: some theoretical considerations

The previous sections have shown that size and past growth have no strong influence on the average growth of companies. As noted in the first chapter, there are a large number of other factors which would be expected to exercise an influence: a firm's current market environment, past decisions regarding investment in physical assets, in research and development and in advertising, the internal organisation of the firm, managerial response to constraints and opportunities. All these factors, and many others, would affect a firm's growth. There are, of course, a number of variables which could reflect or capture the influence of one or more of these factors. One of the more important ones is firm profitability. As well as acting as a surrogate for a number of other factors, it also exercises an independent influence on growth. Consider the likely direction, and the magnitude of this influence. In the perfect competition framework, firms would grow only in order to reach the 'optimum size' at which they maximise profits, and so in equilibrium there is, in fact, no expectation of any relationship between profitability and growth

40

Table 3.6 *The persistency of firm growth*

Industry	I 1960–1965 and 1966–1971					II 1966–1971 and 1972–1976				
	No. of firms	a	b	SE(b)	$\overline{R}^2$	No. of firms	a	b	SE(b)	$\overline{R}^2$
21 Food	24	4.75	0.46	0.36	0.07	18	13.0	0.10	0.11	0.05
23 Drink	43	5.74	0.07	0.15	0.01	37	9.4	0.28*	0.10	0.19
26 Chemicals	41	8.08	-0.09	0.18	0.01	33	13.8	0.27*	0.11	0.16
31 Metal manf.	39	3.81	0.39	0.22	0.08	27	15.4	-0.01	0.10	0.001
33 Non-elec. eng.	88	4.87	0.17*	0.08	0.05	65	15.1	0.05	0.16	0.002
36 Elec. eng.	47	6.45	0.12	0.11	0.02	39	12.8	0.14	0.14	0.03
38 Vehicles	28	5.31	0.29*	0.12	0.18	20	9.3	0.13	0.27	0.01
39 Metal goods	75	3.20	0.32*	0.14	0.07	54	16.5	0.45*	0.14	0.02
41 Textiles	65	3.00	0.27*	0.09	0.13	56	16.7	0.15	0.10	0.04
44 Clothing etc.	31	6.11	-0.16	0.10	0.08	19	13.8	0.07	0.18	0.01
46 Bricks etc.	36	11.29	-0.13	0.16	0.02	37	11.8	0.19	0.10	0.10
47 Timber etc.	24	2.34	0.29	0.18	0.10	20	14.7	0.28	0.30	0.05
48 Paper etc.	53	6.43	-0.02	0.13	0.00	45	12.3	-0.24	0.13	0.07
49 Other manf.	23	6.51	0.61*	0.21	0.03	23	10.2	0.51*	0.25	0.10
All manufacturing	635	5.06	0.17*	0.04	0.03	510	13.0	0.14*	0.04	0.03
50 Construction	30	8.71	-0.01	0.34	0.00	31	22.0	-0.35*	0.14	0.18
70 Transport	18	8.84	0.03	0.19	0.002	13	15.4	-0.24	0.31	0.05
81 Wholesale	56	7.34	-0.02	0.08	0.00	54	18.9	0.14	0.17	0.01
82 Retail	67	4.00	0.13*	0.06	0.07	56	9.9	0.71*	0.24	0.14
88 Misc.	26	6.90	-0.01	0.11	0.001	30	7.8	0.24	0.15	0.08
All non-manufacturing	197	6.40	0.04	0.05	0.005	184	15.5	0.07	0.09	0.003
All industries	832	5.50	0.12*	0.03	0.02	694	13.6	0.13*	0.04	0.02

Notes: In I, only firms surviving over the period 1960–1971 are examined; in II, only those surviving over the period 1966–1976. * denotes significantly different from 0 at the 5 per cent level.

Fig. 3.1 *The relationship between growth and profitability*

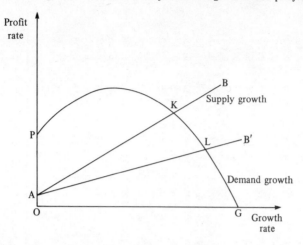

simply because firms will not be growing. If, however, some firms are not in equilibrium but are assumed to be moving towards it, there may be some relationship
between growth and profitability in a cross section of firms. However, the precise
nature of this relationship seems to be in general indeterminate, depending on the
causes of disequilibrium and the speed of adjustment (see Marris, 1964, Ch. 1).

A more fruitful approach lies in the framework studied earlier, where one can
relate the role of profitability to a firm's ability and willingness to grow. The ability
to finance growth is related to a firm's profitability for two reasons. First the higher
the level of profitability, the more would the firm be in a position to grow from
retentions. Second a high level of current profitability may be taken by potential
investors as an indication that the future level of profitability will be high, so the
firm will be able to raise external funds on favourable terms. (These are the reasons
assumed by Marris (1964) for the direct relationship between profitability and
growth summarised by his 'supply-growth' curve noted above.)

A firm's willingness to grow may not depend entirely on profitability. Profitability would provide an incentive for growth, but there are other factors, such as
technological opportunities, the preferences of consumers, the degree of competition and the quality of management, which will also exert an influence. For
example, for the same rate of profit, a firm operating in an industry with buoyant
demand may be expected to grow more than a firm which operates in an industry
with static demand.

This brings us to a consideration of Marris's 'demand growth' curve. It has an
inverted U shape: the demand growth–profitability relation is expected to be
positive in the lower range of growth rates, but negative in the upper range. At low
growth, an increase in growth causes profitability to rise; above a certain growth
rate, however, increases in the growth cause profitability to decline (this is due to
additional demand generating expenditures and managerial constraints – see
Chapter 1). The simultaneous relationship between growth and profitability is
summarised in Fig. 3.1.

It is generally argued that a scatter of observations on the growth and profit
rates of firms will trace not the 'demand growth' curve but the 'supply-growth'

curve, AKB. This is because all firms are thought to face a common capital market which sets a limit on attainable growth for a given profit rate. Two related factors determine this limit (cf. Meeks, 1977, p. 26): the proportion of profit that is retained, and the quantity of external finance that the market will subscribe on acceptable terms as a proportion of current profit. It is argued that this limit is similar for most quoted firms.

The factors which affect a firm's capacity to grow are thought to vary in different industries at different time periods. These factors may also for example be different for large and small firms in the same industry. Marris (1967) therefore argued that there is greater variance of the error term in the 'demand growth' relationship as compared with the variance of the error term in the 'finance limit' one. Hence a scatter of observations would identify the conventional profitability to growth relationship.[7]

There is some evidence, however, which suggests that all quoted firms may not face the same limit on the growth which may be achieved for a given profit rate. The Wilson Report (1980) noted that institutional investors such as pension funds and insurance companies favoured larger firms; earlier, Meeks and Whittington (1975b) had shown that the largest firms were able to rely more on the capital market even though their profitability was lower than that of the rest (see also Kumar, 1983). In terms of Fig. 3.1, this suggests that the 'supply-growth' curve for larger firms may move to the right as compared to that for the smaller firms. In this case, if we examine a cross section of firms, the positive relationship between growth and profitability may be dampened, or indeed obscured, because of the concomitant movement of the 'supply-growth' curve. (In terms of the above diagram there may be several 'supply-growth' curves which together with varying 'demand growth' curves generate a scatter of observations of the form which may not allow us to identify the relationship uniquely.) To see if this may have been the case, we carry out regression analysis using a model which provides estimates of the overall growth–profitability relationship, as well as the relationship for large and small firms separately.

3.5 Growth and profitability: empirical analysis
The main equation tested was the following:

$$g_{i,t} = \alpha + \beta p_{i,t} + \epsilon_{i,t} \tag{3.4}$$

This tests the hypothesis that growth rate is a linear function of profitability. This has the advantage over any logarithmic formulation in that it can be applied to the full population of firms.[8] The results are presented in Table 3.7. The impression for the first period is that current profitability has a positive influence on current growth, i.e. β is positive and it is statistically significant in 16 of the 19 industries. The degree of variation explained by profitability varies considerably from negligible in Food and Drink to nearly fifty per cent in Chemicals and Other manufacturing. In general the explanatory power of profitability is higher for manufacturing than for non-manufacturing firms.

In the second period there is some change from this pattern. The regression coefficient is smaller in 12 of the 19 industries, with a negative sign in one. It is significant in only 14 industries. Further $\bar{R}^2$ generally has a lower value for manu-

Table 3.7 *The impact of profitability on growth*

Industry	1960–1965					1965–1971					1972–1976				
	No. of firms	a	b	SE(b)	$\bar{R}^2$	No. of firms	a	b	SE(b)	$\bar{R}^2$	No. of firms	a	b	SE(b)	$\bar{R}^2$
21 Food	53	0.07	0.21	0.20	0.02	30	0.26	-0.63	0.93	0.02	20	0.10	0.53*	0.21	0.26
23 Drink	67	0.07	0.09	0.14	0.01	49	-0.03	0.72*	0.28	0.11	39	0.02	0.67*	0.22	0.20
26 Chemicals	77	-0.10	0.52*	0.06	0.49	49	-0.01	0.70*	0.13	0.37	40	0.08	0.63*	0.13	0.40
31 Metal manf.	88	-0.04	0.72*	0.11	0.33	46	0.06	0.39	0.44	0.02	33	0.70	0.63*	0.10	0.55
33 Non-elec. eng.	194	0.00	0.55*	0.09	0.16	105	0.03	0.37*	0.11	0.10	77	0.01	0.97*	0.20	0.24
36 Elec. eng.	89	0.03	0.38*	0.11	0.12	55	0.09	0.14	0.17	0.01	44	0.04	0.54*	0.08	0.55
38 Vehicles	51	-0.01	0.68*	0.15	0.28	32	0.03	0.51*	0.15	0.27	26	0.07	0.54*	0.07	0.69
39 Metal goods	135	0.02	0.37*	0.07	0.20	81	0.04	0.32*	0.14	0.06	59	0.07	0.62*	0.17	0.19
41 Textiles	177	-0.01	0.63*	0.08	0.26	72	0.03	0.45	0.28	0.03	60	0.03	0.71*	0.09	0.53
44 Clothing etc.	60	-0.01	0.51*	0.12	0.22	34	-0.14	1.25*	0.23	0.48	27	0.06	0.58*	0.25	0.18
46 Bricks etc.	85	0.09	0.70*	0.16	0.18	42	-0.06	1.25*	0.32	0.28	44	-0.02	1.06*	0.15	0.53
47 Timber etc.	50	-0.02	0.68*	0.11	0.43	31	-0.07	0.49*	0.15	0.28	22	1.0	0.46*	0.15	0.31
48 Paper etc.	91	0.05	0.20*	0.08	0.06	58	0.03	0.36*	0.10	0.19	52	0.04	0.61*	0.11	0.36
49 Other manf.	50	-0.03	0.69*	0.10	0.49	34	0.04	0.42*	0.18	0.14	26	0.02	0.75*	0.12	0.61
All manufacturing	1308	0.01	0.51*	0.03	0.21	740	0.03	0.44*	0.06	0.07	587	0.06	0.63*	0.04	0.33
50 Construction	56	0.04	0.38*	0.13	0.15	53	-0.01	0.81*	0.25	0.17	50	0.07	0.81*	0.20	0.25
70 Transport	39	-0.07	1.23	0.30	0.31	20	0.04	0.40	0.23	0.15	13	0.02	0.84*	0.25	0.50
81 Wholesale	155	-0.01	0.56*	0.09	0.22	81	0.03	0.54*	0.09	0.31	62	0.06	0.75*	0.16	0.26
82 Retail	123	0.02	0.56*	0.23	0.04	87	-0.01	0.51*	0.08	0.30	63	-0.01	0.96*	0.15	0.40
88 Misc.	66	0.07	0.33*	0.15	0.07	40	-0.11	1.72*	0.36	0.38	49	0.11	0.36*	0.15	0.11
All non-manufacturing	439	0.02	0.51*	0.08	0.09	281	-0.02	0.74*	0.09	0.21	237	0.06	0.71*	0.08	0.27
All industries	1747	0.01	0.51*	0.03	0.16	1021	0.02	0.52*	0.05	0.10	824	0.06	0.67*	0.03	0.31

Note: * denotes significantly different from 0 at the 5 per cent level.

facturing firms, and a higher value for non-manufacturing firms. The constant term (α) reflecting variations both in the regression coefficient and in the average profitability of different industries, is also different in a large number of cases between the two periods.

The pattern in the most recent period is closer to the first period. The value of the coefficient is quantitatively greater than in the second period in 12 industries, and it is the same in 2 others. More importantly, the coefficient is statistically significant in all industries. Further, whilst there is still a noticeable diversity in the degree of variation in growth rates across firms which can be explained by profitability, in general the explanatory power is greater. For all firms it is over three times as great, whilst compared to the first period it is nearly twice as great. The difference in the explained variations in firms in manufacturing and non-manufacturing industries is the smallest of the three periods, although the actual coefficient is only slightly smaller for manufacturing firms.

Some extensions. The above regression analysis is based upon the hypothesis of a linear relationship. As the results indicate, it gives a reasonable fit for the first and the third period. Mainly for the second, but also for the other two, it is possible that there is a non-linear relationship between current growth and current profitability so that the specification is incorrect. A simple test of non-linearity can be obtained by scatter diagrams, which were drawn for a number of industries. In general they did not indicate that a non-linear function would fit the data better.

More interestingly results were also obtained for the regression equation 3.4 using two separate sets of firms – the largest, and the rest combined – for each of the three periods. The results indicated that the hypothesis noted in Section 3.4, that the 'supply-growth' curve may differ between the largest firms and the rest, finds some support. For each of the two sets of firms the degree of variation in growth rates explained by profitability was considerably greater than when all firms are considered together. For example, for 1966–1971, for firms greater than £16m in 1966, $\bar{R}^2$ was 0.18, and for the rest 0.16. For 1972–1976, $\bar{R}^2$ had values of 0.38 and 0.46 respectively.

3.6 The birth and death process

The analysis in the previous sections has been confined to companies continuing in the DI databank. In this section we carry out an investigation into companies which 'died' (i.e. disappeared from the population) or which were 'born' (added to the population) during the period under consideration. This investigation is interesting in its own right, but also has a direct bearing on the stochastic framework used earlier, as well as a bearing on the cases of increases in concentration. The evidence given in Table 3.8 refers to a limited range of births and deaths, i.e. companies which were born in 1960–1965 (or 1966–1971) and subsequently continued throughout the period 1966–1971 (or 1972–1976), and companies which died in 1966–1971 (or 1972–1976) and had previously continued throughout the period 1960–1965 (or 1966–1971). They show a number of important features of the birth and death process:

(i) In both time periods, the majority of deaths occurred in smaller size classes and the incidence of death declines almost systematically with an increase in firm

Table 3.8 *Births and deaths of firms, all industries*

A 1960–1971

Size in 1960(a)	1 Deaths 1966–71	2 Births 1960–65	3 Net change (Col.2–Col.1)	4 Cont.(b) 1960–71	5 Col.1 as % of Col.4	6 Col.2 as % of Col.4	7 Deaths by takeovers	8 Col.7 as % of Col.4	9 Col.7 as % of Col.1
<1/2m	70	10	-60	71	98.6	14.1	61	85.9	87.1
<|V| 1m	129	52	-77	150	86.0	34.7	108	72.0	83.7
V| 2m	139	57	-82	186	74.7	30.6	117	62.9	84.2
V| 4m	112	36	-76	149	75.2	24.2	90	60.4	80.4
V| 8m	63	17	-46	100	63.0	17.0	53	53.0	84.1
V| 16m	29	12	-17	55	52.7	21.8	19	34.5	65.5
V| 32m	20	1	-19	77	26.0	1.29	17	22.8	85.0
>| 32m	15	2	-13	44	34.0	4.54	5	11.4	33.3
Total	577	187	-390	832	69.4	22.5	470	56.5	81.4

Table 3.8 Continued.

B 1966-1976

Size in 1966(a)	10 Deaths 1972-76	11 Births 1966-71	12 Net change (Col.11-Col.10)	13 Cont.(b) 1966-76	14 Col.10 as % of Col.13	15 Col.11 as % of Col.13	16 Deaths by takeovers	17 Col.16 as % of Col.13	18 Col.16 as % of Col.10
<1/2m	6	0	-6	5	120.0	0	5	100.0	83.3
≤ 1m	34	10	-24	57	59.6	17.5	25	43.9	73.5
≤ 2m	53	41	-12	129	41.1	31.8	38	29.5	71.7
≤ 4m	48	35	-13	169	28.4	20.7	38	22.5	79.2
≤ 8m	27	20	-7	137	19.7	14.6	19	13.9	70.4
≤ 16m	22	14	-8	66	33.3	21.2	10	15.2	45.5
≤ 32m	8	2	-6	62	12.9	3.2	6	9.7	75.0
> 32m	6	8	2	69	8.9	11.6	4	5.8	66.7
Total	204	130	-74	694	29.4	18.9	145	20.9	71.0

Notes: 'Deaths' exludes those firms removed from the DI population on size criteria.
(a) Measured by net assets.
(b) Firms continuing in the DI Databank.

47

size (see columns 5 and 14). (It should be emphasised that the deaths category excludes those companies which were removed from the DI databank on the basis of size criteria, e.g. in 1969. Thus this category includes only those companies which actually ceased to exist as independent entities.)

(ii) The majority of deaths were due to takeovers. For instance, in the period 1966–1971, of the 577 deaths, over 80 per cent were due to takeovers. Whilst in 1972–1976 this proportion was lower, they still accounted for over 70 per cent of the disappearances. Although the incidence of death due to takeovers also declines almost systematically with size, a more significant finding is that this incidence as a proportion of total deaths exhibits no such relationship. Some earlier studies had led us to expect that the proportion of deaths by takeover would be smaller for larger firms as compared to smaller firms (for a further discussion, see Hughes, 1978). Thus in the first period, for firms with an opening size of less than £1 million in 1960, the proportion of deaths due to takeovers is almost the same as the proportion in the £4–8 million size class or the £16–32 million size class. In the second period there is a tendency for this proportion to decline with size but it is by no means pronounced. The exception to this are the firms in the largest size class. In the first period, the proportion for these firms is considerably lower than that for smaller firms but in the second period this difference is not so pronounced.

(iii) As columns (2) and (11) indicate, whilst there are some births in the larger size classes the majority occur in smaller size classes, although by no means the smallest. This is partly due to the fact that quoted companies are often in existence as unquoted companies for a number of years before achieving a quotation and so being born into the population. Again, this is because new quoted companies are often formed as a result of mergers; thus the new company will be as large as the sum of the merging companies. (Companies are 'born' into the DI population only periodically in the rebasing years, e.g. 1969, 1973. This does not, however, affect the averages over the period.)

(iv) There was a serious net impact of births and deaths on the company population. As a proportion of continuing companies, there was a net loss in both time periods. In the first period it amounted to nearly 46 per cent (net change as a percentage of continuing firms) and in the second period 12 per cent. It was spread more or less evenly over all size classes except the smallest in the first period and, in addition, the smallest but one in the second period, in which there was a much higher net loss.

3.7 Summary of main findings

This chapter has investigated a number of issues bearing upon the interrelationship between the size, growth and profitability of firms. The main findings can be summarised as follows:

(i) A detailed regression analysis showed a mild negative relationship between size and growth. Further the larger size classes were shown to have a somewhat lower mean growth rate than firms in the smaller size classes. This finding suggests a revision of an important conclusion of some studies in this area – that during the last two decades the larger firms in the UK have been growing faster than small ones.

(ii) The dispersion of growth rates declined with an increase in size. This confirms findings for an earlier period.

(iii) The degree of persistency, examined over two sets of time periods, is quite low and in some industries absent altogether.

(iv) The relationship between growth and profitability was much weaker than expected, with profitability explaining, on average, less than a third of the variation in growth rates. The results showed however that there were significant differences in the regression coefficients relating profitability to growth in different industries and over different time periods.

(v) The relationship between growth and profitability was reexamined separately for the largest firms, and for the rest. The results showed that the variation in growth rates explained by profitability was considerably increased, lending support to the hypothesis of the variation in 'supply-growth' curve for quoted firms of different sizes.

(vi) An analysis of the births and deaths showed that a high proportion of deaths occurred due to takeovers, and that the incidence of death, whether or not due to takeovers, declined sharply with an increase in firm size. Although the incidence of birth declines with firm size, a number occur in all size classes. The impact of the birth and death process together was a high net loss of companies in the period 1960–1971, and somewhat smaller net loss in the period 1966–1976.

The growth–profitability relationship indicates that although profitability is important there are a number of other important factors influencing growth. As the correlation analysis in Chapter 2 suggested, another possibility is that profitability may influence one main component of growth – that due to new investment – more heavily than the other main component – that due to acquisition. This strongly suggests that one should study these two main components of growth separately. Even from the point of view of the size–growth relationship, it would be interesting and useful to investigate the relationship of size with alternate forms of growth. We attempt to carry out these two exercises and further extensions of them in the next chapter.

4

Methods of growth

This chapter extends the analysis in Chapter 3, which studied firms' growth as a whole, by distinguishing between growth by new fixed investment and growth by acquisition. An examination is undertaken of the relative importance of these two forms of growth, and of the relationship between them. Whilst the intense acquisition activity in the UK during the last two decades has prompted a large literature on the motives for merger and their implication for firms' efficiency, as well as their impact on industry and overall concentration, there has been surprisingly little published on the relationship between acquisition and investment. The investigation in this chapter attempts to fill part of this gap by studying the following issues: the average contribution of the two forms of growth to firms' total growth in the period 1960–1976; the relationship between size and acquisition growth; the impact of profitability and acquisition on new fixed investment; the relationship between acquisition growth and external growth (for the distinction between these see Section 4.5); and the persistency of both forms of growth.

In an earlier study, the Monopolies Commission (1970) provided evidence of a positive relationship between size and acquisition activity. This study suffers from methodological biases which are discussed later. Meeks and Whittington (1975b) also provided incidental evidence on this which suggested a positive relationship. The investigation below, whilst presenting new evidence, also reconciles these studies. Meeks (1977) has evidence on the third issue – we extend his analysis by examining the impact of acquisition on investment taking into account the impact of profitability.

The rest of this chapter is arranged as follows: Section 4.1 discusses some aspects of the choice between acquisition and investment growth. Section 4.2 provides evidence on growth by acquisition and by new investment, whilst Section 4.3 discusses the relationship between profitability and the two forms of growth. Section 4.4 distinguishes growth by acquisition from external growth, whilst Section 4.5 provides evidence on serial correlation between the two forms of growth. Section 4.6 provides a summary.

4.1 Investment and acquisition: *a priori* considerations

What factors determine the choice between internal and external growth? If a firm undertakes the expansion of its assets, by say setting up a new plant, it entails not only the planning and commissioning of new capacity, but also the hiring of a new management team and other personnel, as well as the allocation of resources needed to market the products. If the firm has insufficient funds, recourse to the capital market would also be required. On the other hand, if a firm purchases another firm, it will acquire not only the production capabilities but also the labour resources and the product markets of the acquired firm. This process may be much quicker and less risky than the first one (cf. George and Joll, 1981).

However, there are a number of important considerations which militate against acquisition as a method of expansion. These relate to the valuation of the acquired firm and its, and the acquirer's, particular circumstances. Assessing the purchase price of a firm is a much more complex and hazardous matter than assessing an internal investment project: it is different in degree and also in kind (see Merret and Sykes, 1965). This is so for the following reasons: it is rare to find a firm suitable for acquisition which has exactly the assets desired, neither more nor less. Almost all firms engage in more than one simple activity. When investing in an internal investment project, a firm can often avoid expanding into activities which it has not chosen. A related problem is that the assets of a going concern usually include goodwill, which gives the concern value over and above the value of its physical assets, but which is by no means easily quantifiable. This is seldom the case with any internal investment project.

This suggests that there may have to be considerable technical and marketing appraisals of the acquired firm to disclose its long-term prospects. Past performance is not necessarily the best guide to future potential. Obviously in this respect there may be considerable risks involved. A major factor is the wrong timing of an acquisition. Management may make the error of acquiring a firm when the demand for its products has just passed its peak – that is when the financial results are brightest. An equally bad error might be made when the development of the products is so early that acquisition is premature.

Existing firms always embrace established contractual obligations or traditional obligations to customers, suppliers and, of course, personnel. Certain customers may have received special terms, and to terminate them might prove costly in terms of public relations, yet to continue them may cause the existing customers of the acquiring firm to object to what they consider discrimination. The relationship with suppliers can be similarly complicated. Acquisitions may also entail special problems with regard to personnel. If acquisition involves significant redundancies, the question of compensation arises (whether from a moral or a legal obligation). The question of redundancy may also arise within the acquiring firm if some of the staff of the acquired firm are more capable or experienced. This problem can also arise with internal investment, say because of greater mechanisation, but it seldom arises in such an acute form, or with so many people (and no people with whom the firm's personnel department is unfamiliar).

Other major problems arising with acquisitions are the settling of outstanding financial obligations, and arranging the form of purchase, the rights of existing shareholders and so on. There is the basic problem of settling the terms of the acquisition itself, whether the shares will be paid for in cash, or with the shares of the purchasing firm, or some combination of the two. These complications do not exist in the case of internal investment. Consideration must also be given to the tax consequences of acquisitions, which are often considerable. The tax consequences of internal investment are usually straightforward and limited to obtaining some sort of investment allowance or accelerated depreciation.

Apart from these considerations which need to be fully examined when undertaking any acquisition, for the following types of expansion internal investment would in any case be the most appropriate: that which is stimulated by the prospect of introducing new products or of using new technology already developed by the expanding firm, and that which arises from special know-how in the organisation of production and in the operation of particular processes. Large firms in particular, undertaking their own research and development, may develop new products and technological processes which may only be best exploited if the firm itself undertakes new investment; this may indeed decrease their desire to grow through acquisition. Similarly, the introduction of new activities into new geographical areas may require new investment (see Parker, 1978).

What is likely to be the relationship between acquisition growth and firm size? To the extent that there are high fixed costs involved in undertaking technical, marketing and financial appraisals, large firms may be more active than smaller firms. They may also have greater organisational resources and may be able to exploit more fully the assets of the acquired firm. But even if large firms do make more acquisitions than smaller firms, it need not mean that acquisition is a more important source of growth for them than for small ones. In general, of course, it can be argued that the larger the acquiring firm in relation to the acquired firm, the less the managerial difficulties of integration; conversely, for a given amount of expansion through acquisition, the smaller the acquiring firm, the greater proportionately the managerial input required to incorporate the acquired firm. But the larger the number of firms to be acquired in a given period, the greater again the effort to discover and to assimilate their operations.

Penrose argues (1959, p. 212) that acquisition as a means of increasing growth may become, after a point, less important. As a firm's size increases, larger firms, or a larger number, have to be acquired to maintain a given growth rate. There would be an increasing scarcity of large firms that can be acquired and the consequent difficulties of discovering suitable small firms in sufficient numbers and absorbing them. Thus the possibility of acquisition may raise the maximum rate of growth for medium-sized and moderately large firms but will probably become less important for the very large firms.

4.2 Size, investment and acquisition

A description of firms' growth by acquisition and by new fixed investment is given in Table 4.1. For each of the three periods, we have computed the average growth rates for all firms in individual industries as well as for the main sectors. Consider, for example, Chemicals: for the 77 firms which continued in independent existence in the first period, the average growth by acquisition was 2.7 per cent per annum, and that by new fixed investment 4.1 per cent per annum (see row 3). In the second period, the number was reduced to 49 firms which had an average growth by acquisition of 3.9 per cent and by new investment of 4.5 per cent.

The noticeable feature of this table is the sharp increase in growth by acquisition relative to new investment in the period 1966–1971. In the first period, the latter was greater in most industries and this is reflected in the average acquisition growth of all firms being 3.4 per cent per annum compared to investment growth of 4.5 per cent. In the third period a similar pattern is found. However, in the second period,

Table 4.1 Growth by acquisition and by new fixed investment, 1960–1976

Industry	1960–1965					1966–1971					1972–1976				
	No. of firms	Acqui-sition	S.D. acqui-sition	Inve-stment	S.D. inve-stment	No. of firms	Acqui-sition	S.D. acqui-sition	Inve-stment	S.D. inve-stment	No. of firms	Acqui-sition	S.D. acqui-sition	Inve-stment	S.D. inve-stment
21 Food	53	4.9	8.0	4.8	5.7	30	11.0	39.7	4.9	4.5	20	3.1	3.8	5.0	6.9
23 Drink	67	2.1	4.5	5.2	3.8	49	2.7	9.4	3.3	2.5	39	1.0	2.8	5.7	3.8
26 Chemicals	77	2.7	5.4	4.1	4.5	49	3.9	18.1	4.5	4.7	40	3.1	6.8	5.2	6.7
31 Metal manf.	88	3.0	6.8	4.7	5.8	46	6.8	22.3	4.3	4.8	33	3.1	4.4	5.0	5.5
33 Non-elec. eng.	194	2.9	9.3	3.4	4.9	105	3.9	7.3	2.9	3.4	77	4.6	11.0	2.9	4.1
36 Elec. eng.	89	3.8	9.8	3.6	3.7	55	5.2	11.2	3.2	4.1	44	3.5	12.5	3.9	5.0
38 Vehicles	51	3.5	6.0	3.9	4.8	32	4.3	7.1	4.3	6.3	26	1.5	4.6	4.5	6.0
39 Metal goods	135	3.1	5.3	4.4	4.5	81	4.0	8.0	2.9	4.1	59	4.4	8.1	4.2	3.0
41 Textiles	177	3.3	8.0	2.9	3.7	72	4.0	7.7	3.4	3.4	60	2.1	3.9	3.4	4.4
44 Clothing etc.	60	4.5	9.6	3.6	4.5	34	5.1	13.7	2.0	4.2	27	6.5	14.6	3.8	3.9
46 Bricks etc.	85	5.6	9.3	8.5	7.8	42	8.1	12.6	5.0	5.6	44	2.1	3.8	5.8	7.0
47 Timber etc.	50	1.9	3.4	4.2	6.3	31	3.2	6.5	4.9	5.5	22	3.2	6.7	7.0	4.9
48 Paper etc.	91	2.8	6.1	4.6	4.5	58	2.7	5.3	2.7	5.6	52	3.0	5.0	4.1	8.0
49 Other manf.	50	2.6	5.8	3.6	5.6	34	5.3	10.5	4.7	4.9	26	4.5	7.4	5.3	6.4
All manufacturing	1308	3.26	7.51	4.17	5.07	740	4.66	13.46	3.54	4.57	587	3.37	7.96	4.51	5.49
50 Construction	56	2.0	5.1	4.5	5.6	53	8.1	20.1	5.3	8.5	50	5.2	12.1	7.9	7.4
70 Transport	39	3.9	8.0	5.9	6.1	20	4.3	7.6	5.6	4.9	13	3.4	5.3	8.6	7.4
81 Wholesale	155	3.0	7.4	3.7	5.8	81	4.5	6.6	4.5	7.0	62	5.1	11.5	6.9	7.6
82 Retail	123	5.3	18.0	5.8	8.3	87	2.8	5.5	4.2	7.5	63	3.4	9.5	7.5	9.9
88 Misc.	66	4.9	8.5	10.1	12.8	40	11.2	28.7	7.5	6.4	49	6.9	13.8	5.7	13.8
All non-manufacturing	439	3.87	11.44	5.55	7.36	281	5.49	14.96	5.04	7.30	237	4.92	11.40	7.10	9.70
All industries	1747	3.41	6.54	4.51	6.04	1021	4.91	13.89	3.95	5.50	824	3.82	9.11	5.27	7.07

Note: Acquisition and investment growth are average % per annum.

Table 4.2 *The effect of size on growth by acquisition*

	I			II			III		
	No. of firms	b	SE(b)	No. of firms	b	SE(b)	No. of firms	b	SE(b)
1960–65									
Manufacturing	1308	−0.21	0.15	1308	0.14	0.16	873	−0.91*	0.20
Non-manufacturing	439	−1.18*	0.46	439	−0.15	0.07	287	−2.21*	0.63
All industries	1747	−0.42*	0.16	1747	0.08	0.16	1160	−1.20*	0.21
1966–71									
Manufacturing	740	−0.17	0.37	740	0.03	0.11	510	−0.83	0.47
Non-manufacturing	281	−1.35	0.72	281	0.04	0.06	193	−2.37*	0.99
All industries	1021	−0.48	0.33	1021	0.02	0.09	703	−1.21	0.43
1972–76									
Manufacturing	587	−0.63*	0.23	587	−0.18	0.52	407	−1.26*	0.29
Non-manufacturing	237	0.33	0.60	237	0.11	0.11	173	−0.50	0.74
All industries	824	−0.43	0.23	824	−0.13	0.39	580	−1.11*	0.30

Note: * denotes significantly different from 0 at the 5 per cent level.

in most industries and in the aggregate, firms' acquisition growth exceeded that by new investment for an average of *six* years. Although it is well known that this period saw intense acquisition activity, the evidence presented in Table 4.1 is nevertheless remarkable for its pervasiveness.

The variation around the average for acquisition growth is generally greater than that for growth by investment. This illustrates the propensity of firms in a cross section to vary relatively more in their reliance on acquisition. The relative variation seems particularly marked in the non-manufacturing sector in the first period, and in most industries in the second period. Further, the distribution by acquisition is more skewed. For firms in each industry, and for the aggregate, a simple measure of skewness was calculated (the so-called third moment).[1] For all firms in the first period, skewness for acquisition was 6.54 and that for investment 2.96. For the second and third periods the values were 7.05 and 1.55, and 4.51 and 0.88, respectively.

Next, consider the extent to which growth by acquisition was undertaken mainly by large firms.[2] If it was mostly undertaken by large firms, one would have to discover the factors favouring their ability and willingness to grow by this method. This has been examined firstly by regression analysis. The following equation was fitted:

$$g_{i,t}^A = \alpha + \beta \log S_{i,t-1} + \epsilon_{i,t} \qquad (4.1)$$

where $g_{i,t}^A$ denotes acquisition growth of the ith firm during period t, $S_{i,t-1}$ denotes the size of firm at the beginning of period t and $\epsilon_{i,t}$ is the stochastic error term; α and β are the parameters. This semilogarithmic equation rests on the hypothesis that a given *proportionate* change in opening size causes the same absolute change in acquisition growth for *all* sizes of firm.[3]

The results are given in section I of Table 4.2. There is in general a negative relationship between opening size and acquisition growth. This is statistically significant in three cases but the degree of explanation provided by size (as measured

54

by $\bar{R}^2$ – not reported here) was very low, seldom being greater than 2 per cent. Nevertheless eight out of the nine values in this section are negative, indicating that acquisition growth tended if anything to decline with size.

An interesting question arises as to the *proportion* of growth undertaken by acquisition by firms of different size. Even if in absolute terms it was negatively related, if larger firms relied proportionately more on acquisition, there could be a positive relationship. This was tested using the same equation in Table 4.1, but this time replacing absolute acquisition growth by acquisition growth as a proportion of total growth.

The results using this variable are shown in section II of Table 4.2. There is a reversal in the pattern found above. In the second period the sign is reversed for the population of all firms whilst for the other two periods there is either a reversal or at a minimum an increase (the absolute value of the coefficient is lower). The results suggest that in general the larger firms relied relatively more on growth by acquisition as a proportion of total growth than the smaller firms but, rather surprisingly, in absolute terms this ranking was reversed. The degree of variation in acquisition growth as a proportion of total growth explained by firm size was again very small – under 2 per cent in most cases.

Finally we examined this relationship by reestimating the original equation, but with a restricted population. The new population consisted of only those firms which undertook at least one acquisition. This reduced the number by over a third in the first two periods, and by somewhat less in the third period.[4] The results are in section III. Compared to section I, the value of the regression coefficient is lower, and although the degree of variation in acquisition explained by size was not much improved, the coefficient itself is significantly different from zero in most cases. These estimates indicate that amongst the smaller firms, there is likely to be a greater proportion which undertake no acquisitions at all. However, when a comparison made between those which do undertake some acquisition, smaller firms are more active than larger firms.

Next we investigated whether there are any marked non-linearities by computing acquistion growth for firms in different size classes. In addition we have computed growth by new fixed investment (Table 4.3). Consider the period 1972–1976. As section C indicates, the smallest but one size class has an edge over the bigger firms, for *both* forms of growth. (The smallest size class has only a few observations.) These firms had an average growth of 4.6 per cent by acquisition and 7.0 per cent by new investment, against the average for all of 3.8 per cent and 5.3 per cent respectively. A similar pattern was found in the first two periods. During 1960– 1965, companies with assets of less than £1/2m excelled others in both forms of growth, whilst during 1966–1971 companies with assets of less than £1m were in that category. (The smallest size classes were combined because of the small number of observations.)

There is a non-linear relationship between size and the other two variables. During 1972–1976, firms in the £8–16 million size class had higher growth by both variables than the size classes on either side, but lower than say the firms in the £1–2m size class. The statistical significance of the differences in size classes was tested by using the Welch–Aspin test.[5] This showed that, apart from the smallest size class, there were no significant differences between the average growth rates in other size classes.

Table 4.3 *Ranking of the two forms of growth by firm size*

Opening size class	A 1960–1965					B 1966–1971					C 1972–1976				
	No. of firms	Acquisition m	s	Investment m	s	No. of firms	Acquisition m	s	Investment m	s	No. of firms	Acquisition m	s	Investment m	s
≤ 0.5m	291	5.2	13.0	6.8	8.8	144	7.2	19.0	6.6	7.7	17	7.4	13.2	9.1	4.7
≤ 1m	439	3.5	10.3	4.3	6.2										
≤ 2m	375	2.7	5.8	3.7	5.0	236	4.2	12.8	4.0	5.4	126	4.6	10.8	7.0	9.2
≤ 4m	268	2.7	6.1	4.1	4.8	242	4.5	11.9	3.8	5.3	203	4.0	10.4	5.7	6.3
≤ 8m	164	3.2	6.8	4.7	5.3	164	5.2	18.2	2.5	4.0	176	3.5	9.3	4.4	7.5
≤ 16m	84	3.2	4.5	3.4	3.3	89	4.2	8.1	3.8	5.8	118	3.6	7.1	5.1	7.8
> 16m	126	3.0	4.7	3.8	3.6	146	4.5	8.9	3.3	3.1	184	3.1	6.4	4.0	4.9
All firms ≤ 16m	1621	3.4	8.9	4.6	3.8	875	5.0	14.5	4.1	4.8	640	4.0	9.7	5.6	7.5
All firms	1747	3.4	8.7	4.5	6.0	1021	4.9	13.9	4.0	5.5	824	3.8	9.1	5.2	7.1

Notes: m = average growth rate (% per annum).
        s = standard deviation.

So whilst there is a non-linearity it is not statistically significant. When one compares the largest size class with the rest, in all three periods, and for both variables, the rest of the firms do somewhat better (although the difference is not significant).

It may be worth summing up the results of this section at this point: we have shown that average growth by acquisition was very high, and that in the period 1966–1971 it exceeded growth by investment. There was no evidence, however, that acquisition growth was positively related to firm size.

Two earlier studies came to rather different conclusions regarding the latter finding. The Monopolies Commission's Survey (1970) investigated, *inter alia*, the importance of mergers in the period 1954–1965 and concluded that they played a relatively greater role in the growth of the largest companies. The population of firms consisted of the quoted companies with the same characteristics as those of our population. The methodology used by the survey, however, gives rise to a systematic bias. As Utton (1972) argued, the survey falls into the 'regression fallacy' ('regression' as used in its original Galtonian sense). This is the result of using end-year rankings for the comparison of total as well as of acquisition growth for companies of different sizes. The largest group when ranked by end-year size is likely to contain some companies who achieved their ranking by merger as well as those who kept their place or who grew rapidly by internal means. Other size groups will contain, in addition to medium or fast-growing firms (previously in lower size classes), those of slow growth who are unlikely to have made many acquisitions.

Therefore this methodology is likely to yield a spurious positive association between size and dependence on merger. Utton used a sub-sample of the top 320 quoted firms to re-examine the issue – but this time ranking firms according to their opening size. Arranged this way he found an inverse correlation between opening size and growth by merger (rank correlation coefficient of -0.50).

There is also a difference between our results and those obtained by Meeks and Whittington (1975b) (MW). We have already noted in Chapter 3 the reasons for the discrepancy in growth of net assets. Similar reasons may hold for the present discrepancy. MW show that the largest firms in 1948 which survived the period 1948–1964 had a slightly lower acquisition growth compared to the rest of the population (1.9 per cent for the 'giants'; 2.0 per cent for the rest (MW, p. 380, Table 2)). However, for 1964–1969 the 'giants' had acquisition growth of 5.4 per cent compared to 3.7 per cent for the rest.

There are two differences between their analysis for 1964–1969 and ours. First they consider the largest 100 in 1964 which survived till 1969 – this gives 75 firms which are compared with 1620; second their period starts two years before our second period and it also ends two years earlier. Because their period ends in 1969, a number of the smallest firms which were excluded in that year on the size criterion would still be part of their population, as well as the firms taken over in 1970–1971, whereas both these groups of firms are excluded from our sample.

This second difference is similar to that noted in Chapter 3, and a similar exercise was carried out to allow for it. We examined the population surviving the period 1966–69 and reconsidered the size–acquisition growth relationship by regression analysis. The results now indicated a slightly lower negative relationship compared to that obtained in Table 4.2 for the period 1966–1971. To see the effect of the first difference, we selected the continuing firms which had opening assets greater than £32 million in 1966 – the largest 76 firms. These were compared with the rest – in all 945 firms. For both sets average acquisition growth was calculated. Surprisingly, the results were very similar – 4.94 per cent for the largest and 4.86 per cent for the rest. (However the standard deviation for the two sets of firms was 8.8 per cent and 14.2 per cent respectively. The difference in this was significant at the 1 per cent level.)

Taking the very largest firms, therefore, and considering the period 1966–1969 accounts for part of the discrepancy between our results and those of MW. One explanation for the remaining discrepancy may lie in the different time period. It is possible that the activities of the 'giants' and the 'rest' in the years 1964 and 1965 exercised a sufficiently strong influence to make the reliance of the giant companies on acquisition greater than that of smaller companies. (This seems plausible since MW find an average of 5.4 per cent for their largest firms of 1964–1971 as opposed to our 4.94 per cent for 1966–1971.)

This exercise also supplements earlier results – Table 4.3 showed that firms with assets greater than £16m (the largest 126 firms) had average acquisition growth of 4.5 per cent during 1966–1971. These results suggest that this set consists of two groups – and that the group of the very largest firms relied considerably more on acquisition than the second group.

These results have a number of implications for size and acquisition activity. The literature on the separation of ownership from control suggests that larger firms are likely to be much more managerially controlled than smaller firms.[6] The motivation of these firms is often assumed to be quite different from the owner-controlled ones, with managers placing more emphasis on size and growth than on profitability as such. This is partly because whilst the influence of profitability on managerial remuneration (and prestige etc.) is not negligible, size and firm growth play a greater role (Meeks and Whittington, 1975a; Cosh, 1978). Our results suggest that whilst management in the larger firms may indeed gain proportionately more from acquisition (*via* an increase in size and growth), there are a sufficient number of other factors which lead smaller firms to engage in similar, if not greater, acquisition activity in relation to their size. In this context, it would be interesting to consider the direction of acquisition activity, horizontal or non-horizontal, across firms in different size classes, and also the proportion of acquisitions which occur outside the domestic economy. We provide some evidence on horizontal acquisitions in the next chapter; unfortunately there is little information by size class on foreign acquisitions. Some aggregate data are provided in the *Business Monitor, MQ7 Series* (third quarter, 1981, Table 4). It shows that whilst the acquisition expenditure overseas was a small proportion of total expenditure in the period 1969–1976 it was not negligible (the average was of the order of 5 per cent). In recent years, however, the proportion has been much higher – about 15 per cent in 1980. This is an interesting development and it is explored further in Chapter 9 where we discuss the foreign production activities of UK firms.

4.3 Profitability and the two forms of growth

This section investigates two related issues: first, the relationship between profitability and the two forms of growth and, second, the impact of acquisitions and profitability on new fixed investment.

Consider first the impact of profitability on growth by acquisition. Do firms which have above average profitability also tend to have above average acquisition growth? In a cross section, there are a complex of factors linking these two variables. Acquisitions would be expected to affect firms' future profitability, as well as to be affected by past profitability. They may lead to a certain relaxation of the growth–profitability trade off; the constraint on management may be relaxed, fewer 'growth promoting' expenditures may have to be incurred, and so on. But in view of the considerations noted in Section 4.1 this is likely to differ considerably according to such factors as the firms' management, market opportunities, the responses of competitors, etc. It may be argued, however, that profitability may exert a more systematic influence on acquisition (cf. Chapter 3 on the growth–profitability relationship in a cross-section analysis). Firms with above average profitability, if it is due to greater productive efficiency, may be more willing and able to acquire less efficient firms in the expectation of improving their efficiency. Even if profitability is the result mainly of monopoly power, the capital market may be more willing to supply funds, if it takes current profitability as an indication of future performance. Higher profitability, by obtaining higher market valuation for shares, may also exercise a positive influence.[7]

The following equation was used to test the influence of profitability:

$$g_{i,t}^A = \alpha + \beta P_{i,t} + \epsilon_{i,t} \tag{4.2}$$

where α and β are the parameters, $g_{i,t}^A$ denotes growth by acquisition, $P_{i,t}$ denotes the firm's profitability and $\epsilon_{i,t}$ is the error term. It is worth noting that, as for the earlier analysis, both profitability and acquisition growth are averages over at least five years. Profitability is therefore likely to be an average of pre-merger and post-merger values. (In order to estimate the effect of acquisitions on profitability, pre-merger and post-merger values have to be distinguished. This is attempted in the next chapter.) The results are given in Table 4.4. The coefficient b is positive and significantly different from zero for the first two periods, whilst in the last period it is only just positive for firms in the manufacturing industries.

In most cases the value of b is small. For example, for the second period it is 0.21 – indicating that across firms an increase in profitability of 1.0 per cent was associated with acquisition growth of 0.21 per cent. Further, the degree of variation explained by profitability is very small – the maximum $\bar{R}^2$ being 0.07 per cent for non-manufacturing firms in the second period; this suggests that there are other variables which collectively exert a more important influence on acquisition growth.

Next consider the influence of profitability on new fixed investment. Here it seems more likely that a higher degree of variation in new investment across firms would be explained by profitability. This is because there would be a more direct influence on investment. Internal funds play an important role in financing new investment (see, for example, Kaldor, 1972; and Thomas, 1978) and profitability may be a rough indicator of the ability of the firm to finance it by retentions.

This was examined by reestimating equation 4.2, but replacing $g_{i,t}^A$ with growth by investment (Table 4.4). The coefficient b is positive and significantly different from zero at the one per cent level in all cases. Furthermore, the degree of variation in investment growth explained by profitability, although still small, is considerably greater than for acquisition.

Table 4.4 *The effect of profitability on new fixed investment and on acquisition*

	No. of firms	Acquisition			Investment		
		b	SE(b)	$\overline{R}^2$	b	SE(b)	$\overline{R}^2$
1960–1965							
Manufacturing	1308	0.10*	0.02	0.01	0.22*	0.01	0.14
Non-manufacturing	439	0.14*	0.07	0.01	0.26*	0.05	0.07
All industries	1747	0.11*	0.02	0.01	0.23*	0.02	0.11
1966–1971							
Manufacturing	740	0.21*	0.05	0.02	0.17*	0.02	0.13
Non-manufacturing	281	0.40*	0.09	0.07	0.30*	0.04	0.16
All industries	1021	0.27*	0.04	0.04	0.21*	0.02	0.14
1972–1976							
Manufacturing	587	0.01	0.03	0.001	0.09*	0.02	0.03
Non-manufacturing	237	-0.04	0.06	0.001	0.21*	0.03	0.11
All industries	824	-0.02	0.02	0.001	0.18*	0.02	0.08

Note: * denotes significantly different from 0 at the 5 per cent level.

The above two exercises have allowed us to distinguish the differential impact of profitability on acquisition and investment and provided hitherto unavailable evidence on this. This is important in its own right, but it is also necessary for the analysis we next undertake into the effect of acquisition on new investment.

4.4 Acquisition and investment: cross-sectional analysis

In analysing business behaviour, it is important to consider whether firms undertaking investment and acquisition do so as alternative or complementary activities. If it turns out that there is a trade-off between them, one may be able to make some inferences about the managerial and financial constraints facing the firms. As noted in Chapter 1, the issue is also important from the point of view of the economy as a whole. Growth of the economy results mainly from new investment undertaken, and not from the transfer of assets from one firm to another. Further, as Kaldor (1959) and Salter (1966) emphasised, new vintage capital stock is the main vehicle for technical change for improving factor productivity. Kalečki (1971) also noted the important role which 'embodied' technical change plays in generating economic growth.[8]

It may be argued that both acquisition and investment are likely to compete for various resources, and if they can both satisfy firms' objectives equally, there may be substitution between them. The elasticity of substitution may be higher, the lower the degree of specificity of resources at the firm's disposal. For example, if funds raised from a particular source can be used equally well for the two activities, there may be a strong trade-off between them.

However, the differences in the nature of the two activities suggest that this need not be so. Acquisition brings with it managerial resources, and whilst the acquiring firm may have to devote some effort to assimilating these resources, this need not deter investment. (It may be perfectly rational, even from a profit maximising point of view, to make an acquisition without assimilating the new operations, e.g., to take advantage of a larger financial unit – see Lynch, 1971). As regards finance, if acquisitions were financed by cash outlays, they might pre-empt funds available for new investment. However, during the period under consideration, acquisitions have been undertaken mainly by share exchange. This may not reduce the existing liquidity and it may not affect the ability of the firm to raise new funds (see Chapter 7 for further discussion). More positively, there are dynamic factors suggesting complementarity between the two activities. If acquisition leads to a decline in the uncertainty which may have been inhibiting investment, there may be a positive relationship between the two (Kamien and Schwartz, 1972).[9] Similarly, a risk-averse firm may prefer to undertake diversification *via* acquisition and, once it is more familiar with production and marketing in its new industry, may proceed with new investment, which in the absence of acquisition might not have been forthcoming from either firm (cf. Chung and Weston, 1981. For the role of merger in diversification, see Cowling *et al.*, 1980; and Goudie and Meeks, 1982).

The theoretical expectations are therefore compatible with the absence of any trade-off between the two activities. The rest of this section and Chapter 5 investigate this issue empirically. It must be emphasised that there are two, albeit related, questions here. The first is, given a cross section of firms, do those with above average acquisition growth also have above average investment growth? If the firms have a similar willingness and ability to grow by both means, we can estimate from cross-sectional observations their reliance on the two forms of growth. However, these do differ across firms. It is possible, to some extent, to taken into account factors reflecting differential ability. A cross-sectional regression analysis can then provide a reasonable estimate of the possible investment–acquisition trade-off.[10]

The second question is more direct: what is the *effect* of acquisition on new investment? To clarify the difference between the two questions, note that a positive cross-sectional relationship between acquisition and investment need not imply that the impact of the former upon the latter is positive. A firm may undertake above average of both because it possesses, say, capable management, or some other superior asset; yet had it *not* undertaken acquisition, investment could have been higher still. This second question we examine in Chapter 5. Here we study the cross-sectional relationship.

It might be argued that rather than consider the relationship with net investment, a better variable would be gross investment. In an inflationary environment with growth, depreciation provisions typically finance not just the replacement of the retired capital stock but also contribute towards new capital (Meeks, 1974). Net investment (gross investment *minus* depreciation provisions) may therefore give an underestimate of the new capital stock being created. In Chapter 5 we indeed carry out the bulk of the analysis using gross investment. Here we continue to use net investment. One reason for this is that in considering firms' *growth*, it is the net addition to capital stock which is relevant. Further, Meeks (1977) has estimates of the acquisition–gross investment relationship for a period which corresponds with our second period. Although our analysis is somewhat different from his, it is, nevertheless, useful to enquire whether using net investment complements his results.

The equation used to examine this is the following:

$$g_{i,t}^I = \alpha + \beta g_{i,t}^A + \gamma P_{i,t} + \epsilon_{i,t} \tag{4.3}$$

Here α, β and γ are the parameters of the equation. $g_{i,t}^I$, $g_{i,t}^A$ and $P_{i,t}$ denote investment, acquisition growth and profitability respectively, of firm i in period t. $\epsilon_{i,t}$ is the error term. The rationale for introducing $P_{i,t}$ is this: we have seen that it exerts a considerable positive influence on investment. Since it varies greatly across firms the ability to finance investment may also vary; it is appropriate therefore to take explicit account of this. The model was estimated using OLS for firms in individual industries as well as for the aggregate.

The results are given in Table 4.5. Consider the period 1960–1965. The noticeable feature is the positive sign of the coefficient b, indicating the absence of any trade off between acquisition and investment. For firms in the chemical industry (Industry 26), for example, b has a value of 0.26 and it is statistically significant. Profitability is also significant and in addition the degree of variation explained by the equation is quite considerable (30 per cent). This pattern is repeated across most industries. (The main exception is Industry 21.) In the manufacturing sector as a whole, the explanatory power is almost twice as great as was obtained with profitability alone.[11] Over all, the results for the first period indicate that, in a cross section of firms, above average acquisition growth and profitability were associated with above average investment growth.

For the second period the evidence is more complicated. Although b is still positive for firms in most industries, its value is smaller and it is statistically significant in only eight industries. $\bar{R}^2$ is also in general lower. The effect of profitability, however, is still positive and significant. These estimates indicate that although there is no evidence of any substitution, the degree of complementarity obtained earlier is not maintained. One speculative explanation is that in a period of rapid acquisition growth such as 1966–1971, the constraints on firms do become more important than in a period of mild growth. There may thus be a threshold above which acquisition and investment growth cease to be complementary.[12]

A similar situation pertains for the last period. Here b is negative for firms in five industries, although it is statistically significant for only two. There is a significant positive association for six industries (out of 19) as well as for the manufacturing sector, and for all firms taken together. Whilst the average rate of merger activity in this period was considerably lower, the pattern of financing of acquisition was rather different. (The impact of this on investment is examined in Chapter 6.) A higher proportion of acquisitions were financed by cash, rather than by share exchange. This may have pre-empted funds for new investment.

Table 4.5 *The impact of acquisition and profitability on new fixed investment*

Industry	1960–1965					1966–1971					1972–1976				
	b	SE(b)	c	SE(c)	$\bar{R}^2$	b	SE(b)	c	SE(c)	$\bar{R}^2$	b	SE(b)	c	SE(c)	$\bar{R}^2$
21 Food	-0.02	0.09	0.37*	0.11	0.18	-0.06	0.02	0.21*	0.08	0.47	-0.33	0.38	0.37*	0.15	0.31
23 Drink	0.06	0.11	0.14*	0.09	0.04	0.02*	0.04	0.15*	0.07	0.12	-0.05	0.14	0.27*	0.14	0.05
26 Chemicals	0.26*	0.09	0.16*	0.05	0.30	0.05	0.04	0.12*	0.05	0.29	0.11	0.15	0.20*	0.10	0.28
31 Metal manf.	0.23*	0.08	0.27*	0.06	0.30	0.02	0.03	0.27*	0.07	0.25	0.05	0.23	-0.14	0.11	0.08
33 Non-elec. eng.	0.31*	0.03	0.16*	0.03	0.46	0.19*	0.04	0.16*	0.03	0.32	-0.23*	0.04	0.21*	0.06	0.18
36 Elec. eng.	0.10*	0.04	0.15*	0.04	0.23	0.05	0.05	0.07*	0.05	0.05	0.21*	0.06	0.04	0.04	0.28
38 Vehicles	0.36*	0.09	0.23*	0.06	0.48	0.30*	0.14	0.21*	0.08	0.36	0.29	0.23	-0.20*	0.05	0.40
39 Metal goods	0.37*	0.07	0.19*	0.04	0.34	0.08	0.06	0.16*	0.06	0.12	0.07	0.05	0.10*	0.05	0.08
41 Textiles	0.12*	0.03	0.19*	0.03	0.26	0.03	0.04	0.19*	0.05	0.19	0.24	0.14	0.16*	0.07	0.18
44 Clothing etc.	-0.01	0.10	0.24*	0.05	0.31	0.05	0.09	0.27*	0.09	0.24	0.15*	0.04	0.13*	0.06	0.45
46 Bricks etc.	0.27*	0.06	0.12*	0.07	0.25	0.12*	0.05	0.14*	0.09	0.34	0.10	0.21	0.80*	0.14	0.58
47 Timber etc.	0.20	0.19	0.62*	0.17	0.30	0.27*	0.07	0.44*	0.09	0.73	0.45*	0.11	0.11*	0.05	0.58
48 Paper etc.	0.25*	0.08	0.15*	0.06	0.15	0.31*	0.12	0.27*	0.07	0.26	0.21	0.19	0.38*	0.13	0.18
49 Other manf.	0.52*	0.11	0.53*	0.05	0.36	-0.02	0.12	0.25*	0.67	0.35	0.48*	0.16	-0.02	0.09	0.25
All manufacturing	0.22*	0.02	0.19*	0.01	0.25	0.03*	0.01	0.16*	0.02	0.14	0.11*	0.03	0.09*	0.02	0.08
50 Construction	0.15	0.12	0.30*	0.07	0.24	0.09*	0.04	0.17*	0.06	0.21	-0.23*	0.09	0.22*	0.10	0.08
70 Transport	0.74*	0.19	0.19*	0.14	0.67	-0.01	0.27	0.55	0.45	0.16	0.61*	0.29	0.55*	0.15	0.55
81 Wholesale	0.20*	0.06	0.27*	0.06	0.19	0.01	0.10	0.27*	0.08	0.14	-0.03	0.07	0.44*	0.09	0.3?
82 Retail	0.16*	0.03	0.28*	0.06	0.15	0.05	0.13	0.49*	0.07	0.43	0.11	0.12	0.34*	0.10	0.17
88 Misc.	0.40*	0.10	0.26	0.17	0.20	0.13*	0.05	0.42*	0.10	0.14	0.08	0.14	0.34*	0.12	0.14
All non-manufacturing	0.17*	0.03	0.24*	0.04	0.12	0.06*	0.02	0.27*	0.04	0.17	0.03	0.05	0.33*	0.05	0.18
All industries	0.20*	0.02	0.20*	0.01	0.19	0.04*	0.01	0.20*	0.02	0.15	0.08*	0.03	0.18*	0.02	0.05

Notes: Number of firms is as given in Table 4.1. * denotes significantly different from 0 at the 5 per cent level.

63

From the above evidence there is no indication of a general trade-off between the two forms of growth in the period since 1960. There are, however, two caveats which should be noted. First we have considered expenditures on acquisition and investment across firms. In this, we have followed other researchers in this area. However, it is possible that this may exaggerate the positive relationship. This is because a firm which undertakes acquisition will automatically be credited with having carried out new investment, if the *acquired* firm itself carried out invest- ment. This is so since its opening assets are not included in the acquirer's opening assets in the year of acquisition. The greater the value of the acquisition, the higher may be the 'investment' due to such an effect. Since we have examined the invest- ment of the acquiring and acquired firms combined, there may be some positive relationship between the two activities due to this factor alone. In subsequent years the assets of the acquired firm would form part of the denominator, and so the procedure would be quite appropriate. However, since we are averaging over a num- ber of years, it is possible that the bias imparted by the procedure may be of some significance.[13] An additional exercise was therefore carried out which took this into account. For firms in three industries – Chemicals, Electrical and Non-electrical engineering – for 1960–1971, for quoted companies' acquisitions, the assets of acquired firms were added to those of the acquirer and the investment growth variable recalculated. The results showed that the relationship was now weaker – although it was still positive and significant. It should be noted that this procedure assumes that all acquisitions occur at the beginning of the year. Since this is obviously not the case, the procedure is biased *against* finding a positive relation- ship. (It would in fact have been more appropriate to take half of the assets of the acquired company.) Since it does not lead to a reversal of the results, one can be reasonably sure that they do provide an accurate indication of the cross-sectional relationship between the two activities.

As noted at the beginning of this chapter, Meeks (1977) examined the investment– acquisition relationship for the period 1964–1971. His explanatory variable was gross investment, and he did not use profitability as an additional independent variable. Nevertheless, his analysis provided results which are in accord with those obtained above – that there is no evidence of a systematic trade-off between acqui- sition and investment. (This result was not unduly affected by bias in method- ology.)

The results suggest a complex and dynamic process of firm behaviour in which high investment and high acquisition need not be substitutes. However, the empirical methodology adopted above needs to be supplemented before one can accept fully the results based on it. This, together with an analysis of a number of other issues arising from the above discussion, is undertaken in the next chapter.

4.5 Acquisition expenditure and growth by acquisition

A second caveat relates to the following: it may be argued that to dis- tinguish properly between acquisition and investment growth, and to study the association between them, one has to consider not just the initial effect of acqui- sitions, but also their subsequent contribution to firm growth (see Weston, 1957). This is also important when studying the role of mergers in increases in industrial concentration (see George, 1971). The problem arises in making assumptions about the growth rate to credit to acquired assets, since it is virtually impossible to get data on this separately from the growth of the firm as a whole.

One may assume either that a taken-over firm continues to grow at the same rate as when it was independent, or that the acquiring firm exerts some influence and grows at a rate corresponding more to that of the acquirer. Clearly one has to make some assumption in order to trace the impact of this growth. We assumed the latter.

There were three reasons for this. First, we had no data on the past performance of non-quoted acquired firms. Second, for a large number of quoted firms, records for insufficient numbers of years (previous to their acquisition) were available. Even when records were available, it would have been rather arbitrary to choose an average of some years for projecting future growth. Third, it was considered more satisfactory to have some variable which would influence the acquired firm's *current* performance. The current performance of the acquirer would obviously be an important variable.

Using this assumption we calculated the proportion of an increment in assets due to acquired assets and their subsequent growth, and from this a firm's 'external growth' was computed. The procedure is as follows. Let S_t be the assets at beginning of year t and A_t the assets acquired during year t. Let g_t be the rate of internal growth. Then assuming assets are acquired in the middle of the financial year[14] assets at the beginning of the next year, S_{t+1}, would be given by the following expression

$$S_{t+1} = S_t(1 + g_t) + A_t(1 + g_t/2) \tag{4.4}$$

i.e., assets at the beginning of the year consist of two parts: original assets which have increased due to internal growth (first term on the right), and acquired assets themselves (A_t) and increase in them due to internal growth $(A_t(g_t/2))$. Rearranging equation 4.4 gives

$$g_t = (S_{t+1} - S_t - A_t)/(S_t + (A_t/2)) \tag{4.5}$$

To calculate external growth over a period of T years let the assets at the beginning be B_A and at the end E_A. Then *by internal growth* assets at the end of the period I_A would be given by the following:

$$I_A = B_A \prod_{t=1}^{T}(1 + g_t) \tag{4.6}$$

where $\prod$ is the multiplication operator. Once we have calculated assets due to internal growth we can calculate the proportion which is due to acquisitions (acquired *plus* their growth). Denoting this proportion by A_P we have

$$A_P = (E_A - I_A)/(E_A - B_A) \tag{4.7}$$

(i.e. the acquisition proportion over the period is equal to the change in assets over this period due to acquisition divided by the total change in assets). External growth can then be calculated by multiplying the acquisition proportion by total growth; and internal growth is total growth *minus* external growth.

For each firm in the population, and for each of the three periods, we computed the acquisition proportion as well as internal and external growth (see Table 4.6). A comparison of 'external growth' and 'acquisition growth' shows that once growth

Table 4.6 *A comparison of acquisition growth and 'external' growth*

Industry	1960–1965			1966–1971			1972–1976		
	External growth	Acquisition growth	Correl. coeff.	External growth	Acquisition growth	Correl. coeff.	External growth	Acquisition growth	Correl. coeff.
21 Food	5.4	4.9	0.95	10.5	11.0	1.00	4.6	3.1	0.80
23 Drink	2.9	2.1	0.98	3.0	2.7	0.98	2.5	1.0	0.87
26 Chemicals	3.2	2.7	0.94	6.3	3.8	0.79	4.6	3.1	0.74
31 Metal manf.	4.2	3.0	0.93	7.6	6.8	1.00	5.1	3.1	0.90
33 Non-elec. eng.	3.5	2.9	0.95	4.4	3.9	0.99	6.4	4.6	0.98
36 Elec. eng.	4.4	3.7	0.99	3.7	5.2	0.60	5.7	3.5	0.99
38 Vehicles	4.4	3.5	0.96	5.7	4.3	0.98	2.8	1.5	0.95
39 Metal goods	3.8	3.1	0.83	4.9	4.0	0.98	6.5	4.4	0.97
41 Textiles	3.9	3.3	0.97	4.8	4.0	0.96	3.1	2.1	0.94
44 Clothing etc.	5.6	4.5	0.97	6.0	5.1	1.00	8.2	6.5	0.98
46 Bricks etc.	7.0	5.6	0.98	8.7	8.1	0.99	4.0	2.1	0.81
47 Timber etc.	2.9	1.9	0.80	2.0	3.2	0.41	4.7	3.2	0.95
48 Paper etc.	3.7	2.8	0.98	2.7	2.7	0.55	4.9	3.0	0.50
49 Other manf.	3.1	2.6	0.97	6.3	5.3	0.97	7.1	4.5	0.97
All manufacturing	4.01	3.26	0.95	5.16	4.66	0.90	5.13	3.37	0.92
50 Construction	2.1	1.9	0.72	9.3	8.1	0.99	7.8	5.2	0.98
70 Transport	2.1	1.9	0.72	9.3	8.1	0.99	7.8	5.2	0.98
81 Wholesale	4.0	3.0	0.97	5.5	4.5	0.97	7.6	5.1	0.95
82 Retail	6.6	5.3	0.99	3.4	2.7	0.95	6.8	3.3	0.88
88 Misc.	6.2	4.9	0.94	12.2	11.2	0.98	7.6	6.9	0.85
All non-manufacturing	4.89	3.87	0.97	6.51	5.58	0.98	7.26	4.92	0.88
All industries	4.23	3.41	0.96	5.53	4.91	0.92	5.74	3.81	0.89

Notes: External growth takes into account the growth of acquired assets.
Acquisition growth is as before. (Both are % per annum.) No. of firms is as in Table 4.1.

of acquired assets is taken into account, the former is considerably greater than the latter. For example, in 1972–1976 for all firms, average external growth was 5.74 per cent compared to 3.81 per cent for acquisition growth. This result is of significance in examining the role of acquisition in changes in concentration. However, in a cross-sectional framework what is more interesting is the degree of association between these two variables across firms. Spearman's rank correlation coefficient was calculated for each industry, and the results indicated a high degree of association between them (Table 4.6). This suggests that results obtained in Section 4.3 may continue to hold. Whether this is so can be seen by reestimating two of the equations used earlier. Equation 4.1 was reestimated using external growth as the dependent variable, and for equation 4.3 internal growth was used as the dependent variable and external growth as the independent one. In both these cases the earlier results were sustained – there was a negative relationship between size and external growth, and a positive one between internal and external growth.

4.6 Persistency of the two forms of growth

The final question we turn to in this chapter is whether acquisition growth persists over time. For small firms the opportunities for acquisition may be maintained from one period to the next because of an ample supply of suitable 'victims' including new firms which are born into the smaller size classes. For larger firms, however, the availability of suitable firms in their own or allied industries may after a time become a constraint. However, for these firms the possibilities of conglomerate acquisitions, or acquisitions outside the domestic economy, may mean that this constraint need not be too severe. Concerning firms' ability to acquire, there may be learning from experience in searching for opportunities, in financing, as well as in the technique of incorporating the operations of acquired companies. There may not be a continued desire to acquire, however. The results of past acquisitions may have been unsatisfactory; even if they were successful, the firm may subsequently have become more concerned with internal investment, for example to exploit the potential of some newly acquired product, or with process innovation (cf. Mueller, 1969).

Nevertheless, in view of the serial correlation in total growth, the hypothesis of persistency in acquisition is not unwarranted. We tested this using the following equation:

$$g_{i,t}^E = a + b g_{i,(t-1)}^E + E_{i,t} \tag{4.8}$$

Here $g_{i,t}^E$ and $g_{i,(t-1)}^E$ refer to the external growth of a firm in consecutive periods. (External growth is as calculated in the previous section. The results of using acquisition growth were similar and are not reported.) We examined the firms which continued in independent existence at least over either the period 1960–1971, or 1966–1976. The results given in Table 4.7 suggest that external growth does persist over time. Firms which had above average external growth in one period had above average external growth in the subsequent period, although this relationship was significant only for 1960–1971. This is all the more interesting since it is persistence over a medium-run period. It is likely that over shorter periods the relationship would have been stronger still. By the same token, it might be expected that it would be weaker over a longer period. For a sample of firms surviving over the

Table 4.7 *The persistency of the two forms of growth*

	I 1960–1965 and 1966–1971				II 1966–1971 and 1972–1976			
	No. of firms	b	SE(b)	$\bar{R}^2$	No. of firms	b	SE(b)	$\bar{R}^2$
A. ACQUISITION								
Manufacturing	635	0.32*	0.05	0.06	510	0.03	0.03	0.001
Non–manufacturing	197	0.01	0.04	0.001	184	0.10	0.07	0.01
All industries	832	0.17*	0.04	0.03	694	0.05	0.03	0.005
B. INVESTMENT								
Manufacturing	635	0.12*	0.04	0.01	510	0.06	0.06	0.002
Non–manufacturing	197	0.07	0.05	0.01	184	0.43	0.12	0.07
All industries	832	0.10*	0.03	0.01	694	0.20*	0.06	0.02

Notes: In I, only firms surviving over the period 1960–1971 are examined; in
II, only those surviving over the period 1966–1976.
* denotes significantly different from 0 at the 5 per cent level.

period 1960–1976, above average growth in the period 1960–1965 was very weakly related to above average growth in the period 1972–1976.

It is worth noting that for the first period the b coefficient is greater than that found for total growth in Chapter 3 (see Table 3.3). Since the population of firms is the same, this indicates that there may not be *similar* persistency in internal growth. Typically, new investment requires greater gestation lags than does acquisition for producing a given flow of output, and this may lead to firms which have above average new investment in one period not maintaining their ranking subsequently.

We examined this by reestimating equation 4.8 but this time using internal growth. The results given in Table 4.7 section B show this to be the case for the first period; it is not so, however, for the period 1966–1976. Interestingly, firms in non-manufacturing have a high persistency which makes the results for the whole population significant.

4.7 Summary of the findings

This chapter has examined some aspects of growth by acquisition and growth by new investment. The following five main results were obtained.

(i) Over the period 1960–1976, the average contribution of acquisitions to firms' growth was quite considerable, exceeding that of new investment in the period 1966–1971.

(ii) There was a mild negative relationship between firm size and acquisition growth.

(iii) In a cross section, there was no trade-off between acquisition growth and growth by new investment.

(iv) An examination of 'external growth', that is taking into account the growth of assets subsequent to their acquisition, showed that it was considerably greater than 'acquisition growth' (without considering growth of acquired assets). The relative ranking of firms according to these two measures was, however, the same.

(v) Acquisition growth was found to be persistent from one period to the next. Firms which had above average acquisition growth in one period also had above average acquisition growth in the subsequent period, although this relationship was significant for 1960–1971 only, and even then there was regression towards the mean.

5

The impact of acquisition on investment and profitability

One main issue examined in Chapter 4 was the cross-sectional relationship between new investment and acquisition expenditure. An extension of this is to examine the impact of acquisitions on investment. Even in the absence of a cross-sectional trade-off across firms, acquisition may have an adverse impact on subsequent investment in the sense that, had acquisition not taken place, investment would have been higher still. This is the main issue investigated in this chapter. The investigation enquires specifically into the impact of the acquisitions of relatively large firms, that is, of quoted firms. This is in contrast to the previous chapter which analysed expenditure on acquisitions. The present exercise also distinguishes between horizontal and non-horizontal acquisitions.

There is scant existing evidence on these issues. In addition to investigating them, we also examine one of the traditional concerns of the effects of acquisitions; *viz.*, their effect on companies' profitability. This exercise, apart from being related to the above questions, is also warranted by the results of two large UK studies which reach different conclusions (Meeks, 1977 and Cosh, Hughes and Singh, 1980). The results of these exercises are also considered together and an attempt is made to provide an interpretation based on both of them. The chapter is arranged as follows: Section 5.1 provides a theoretical discussion on the impact of acquisition on new investment – this section develops and supplements the discussion in the previous chapter. Section 5.2 sets out the methodology whilst Section 5.3 presents the main evidence. Section 5.4 considers the likely impact of acquisitions on profitability whilst Section 5.5 gives evidence for the *same set* of firms as in Section 5.3. The last section presents a summary of the results.

5.1 The influence of acquisition on investment: further theoretical considerations

An appropriate framework for analysing the impact of acquisition is provided by the relatively newer theories of the firm, some of which were discussed in Chapter 1. In an imperfect environment, the adverse influence on investment hypothesised, for example, by Kaldor (1981) and Mueller (1977) may be due to the following well-known factors: although in the long run, as Penrose argued, acquisition is likely to weaken the managerial constraint on growth, in the short run, if the supply of managerial services is relatively inelastic, there may be a deficiency of services for the commissioning of new investment. A similar argument holds if the supply of finance is constrained. The willingness to invest may also be adversely affected if acquisition reduces competitive pressure to install new capacity to maintain or gain market shares.

However, in the context of the effect of acquisitions on market structure and monopoly power, in theory the effect on investment could go either way. Merger(s) may eliminate the competitive investment plans of hitherto independent firms and by monopolising the industry result in a lowering of investment (see also Kamien and Schwartz, 1972, for the argument that rivalry stimulates technical progress and so investment). On the other hand, mergers may reduce competitive uncertainty, restore a more favourable balance between safety (monopoly) and competition, and result in increased investment.[1] Another possibility is that mergers between smaller companies may increase their ability to compete with larger ones, and enhance their willingness to invest.

In Mueller's (1972) 'life cycle' theory, product maturity can slow down growth. The management may try to avoid this by undertaking projects which have lower marginal profitability; but there may then be a conflict between them and the shareholders. In such circumstances acquisition may not only avoid the slowdown in growth that product maturity brings, but may also open up opportunities for further investment. Acquisitions as a means of providing investment opportunities has been studied explicitly in two other theoretical contributions. Cable (1977) argued that a firm may undertake acquisition mainly to obtain information on potential investment opportunities. (This is most likely to be the case in conglomerate mergers.) Assuming profit maximisation, it is argued that firms are continuously engaged in search activity to expand their investment opportunity sets, that is, investment projects capable of implementation.

Merger is considered as a form of search since, *inter alia*, it involves the acquisition of information embodied in a firm. It differs, however, from other methods of search in two ways. First, it permits the acquisition of complete information sets, whereas other search options, such as that of hiring key personnel, involve the piecemeal accumulation of knowledge. Second, the merger search is likely to contain a relatively large fixed cost element, in comparison with other methods, owing to the existence of acquisition-price premia and transaction costs. Nevertheless, the theory suggests that search *via* merger can be efficient, and rational, under some standard assumptions (constant returns and lack of externalities) and that there need be no deleterious effect on subsequent investment.

A similar conclusion is reached by Chung and Weston (1981). Again assuming profit maximisation, they argue that one situation in which a merger may occur is where a firm, in an industry with low demand growth relative to the economy, tries to capture investment opportunities available in a firm operating in an industry with high expected demand growth. Unlike Cable's theory, however, in which less profitable firms would acquire relatively more profitable ones, it is suggested here that the acquired firm would have low profitability relative to the competitors in its industries. The assumption is that because of low existing profitability, the acquired firm would have been unable to undertake any significant investment by itself.

It is worth noting that in both these theories, as well as in the 'life cycle' hypothesis, it is the diversifying or conglomerate merger which is expected to have some beneficial effect on new investment both by providing information on investment opportunities and by leading to a shake up as new management enters the industry.

But the other important considerations noted above, and in Chapter 4, may still outweigh these beneficial effects, and lead to an adverse outcome. In the case of horizontal mergers, even these beneficial effects are much less marked, and in view of the likely monopoly effect, an adverse effect is more likely. Nevertheless, the *a priori* arguments are not conclusive, and it is clearly important to test the alternative hypotheses empirically.

5.2 Methodology and data

Methodology. The main empirical question investigated below is, in which direction and to what extent did merger by UK firms (from 1967 to 1974) affect their subsequent investment performance? The method adopted for studying this is the cross-sectional 'pre-post merger difference' approach which has been used by earlier writers to determine the impact of mergers on other aspects of company performance (see Singh, 1971; Mueller (ed), 1980). The ideal procedure according to this would be to compare the new investment undertaken by firms after the acquisition with the investment that would have been carried out by the participants had the merger not occurred. An approximation to this ideal, which has been attempted here, consists of comparing the investment carried out by the amalgamating firms after merger with their investment prior to it.[2]

To taken into account the systematic influences on investment other than acquisition, allowance has to be made for changes in the firms' environment during the period of comparison. This is because investment has pronounced cyclical fluctuations; and some industries have been more sensitive than others to these fluctuations. Further, the level of merger activity has been highly uneven between years and between industries. One consequence of this is that for reasons not directly associated with merger, years of numerous mergers may have been followed by years of above or below average investment.

These external influences have been taken into account by expressing firms' investment as a proportion of the current year's investment of the industry, or for non-horizontal mergers as a proportion of the sum of the two industries' investment in which the merging firms were operating. Note also that since in general inflation in the post-merger years was higher than in the pre-merger years, any unadjusted comparison of the 'pre-post' merger investment may result in a spurious improvement in investment. The adjustment adopted to 'remove' the effect of other external influences is also likely to eliminate any bias which may otherwise be imparted to the results.[3]

The precise form of the tests which we carried out can be considered by using the following symbols:

Consider two merging firms A and B and denote their pre-merger respective investments at time t as i_t^A and i_t^B and their total as $i_t^{A+B} = i_t^A + i_t^B$. Similarly denote their associated industries' investment as I_t^A and I_t^B respectively and let $I_t^{A+B} = I_t^A + I_t^B$. (For horizontal mergers $I_t^A = I_t^B$.) The pre-merger normalised investment (averaged over five pre-merger years) can then be written as

$$S_0 = \frac{1}{5} \sum_{r=t-5}^{t-1} \left\{ \frac{i_r^{A+B}}{I_r^{A+B}} \right\}$$

where t is the year of merger.

Similarly the post-merger normalised investment averaged over m post-merger years can be written as

$$S_m = \frac{1}{m} \sum_{r=t+1}^{t+m} \left\{ i^{A+B} \Big|_{I_r^{A+B}} \right\} \quad m = 1, \ldots 8$$

Then $C_m = S_m - S_0$ can be taken to represent the merger induced change in the investment share of the firms. If we denote the average value of C_m by C, the main null hypothesis which is tested can be stated as follows:

There is no overall systematic change in investment behaviour due to merger. That is, $C = 0$. The alternative hypothesis is $C \neq 0$.

This interfirm cross-sectional framework for isolating the influence of mergers on new investment is not the only one which may be used for this purpose. It may also be possible to do this by obtaining an investment function for each of the firms separately. Using time series data, and with acquisition as a dummy variable, one could estimate such a function and obtain from it an indication of the impact of merger. However, this approach would be useful only if there were a generally applicable theory of investment for all firms, which is far from being the case. Further, the difficulties involved in obtaining data and estimating an investment function for a large sample of firms would have made this method inappropriate for this investigation.

Data. The data were again obtained from the Department of Industry's Databank for companies in nineteen industries for 1962–1976.[4] The mergers selected took place between 1967 and 1974. Their total number was 354 – of these 264 were in the manufacturing sector and the rest in construction, transport and distribution. These account for a high proportion of acquisitions of quoted companies in this period in the UK.[5] The main variable used was gross fixed investment (net investment *plus* depreciation provisions). It was noted in Chapter 4 that in an inflationary environment with real growth this may be a more appropriate variable for measuring additions to the capital stock than net investment. Moreover, within a non-neoclassical framework, following Kaldor (1957) and others, there has been a considerable emphasis on the crucial role of embodied technical change, so that depreciation provisions do not simply lead to a replacement of old equipment, but also embody more up-to-date technology. For both these reasons, gross rather than net investment was considered the more appropriate variable.[6]

5.3 Empirical results

5.3.1 The pre-merger characteristics of 'victims' and acquirers

For each of the years from 1967 to 1974, Table 5.1 expresses the average size of those who became 'victims' in the following year, and of those who became acquirers in the following year, as a percentage of the population average for the pre-merger year. The typical victim was considerably smaller than the population average; the typical acquirer, on the other hand, was generally bigger than the average. These results accord with those obtained by Singh (1971) for the 1950s and Meeks (1977) for the period 1964–1971. It is noticeable, however, that the percentages are lower for both groups after 1969 than before. This decline is due

Table 5.1 *The average size of those to be acquired, and those to become acquirers*

Year of merger	Acquirer's size	Acquired's size
1967	321	84
1968	181	51
1969	107	49
1970	121	30
1971	150	46
1972	109	35
1973	117	18
1974	118	32
All years	176	61

Note: Net assets are used as the measure of size.
The firms' size is a percentage of the
average for the DI quoted company population.

mainly not to an absolute fall in the size of participants but to the rise in the average size of the Department of Industry's quoted company population after the 1969 rebasing (cf. Meeks, 1977, p. 19).

Table 5.2 expresses, as an average, the investment of victims and acquirers for each of the five years prior to the merger, as a percentage of the investment of their industry. As the typical victim was considerably smaller than the acquirer, so its investment share was also considerably lower than that of the typical acquirer, the difference being statistically significant at the 1 per cent level for each of the five pre-merger years. Note also that there is no indication of a trend in the pre-merger investment share of either the victim, or the acquirer. Had there been such a trend, the *effect* of merger on subsequent investment could not have been isolated from that due to the continuation of the pre-merger trend. As it is, any significant change in the post-merger period can be more confidently regarded as being due mostly to the act of merger itself.

5.3.2 Post-merger performance

Principal results. Table 5.3 reports the typical change after merger in the normalised investment of the whole sample. Consider, for example, Row 4. It shows that for the 203 mergers for which a comparison could be made, the share of the average merging firm in total industry investment in the pre-merger period was 1.70 per cent. For an average of four years after merger, this share increased to 1.99 per cent. The marked feature of these results is that the *average* investment share of merging firms shows an improvement over the pre-merger level for all post-merger years, although it is significant at the 5 per cent level for an average of only two and eight years. (Note that the merger year has been excluded throughout.) The results

Table 5.2 *The pre-merger investment of acquired companies and acquirers*

Year	Acquirer %	Acquired %
Y-5	3.34	0.65
	(0.29)	(0.08)
Y-4	3.33	0.77
	(0.30)	(0.10)
Y-3	3.42	0.74
	(0.30)	(0.09)
Y-2	3.46	0.74
	(0.39)	(0.08)
Y-1	3.22	0.77
	(0.35)	(0.09)

Notes: The standard error is given in brackets beneath the mean.
Y = Year of merger.
The firms' investment is a percentage of their industry for that year.

at least suggest that on average the investment share of firms does not decline after merger. (The number of mergers examined declines over time as data were only available up to the year 1976. The normalisation procedure typically leads to smaller merged firms as t increases for the following reason: after the first merger, the post-merger record of multiple acquirers is examined only up to the year before the subsequent merger. Following this second merger, the records are re-examined with respect to this merger. For single acquirers the record can be examined continuously till the end of the period investigated. Since single acquirers are generally smaller than multiple acquirers, this leads to the above result.)

An analysis using a constant sample – those mergers for which at least five post-merger years could be studied – yielded results similar to the above. For these, and for some results excluding extreme observations, see Kumar (1981).[7]

It is important to note, however, that although on *average* investment performance improves after merger, there is a very substantial *minority* of cases where it worsens. The statistic P_1 (Column 7, Table 5.3) shows the proportion of mergers showing an improvement, regardless of the actual magnitude of the improvement. It shows, for example, that for the average of four years after merger, 46 per cent of the companies showed some decline ($P_1 = 0.54$) and for the average of five years after merger 42 per cent were in this category ($P_1 = 0.58$). The majority of firms only show significant improvement for an average of seven and eight years. (The null hypothesis is that $P_1 = 0.5$, and the standard binomial probability test is used.[8]) This result is not particularly surprising, especially in view of the *a priori* arguments

Table 5.3 *The change in investment after merger: all companies, all years*

Year	n	Pre-merger normalised investment	Post-merger normalised investment	Differ-ence C	Statistical significance t-value	P_1	P_2
Y+1	354	1.99	2.26	0.27	1.64	0.50	0.57
Y+2	291	1.79	2.09	0.30(a)	2.09	0.51	0.59
Y+3	241	1.78	2.04	0.26	1.88	0.54	0.77(b)
Y+4	203	1.70	1.99	0.29	1.90	0.54	0.81(b)
Y+5	186	1.44	1.65	0.21	1.70	0.58(b)	0.75
Y+6	164	1.39	1.53	0.14	1.39	0.57	0.65
Y+7	147	1.40	1.46	0.06	0.65	0.59(b)	0.65
Y+8	93	1.51	1.78	0.27(a)	2.43	0.66(b)	0.68

Notes: (a) denotes significantly different from 0 at 5 per cent level.
(b) denotes significantly different from 0.5 at the 5 per cent level.
Y = year of merger (Y+5 refers to average of five years after merger and so on).
n = number of mergers qualifying for inclusion in that year.
C = difference in post-merger investment (normalised for industry and year) and 5 year average of pre-merger investment (similarly normalised).
P_1 = proportion of firms showing an improvement in investment (irrespective of industry).
P_2 = proportion of individual industries in which the merging firms showed on average an improvement in investment.
Normalised investment refers to firms' gross investment as a percentage of their respective industries' investment.

presented earlier which suggested that the effect of merger on investment could go either way.

A number of objections may be raised to the evidence on which this conclusion is based. One important one is the aggregation bias which may be present as a result of aggregating the results of industries with very different investment performance. To eliminate this bias, the proportion of individual industries was computed in which mergers, on average, showed an improvement. This proportion, denoted by P_2, is shown in Column 8. Consider, for example, Row 4: the value of P_2 is 0.81, indicating that on average mergers in 81 per cent of the industries displayed an improvement over the first four years. (This proportion is in general higher for later years, and if the null hypothesis is that $P_2 = 0.5$, it is significantly different from 0.5 for three and four years.)

A different kind of objection could be made, that the analysis is confined simply to the performance of merging firms. It may be argued that mergers reduced overall investment in their respective industries, but left merging firms doing the same, or more of the smaller total. Of course, there is little one can say, on *a priori* grounds, about the likely effects of the activities of individual firms on the performance of industries in which they operate. At an empirical level, whilst it is indeed true that the UK's investment has been low by internal standards, it is difficult to ascribe this to merger activity. At the simplest level, it may be noted that during the 1950s the relative level of investment in UK industries was still too low even though there was only limited merger activity.

Table 5.4 *The change in investment: horizontal mergers*

Year	n	Pre-merger investment	Post-merger investment	C	t-value	P_1	P_2
Y+1	119	1.32	1.44	0.12	0.85	0.45	0.56
Y+2	107	1.32	1.40	0.08	0.54	0.47	0.47
Y+3	88	1.39	1.41	0.02	0.11	0.53	0.56
Y+4	76	1.25	1.33	0.08	0.47	0.55	0.65
Y+5	71	1.18	1.25	0.07	0.37	0.55	0.71
Y+6	59	1.10	1.13	0.03	0.20	0.49	0.67
Y+7	51	1.05	1.03	-0.02	-0.11	0.53	0.60
Y+8	34	0.96	1.13	0.17	1.35	0.59	0.71

For notes see Table 5.3.

Nevertheless, in view of the importance of the issue, an investigation was undertaken to examine the relationship between acquisition activity and investment at the industry level. This was done in two ways. First, for each industry an examination was undertaken of the time series (1962–1976) of new fixed investment and acquisition expenditures (both adjusted for inflation): a correlation analysis revealed no strong systematic relationship. Second, for all industries we examined whether there were any significant differences in investment between them which could be associated with the intensity of acquisition activity. For each year, the correlation between investment and acquisition expenditure across industries was calculated. There appeared to be some positive relationship across the industries; although it was not statistically significant.

Diversification and investment performance. This section examines whether the pattern of investment after merger differs according to whether the victim and the acquirer are in the same, or in different industries. Consider first the impact of horizontal mergers (Table 5.4).[9] Unlike the results for the whole sample, the investment share of firms in the post-merger period (relative to the pre-merger period) shows very little improvement.[10] Indeed, for the average of seven post-merger years there is a decline, although its magnitude is quite small. The change is not, however, statistically significant in any year (see Columns 5 and 6). In addition, the statistic P_1 (Column 7) showing the proportion of mergers with an increase indicates that on average about half the firms show an improvement, with the proportion generally high for later years. P_2 yields a somewhat similar result for the number of industries in which mergers had a positive impact. These two statistics tend to strengthen the impression that for horizontal mergers, there was on average little impact on investment.

In view of this result, and of the evidence in Table 5.3, it is not surprising to find that the results for non-horizontal mergers show a substantial improvement (Table 5.5). It is noticeable, however, that the pre-merger investment share of firms involved is considerably greater than that of firms involved in horizontal mergers so that their proportionate improvement is comparatively not as great as may appear at first sight. Nevertheless, it is still significant, and it is reinforced when individual firms and industries are studied separately (see the last 3 columns of Table 5.5).

Table 5.5 *The change in investment: non-horizontal mergers*

Year	n	Pre-merger investment	Post-merger investment	C	t-value	P_1	P_2
Y+1	154	2.47	2.97	0.50	1.67	0.52	0.60
Y+2	138	2.08	2.70	0.62(a)	2.46	0.58	0.60
Y+3	129	1.98	2.52	0.55(a)	2.36	0.57	0.70
Y+4	106	1.89	2.44	0.55(a)	2.20	0.58	0.68
Y+5	85	1.42	1.89	0.47(a)	2.00	0.56	0.72
Y+6	80	1.43	1.67	0.24	1.65	0.54	0.67
Y+7	74	1.51	1.65	0.13	1.12	0.57	0.67
Y+8	40	1.84	2.17	0.33	1.71	0.60	0.67

For notes see Table 5.3.

Size and frequency of acquisitions. As noted in Chapter 1, beyond a certain point increases in a firm's growth rate may entail increasing costs. When growth is by acquisition, it may be conjectured that the larger the size of the acquired company (relative to the acquirer), or the greater the number acquired, the more systematically would the effects on subsequent performance differ from those resulting from smaller or fewer acquisitions. This was investigated empirically in two ways.

First, we excluded from the sample those mergers in which the investment of the acquired firm(s) was *less than 20 per cent* of the combined investment of the merging firms. Even though it is quite a weak criterion, the mergers satisfying it account for less than half the full sample. Note also that this criterion excludes some of the largest firms; the pre-merger investment share of the remaining firms is considerably less than that for the full sample (Table 5.6). The effect on investment is also somewhat different from that for the full sample. As the values of C indicate, there was on average some improvement in the post-merger period. However, when we examine the proportion of firms and industries showing an improvement, it is quite low for the first two years, and there is only a gradual subsequent improvement. This confirms what one would expect, that for the average firm undertaking a relatively large acquisition, it takes a considerable time to assimilate the acquisition and re-organise itself. During this time investment shares do decline somewhat. However, after the period of re-organisation, the investment either returns to the pre-merger level or shows an improvement.

Second, we examined the performance of firms making only single acquisitions: if merger does entail substantial assimilation problems, then the expectation would be that for these firms there would be smaller adverse effects than for firms undertaking multiple acquisitions. The evidence shows that, if anything, the reverse is the case. As Table 5.7 indicates, investment declines for the average of the first two years and improves subsequently. The improvement, however, is small compared to the results for the whole sample. The non-parametric statistics P_1 and P_2 also indicate that the change in investment for these firms was generally much less marked than in the earlier results. One explanation for this may be that firms making repeated acquisitions are more likely to become adept at assimilating these acquisitions than those undertaking them only infrequently. Hence the impact on investment may be less adverse for the former set of firms.

Table 5.6 *The change in investment: larger mergers*

Year	n	Pre-merger investment	Post-merger investment	C	t-value	P_1	P_2
Y+1	169	1.16	1.21	0.05	0.27	0.38	0.50
Y+2	152	1.13	1.29	0.16	0.89	0.46	0.48
Y+3	139	1.10	1.28	0.18	1.04	0.47	0.62
Y+7	75	0.97	0.96	-0.01	-0.04	0.52	0.53

For notes see Table 5.3.

There are two essential points to note about these findings. First none of them is unacceptable from an economic point of view. As noted earlier, there seem to be adequate theoretical explanations for them. Second, a number of earlier studies provide some additional empirical support for them. Cosh, Hughes and Singh (1980), using the matched-pair technique (whereby the acquiring and acquired firms were paired with non-acquiring firms, on the basis of industry and size), showed that for a large sample of UK quoted firms which merged in the late sixties, the post-merger growth rates (in terms of net assets and physical assets) of merging firms were not very much different from the corresponding growth rates of the control group of firms (the merging firms slightly improved their relative growth). However, when the merging firms were compared with the non-merging firms in the entire population (in the DI databank), the merging firms showed a definite increase in their growth relative to these companies. It may be argued that acquisition activity subsequent to the particular merger studied may increase proportionately more than any decline in new investment. This could yield increasing total growth with declining investment growth. There is, of course, little theoretical or empirical basis for this. As such, these results are complementary to those obtained above.[11] (But see below for the sample used in the study.)

5.4 The impact of acquisition on profitability

The main reason for examining the impact of acquisition on profitability follows from the evidence presented earlier in Chapter 4. As discussed there, in an imperfect capital market profitability exercises a considerable influence on investment. Therefore, in view of the above results, it is interesting to investigate the concomitant effects of mergers on profitability. This is particularly so since two other studies come to different conclusions regarding the profitability effect. Meeks (1977) showed that on average profitability declined after merger whilst Cosh, Hughes and Singh showed that profitability either increased, or remained the same following merger (see below for details). It is thus important to enquire what the effect is on profitability for our sample.

What is likely to be the effect of merger on profitability? There are a number of motivational factors which would influence the outcome (see Steiner, 1975). If the managers of acquiring firms are trying to maximise profits, they would expect an increase in the profitability of the newly-formed firm, over what the weighted

Table 5.7 *The change in investment: companies making single acquisitions*

Year	n	Pre-merger investment	Post-merger investment	C	t-value	P_1	P_2
Y+1	125	1.36	1.34	−0.02	−0.16	0.44	0.58
Y+2	125	1.35	1.34	−0.01	−0.09	0.48	0.40
Y+3	124	1.36	1.37	0.01	0.09	0.50	0.60
Y+4	116	1.36	1.37	0.01	0.10	0.49	0.60
Y+5	104	1.31	1.37	0.07	0.50	0.51	0.75
Y+6	99	1.25	1.33	0.09	0.86	0.49	0.65
Y+7	90	1.25	1.31	0.05	0.56	0.49	0.65
Y+8	60	1.38	1.60	0.22(b)	2.08	0.58	0.63

For notes see Table 5.3.

average of the profitability of the two combining firms would have been had they not merged. For example, as Hindley (1973) has argued, the sale of a business takes place only when 'the buyer . . . has higher expectations of its future profitability than the seller'. If it is assumed that on average these higher expectations are fulfilled after sale, then an increase in profitability should result. It is worth noting, however, that this is not a sufficient condition, even for a profit-maximising acquirer. Expectations of the profitability of a firm may be the same for buyer and seller. But the acquirer may take the view that the independent existence of the two firms will result in a lower profit for both of them than would be the case if they amalgamated.

The outcome is less clearcut with alternative maximands such as growth. Initially, higher growth and higher profitability may be positively correlated: slow-growing firms relying heavily on old products, with declining markets, may have low profitability. A more active pursuit of markets, together with greater expenditure on research and development, is likely to produce both rapid growth and higher profitability. However, beyond some point the relationship may be inverse: this may be owing to increased marketing or research costs necessary for further growth, or to the problems of assimilating a large number of new additions into the management team. If these problems are acute, profitability may well fall after merger.

In the 'behavioural' theories, where there is no specific maximand, a merger which entailed the expectation of higher profitability, either through increased market power or lower average costs for the combined firm, may not in fact lead to an improvement in profitability. Rather, it may lead to a further relaxation of effort on the part of management, or an increase in 'X-inefficiency' (cf. Leibenstein, 1966). Further, it may be plausibly argued that a firm's performance depends to a considerable extent on managerial aspirations, which are relatively stable in the short run (Cyert and March, 1963). In this case too, a change in the environment which may have the potential of higher profitability may not in the event lead to it; either the firm may not realise the potential benefits, or they may be absorbed in wasteful production or administrative activities.

Next consider the relationship between the *change* in profitability and the *change* in the efficiency of a firm's operations. It is well recognised that in an imperfectly competitive environment, improvement in efficiency, for example, is not a necessary condition for an improvement in profitability. The latter can arise from improved market power, so that an increase in efficiency cannot be inferred from an increase in profitability alone (cf. Hughes, 1978). It has been suggested, however, that in some cases it may be possible to infer changes in efficiency from changes in profitability (Meeks, 1977). For example, assume that market power is unchanged as a result of merger; then the other influence on profitability change, change in efficiency, will determine whether profitability rises, falls or remains unchanged. With constant market power, a decline in profitability would imply a decline in a firm's efficiency.

It may be argued that in a competitive environment the assumption of unchanged market power is highly conservative. A more plausible assumption would be that market power is enhanced by merger. In such a case, a decline in efficiency may be inferred not just from reduced but also from constant profit-ability, whilst even improved profitability would have no unambiguous implication for efficiency. Gains in market power may occur in the capital market and in the market for inputs as well as in product markets. An increase in size accompanying merger may lead to easier, and cheaper, availability of funds. Further, the supply of material inputs may be more certain and may be obtained at a discount. This suggests that the power of the firm in the various markets in which it operates may indeed be enhanced by merger, and therefore if profitability remains constant after merger or even increases, this could still be compatible with a decline in efficiency. Against this, however, there are at least two considerations which suggest that com-petition in the product markets need not automatically decrease following merger. First, a merger between two or more relatively small firms may increase their ability to compete against large competitors. Second, as George and Joll (1981) point out, merging firms may be more heavily engaged in international trade than non-merging ones, and competition there may be fiercer than in the domestic economy. In these cases the assumption of enhanced market power may not be appropriate.

Apart from these considerations relating to the product and capital markets and the markets for material inputs, there is some evidence that the position of merging firms in the labour market may also be affected. The effects upon industrial relations, and the changes in the expectations of employees following merger, may in addition influence the firm's profitability adversely.

To elaborate this point, consider a simple profit function for a firm: $\Pi = pq - C$ where Π = total profit, p = price per unit of output, q = quantity sold, and C is total cost. Assume that the cost function is of the following form: $C = a + bq$, where $a > 0$, $b > 0$. An increase in market power following merger may be thought of as leading to an increase in p and a decrease in the non-labour cost component of C.

With regard to the labour costs, however, the situation may be rather ambiguous. There is some evidence that, *ceteris paribus*, larger firms tend to have poorer indus-trial relations than smaller firms. The number of work stoppages and strikes in larger firms seems considerably higher than in other firms (cf. Prais 1978). More precisely, the evidence indicates that increasing the size of *plant* normally leads to greater industrial conflict and to higher production costs (see Shorey, 1975 and Smith *et al.*, 1978, who provide evidence of the strike incidence (man-days lost per 1000 employees) rising sharply with plant size). However, as Shorey further shows, average costs do not increase automatically with the size of *firm* if plant size is constant. So, whilst acquisitions can lead to a sharp increase in firm size, the effect on industrial relations is not clear. If plant size is in fact increased and this leads to a significant deterioration in industrial relations, this in turn may lead to an increase in the fixed cost component, *a*. If other components of the profit function remain constant, this would be reflected in a decline in profitability. In this case it may be correct to infer a decline in efficiency, since it can be argued that it is precisely the inability of management, in the larger unit, to coordinate labour relations well which has resulted in cost increases. Costs may also increase, however, because employees in the larger units, whether or not this is due to larger plants, have higher expectations of remuneration than they had previously. This is likely to be particularly true in the case where employees in the merging firms differ considerably in their average pay. So there may be pressure after acquisition for some parity in the remuneration – especially if it is thought that the acquiring firm has the ability to pay. This would lead to an increase in average payment to the employees, without any corresponding increases in productivity, and hence an increase in unit costs (for some evidence supporting this see Millward and McQueeney, 1981, pp. 30–34). The ability of a firm to pay increased wage costs is a widely-used argument in pay negotiations and a takeover can clearly affect the ability to pay (Daniel, 1976). As Millward and McQueeney observed: 'Union negotiators within an acquired firm may see the greater financial resources of the parent company as justifying a more favourable settlement.' In addition, there may be a demand for a move towards identical conditions of employment, e.g. in terms of pension schemes and other fringe benefits, which again would raise unit costs.

It seems, therefore, that in some cases, the relationship between changes in profitability and changes in efficiency following acquisition may not be a simple one: even if the market power of merging firms may increase in the product and capital markets, the bargaining situation in the labour market may be such as to reduce or nullify this advantage.

5.5 The impact of acquisition on profitability: empirical evidence

The empirical approach adopted here was similar to that used in isolating the effect of acquisitions on new investment. There are three steps in the methodology. First, for each merger, the pre-merger profitability of the merging firms was calculated in relation to the relevant industries' profitability. The pre-merger reference period was taken to be an average of five years. Second, post-merger profitability was calculated for the amalgamation for an average of up to seven years, again in relation to the relevant industries' profitability. Third, the difference in the pre-merger and post-merger profitability of merging firms was averaged across the firms and tested for statistical significance. Non-parametric tests were also carried out to check the robustness of the results.[12] The sample of mergers was the same as in Section 5.3 and, as before, in the case of firms making more than one acquisition the influence of other acquisitions and their industry environment was also taken into account. This allows the results to be directly comparable to those obtained for investment.

The results for the full sample are given in Table 5.8. In row 5, for example, we see that for an average of five post-merger years records of 186 mergers were

Table 5.8 *The change in profitability: all companies, all years*

Year	n	Pre-merger normalised profitability	Post-merger normalised profitability	Difference C	Statistical significance t-value	P_1
Y+1	354	1. 16	1. 06	−0.10	−1.59	0. 46
Y+2	291	1.20	1.13	−0.07(a)	−2.24	0.44
Y+3	241	1.22	1.14	−0.08(a)	−2.43	0.39(b)
Y+4	203	1.24	1.16	−0.08(a)	−2.16	0.35(b)
Y+5	186	1.22	1.16	−0.06	−1.50	0.40(b)
Y+6	164	1.21	1.14	−0.07	−1.96	0.41
Y+7	147	1.23	1.16	−0.07	−1.71	0.43

Notes: (a) denotes significantly different from 0 at 5 per cent level.

(b) denotes significantly different from 0.5 at 5 per cent level.

The methodology is similar to that used for determining the effect of acquisition on investment. (Firm profitability is examined as a proportion of industry profitability.) For other information see notes to Table 5.3.

Y denotes the year of merger. Y+5=average of five years after merger and so on.

C denotes the average difference between pre-merger and post-merger profitability.

P_1 denotes the proportion of firms which had an increase in post-merger profitability.

Figures are rounded to two decimal places.

examined. The average normalised profitability in the pre-merger reference period was 1.22. For an average of five post-merger years it was down to 1.16 – a relative decline in the post-merger period of − 0.06. Under the null hypothesis of no change in profitability the computed value of the *t*-statistic was − 1.50, which is statistically insignificant at the 5 per cent level. The proportion of mergers for which the normalised post-merger profitability was greater than the pre-merger value was 0.40. Using the binomial test this was found to be significantly different from 0.50. The clear impression given by this table is that on average there was a decline in profitability following acquisition. Whilst this decline is not statistically significant for all years, it is nevertheless persistent. Further, it presents a sharp contrast with the earlier results obtained for investment.

There is one important *caveat*, however, with regard to the role played by the valuation of acquired companies, and its impact on profitability (see Meeks, 1977, Appendix A, pp. 68–73). This can lead to a downward bias in post-merger profitability relative to its pre-merger value, and hence may partly contribute to the above results. The bias arises in the following way: in an inflationary environment, the book value of companies' assets, based on historic cost accounting, usually understates their realisable value. When a company is acquired, the acquirer generally pays more than its book value. It may then enter the acquired company in its books at a value exceeding that in the acquired's books prior to merger. This excess is normally entered in the acquirer's balance sheet under 'goodwill'; the acquired firm's assets are then added to the other components of the balance sheet at historic cost.

In these cases of revaluation, the profitability of the amalgamated company (calculated as profits divided by the average book value of net assets) will be lower than the weighted average profitability for the two separate entities would have been in the absence of merger. This is so since a bigger denominator (incorporating goodwill) is used in calculating profitability. The value of this bias in post-merger profitability is a function of the value of 'goodwill'. Unfortunately, the amount at which the acquisition is recorded in the acquirer's balance sheet is not provided in the DI's Databank for the period since 1964 – and hence one cannot evaluate the goodwill.

However, a procedure was developed by Meeks (1977) for estimating the goodwill arising on consolidation. His calculations showed it to be on average around a third of the book value of the acquired firms for mergers during 1964–1971. It was found to be generally stable across years, so that any bias which it produces in profitability measures is unlikely to vary greatly between mergers undertaken in different years. By subtracting goodwill from the assets of the amalgamation, Meeks obtained the effect on profitability of the goodwill increment. According to his estimates, in the year of acquisition, adjusted profitability (with goodwill removed from the denominator) was on average between 1 per cent and 3.5 per cent higher than unadjusted profitability. In the subsequent year, however, it was higher by between 1.3 and 5.5 per cent.

What is of more interest to us is the extent to which this may affect the conclusions reached in the above investigation. Assuming that the bias is *similar* for our sample of mergers (and in view of the stability of goodwill across years this seems a reasonable assumption) it seems that *had* there been no distortions due to goodwill, the adverse impact on profitability would have been somewhat lower. It is true that the bias is small (a maximum of 5.5 per cent), but then the change in profitability is also rather small. In addition, the estimates of the above bias include the effects of only a single year's acquisition activity – for a persistent acquirer the difference would be cumulative and could exceed the above averages. This is particularly important since more than half the firms in this sample undertook acquisitions in more than one year. In short, it seems likely that the profitability decline shown in Table 5.8 may be exaggerated somewhat due to the inclusion of 'goodwill'.

It should be noted that the existing evidence on the effect of acquisition on profitability is not clear-cut. Meeks (1977) examined a sample of 233 mergers occurring in the period 1964–1972. Despite some differences in the sample and the methodology, the results are quite similar to those obtained in this study.[13] This is not so in the case of the investigation by Cosh, Hughes and Singh (CHS, 1980). They showed, in fact, a slight improvement in the relative profitability of firms merging in the period 1967–1969. Their methodology is different from that used here and in an earlier study we examined these differences in detail (Kumar, 1980). The important difference is that CHS compared the experience of their sample of mergers with that of comparable randomly selected non-merging firms. The sample of non-merging firms was drawn from a population which excluded all firms engaged, to any significant extent, in mergers in the 1960s.

Table 5.9 *Correlations between post-merger change in profitability and investment*

Post–merger year	Sample of mergers	Correlation coefficient	Maximum significance
Y+1	354	0.126	0.025
Y+2	291	0.123	0.030
Y+3	241	0.113	0.051
Y+4	203	0.107	0.077
Y+5	186	0.102	0.105
Y+6	164	0.116	0.098
Y+7	147	0.111	0.127

Notes: Y refers to the year of merger. For other notes see Table 5.3. 'Maximum significance' refers to the level at which the coefficient is significant. For the first year, the results are significant at the 2.5 per cent level, and so on.

In Kumar (1980), the same set of mergers as investigated by CHS was examined, but using the methodology of this chapter. Thus pre-merger and post-merger profitability was normalised using industry profitability figures. There were changes in results using this methodology – the profitability of merging firms declined slightly – although this change was not statistically significant. Some other changes were then made – such as excluding the year of merger and aggregating results in a different form. However, the results were quite robust, and it was concluded that some difference is certainly made to the computed change in profitability by the particular normalisation method adopted. In theory, the method used by CHS and that used by Meeks (and here) seem equally efficient in isolating the impact of mergers. In practice, however, the 'matched-pair' technique may have a drawback since in view of the widespread nature of acquisition activity, it is not always possible to obtain appropriate 'matched' firms. It was for this reason that we used the alternative methodology.

The question naturally arises whether these results are compatible with those we obtained earlier for investment. It was shown there that on average the investment share of firms improved somewhat after acquisition, and that this improvement was maintained for the sample period. Before discussing this, it is worth emphasising again that these results are *averages* over the sample. In the case of profitability, some 40 per cent of the firms in fact showed an *improvement*, whilst in the case of investment there was a *decline* for about 40 per cent of the firms. Since the averages may be due to the influence of a few mergers showing different results (an increase in investment accompanied by a sharp decrease in profitability), it is useful to enquire what is the relationship between the change in profitability and the change in investment for individual firms.

In order to get a measure of the degree of relationship, zero order correlation was computed between the changes in the two variables for 7 post-merger years.

As Table 5.9 (Column 3) indicates there was some positive association in the impact of acquisitions on the two variables. Companies which showed an improvement in investment tended also to have an improvement in profitability. Whilst the relationship is not strong in absolute terms (as is to be expected in view of the earlier results) it is statistically significant. This just indicates the fact that only for a small proportion of mergers did the changes in the two variables tend to go together.

For the rest of the mergers in the sample, we next note some arguments which may reconcile the investment increase and the concomitant decline in profitability. The earlier discussion showed that the development of organisational slack, or 'X-inefficiency', may lead to potential gains due to merger not materialising as actual improvement in performance after merger. As some commentators have suggested, this may be in spite of an increase in investment, or perhaps in some cases, even because of it (O'Brien, 1978). The latter may be the case if a firm's management, feeling less competitive pressure, undertakes investment which may not be optimal for the firm's shareholders, but which may nevertheless contribute to increasing managerial welfare.

It is not possible to gauge the strength of this explanation, but it is unlikely to be very important. A more likely explanation of the lower profitability/higher investment result is that businessmen were simply over optimistic about the outcome, and made mistakes. It is also possible that, in spite of the merger, in these cases competition has intensified, especially if competition from imports is important. These two considerations would also explain the lower profitability/ lower investment result. In the case of higher profitability/lower investment, there may have been some increase in monopoly power, and as noted above this can also have some detrimental effect on investment by removing competitive pressure.

It may be argued that since profitability affects the availability of funds, a fall in profitability should have an adverse impact on firms' ability to undertake new investment. However, this may be offset at least in part if large size brings with it stability in earnings, which is at a premium in the capital market from which the firm can raise fresh funds. In addition to the availability of funds, the cost of funds may also be lower for larger firms.

5.6 Summary

The main results of this chapter, based on an investigation of the records of over 350 acquisitions in the United Kingdom over the period 1967–1974, are as follows:

(i) There was no decline, and in some cases an improvement, in the average share of new fixed investment of merging firms over their pre-merger value. The average value of this improvement was substantial and it was maintained over several post-merger years, although it was generally not statistically significant. This result was not unduly influenced by outlying observations or by aggregation bias. But it should be noted that these are *average* results and that for a significant minority of mergers (around 40%) investment performance worsened after merger.

(ii) The analysis by type of merger showed that for the non-horizontal category there was a clear improvement; for the horizontal, there was no pronounced average effect, with about half the mergers showing an improvement.

(iii) A separate investigation of single acquirers, and of relatively large acquisitions, suggested that the change in investment was much less marked than for the sample as a whole. Even here, however, there was no evidence of a general decline in investment following merger.

(iv) An examination of the profitability of merging firms showed a decline over its pre-merger value. Whilst this decline was small, it was persistent over several post-merger years. In the case of profitability too, the experience of a significant minority of mergers differed from the average result. Here, for around 40 per cent of cases, profitability in the post-merger period was higher than before merger.

Appendix to Chapter 5

In this appendix we consider the following issues: the treatment of the year of merger, trends in pre-merger investment, the procedure for normalisation, and the impact of merger on net investment and total industry investment.

The merger year. The year of merger itself has been excluded throughout the analysis to avoid any ambiguities in interpreting the results. For instance, if we compare two companies, one of which acquired at the beginning of its financial year, and the other towards the end of the same year, it would be inappropriate to place the same interpretation on the 'year of merger'. This is because the former company would have had more time to reorganise and invest subsequent to the merger. This problem would, of course, influence later years' comparison as well, but the averaging procedure adopted would tend to reduce its magnitude. Nevertheless, in view of the possible importance of the performance in the merger year itself, we examined it separately. The results shown in Table 5.A.1 indicate that on the face of it there was a mild improvement in that year.

Trend in the pre-merger period. If there had been an upward *trend* in the pre-merger investment of the merging companies in our sample, this would mean that the post-merger investment share of these firms would on average have been higher, whether or not the merger took place. An investigation of their pre-merger annual investment shares revealed no such trend.

Normalisation procedure. For companies making only single acquisitions, the procedure is as noted in the text. For multiple acquisitions it was extended in the following manner.

For an acquirer undertaking more than one acquisition in any given year, but no *further* acquisition in later years, we considered the sum of the acquirer and acquired companies' investment as a share of their respective industries' investment in the pre-merger period. For the post-merger period, the investment of the merged companies was normalised by the acquirer's industry's investment plus that of the industries of the acquired companies.

Where the acquirer took over another quoted company after the first merger, the following rule was applied: if there was no merger for at least one year after the first one, normalisation was carried out as for single acquisitions up to the year before the second merger and the post-merger analysis was only carried out for that period. The post-merger record for the second merger was examined by normalising

Table 5.A.1 *Results for the year of merger*

No. of mergers	Pre-merger investment	Post-merger investment	Difference	T ratio	p_1	p_2
354	1.98	2.15	0.17	1.48	0.51	0.54

again, this time taking into consideration the industry investment total of the second acquisition as well. Thus if we consider A acquiring B and then C, the analysis for the first merger would be based on comparing normalised A + B investment before and after merger until C was acquired when the analysis would then be based upon normalised A + B + C pre-merger and post-merger investment. If a second acquisition occurred within a year of the first one, the first merger was not considered separately and only the performance after the second merger was examined.

For non-horizontal mergers, as an alternative to the unweighted normalisation procedure reported in this study, a weighted average of the investment of industries was also used, the weights being the proportionate contributions of each of the merging firms' net assets to the amalgamation's net assets. The reason for considering this alternative was that the effect of industry environment may be considered to depend on the *proportion* of the firm's activities in that environment. Since the purpose of normalisation is to adjust for external factors, it was thought necessary to consider this alternative. In the event the results were similar to those reported in the text, and did not affect any of the conclusions reached there.

Effect on net investment. In addition to the economic and accounting reasons for preferring gross rather than net investment, there is a methodological problem when using the latter variable. This is because net investment was negative for several companies in the pre-merger period, yielding a negative share which is obviously meaningless. Nevertheless, in order to study the influence of merger on net investment we repeated our analysis for a sample of companies which had positive investment in the pre-merger and post-merger periods. The results were broadly comparable to those discussed earlier.

Effect of merger on industry investment. A preliminary investigation undertaken to examine the relationship between acquisition and investment expenditure at the industry level presented no strong systematic relationship. For example, Pearson's correlation coefficient between these two forms of expenditure (normalised by industries' total assets) over the years 1962–1976 for some of the industries was as follows: Chemicals − 0.02, Electrical engineering 0.15, Clothing 0.45, Textiles − 0.18, Metal manufacture 0.24, Building materials 0.28, Wholesale 0.06, Retail 0.03 and Construction 0.06. An analysis of the current acquisition expenditure with lagged investment expenditure (lagged by one to three years) produced similar results. In addition, for each year we examined the cross-section correlation between the two forms of expenditures across the 19 industries included in our sample. Typical correlations obtained were as follows: 1964: 0.09, 1967: 0.19, 1970: 0.15, 1972: − 0.07, 1974: 0.03, 1976: 0.28. Although these tests are rather crude they do suggest that there is no simple relationship between mergers and industry investment.

6

The financing of growth

In the last chapter it was shown that, in general, acquisitions had an adverse impact on profitability, but a positive one on investment. This raises a number of issues concerning the financing of both these activities. To what extent were acquisitions financed by external funds raised from the capital market? If these were financed mainly by external funds, why, in view of the decline in profitability, was the market willing to supply these funds? In those cases where they were financed by retentions, is there any significantly different relationship with investment? A number of general questions also arise in this context on the discipline exercised by the stock market on the firms' behaviour. This chapter discusses these questions and provides empirical evidence on them. In addition, a number of questions arising from earlier chapters are investigated. For example, one of the main conclusions of Chapter 3 was that there is a mild negative relationship between growth and firm size. To what extent is this reflected in the reliance on external funds across firms in different size classes?

The rest of this chapter is arranged as follows. Section 6.1 discusses the relationship between internal and external finance, and some aspects of borrowing and equity funding. Sections 6.2–6.5 contain empirical analyses of the above issues. The last section provides a summary and implications of the results.

6.1 Retentions and external finance: preferences and constraints

In the neoclassical theory of the firm, in a world of certainty there is no need for a firm to rely on retained earnings to finance its growth. The firm is able and willing to finance by external funds any project that it would be prepared to finance out of retentions – any project with a positive net present value (Modigliani and Miller, 1958). As Wood (1975) has pointed out, this result rests on two main assumptions: that the firm's objective is to maximise the present value of its future earnings; and, that the capital market is perfect, in the sense that no individual borrower or lender can influence the prevailing interest rate (i.e. there are no transaction costs, no taxes and no constraints on the supply of finance).

In the more realistic world of uncertainty, the above result continues to hold if the following three assumptions are made: that expectations of the future are common to all agents in the capital market; that firms are indifferent between financing a project from retentions and from borrowed money; and that lenders would be willing to provide funds provided they are adequately compensated for the degree of uncertainty involved. As Wood (1975) has argued, these are unrealistic assumptions. For example, expectations are likely to vary considerably among individuals; further, in an uncertain world, borrowing may entail risks and disadvantages which do not generally arise when investment is undertaken out of retentions (such as the possibility of bankruptcy).[1,2]

In Wood's own analysis, retentions are a preferred source of finance. This view is not novel – several earlier writers have emphasised the preference for internally generated funds (Galbraith, 1972; Baran and Sweezy, 1966). There are a number of drawbacks to external finance which prompt this view. There is uncertainty regarding its availability, and it entails a number of costs; management may resent the outside scrutiny associated with any new issue of equity; and the tax system may add a disincentive to distribute profits, by taxing dividends more highly than retentions. An important question arises as to how the preference for retentions may affect the mechanism for allocating funds efficiently between companies. It has been often argued that the process of 'recycling' funds, paying out dividends which are subsequently reinvested, results in more 'efficient' investment than the retention of funds for investment within a given company. The main reason for this is thought to be the one noted above for the managerial preference for retentions: that funds raised on the capital market are subject to market discipline while retentions are subject to less direct control by shareholders (Baumol, 1965; Whittington, 1972). But an alternative view would shift the focus from the source of the funds to the company making use of them. It may be argued that companies which are efficient will use funds efficiently whatever their source, and *vice versa*. This assumes, of course, that the decision to retain funds or distribute them is made according to managerial preferences. The position would be different if companies were compelled by external constraints to retain funds, which they would not themselves have done.

To the extent that firms do have recourse to the capital market, what are the factors which determine their decision to raise loan or equity capital? The incentives for loan finance may lie in tax advantages and advantages due to unanticipated inflation, which may lead to a negligible real rate of interest. But there is the ultimate risk that the firm might be forced into bankruptcy as a result of an unanticipated fall in profits such that it could not meet the fixed interest obligations. But even before that, a high gearing ratio (debt/net worth) would amplify the proportional effect of short-run fluctuations of profits on the level of retentions. This would necessitate better temporary credit facilities, which may not be available since a high gearing ratio would make banks more reluctant to provide additional short-term credit. So there would be some upper limit on the firm's long-run gearing ratio. The precise level of this limit would depend on managerial and market expectations of the firm's future profit stream, and on the extent to which the managers and owners are risk averse.

The ability of large firms to have a higher gearing than small firms is well recognised. The main reason is the lower variability of the income streams of large firms, so that the danger of insolvency is lower than for smaller firms (see Utton, 1982, pp. 44–46).[3] In this context merger can play an important role: as the result of merger even between two similar firms, the relative variability of their joint income stream is likely to be reduced, permitting an increase in loan funds. More interestingly, as Prais (1976) has noted, merger may be used in restructuring a company's capital to have higher gearing. Any change in capital structure which may be intended to yield a tax advantage is legally prohibited, but the issue of debentures to provide finance for the acquisition of the equity of another company, is not subject to such restrictions.

What are the factors influencing the decision to raise equity capital? Consider first the 'new money' issues – those which increase the amount of finance available. On average new issues are a minor source of finance (see, e.g., *Business Monitor, M3*, 1984, p. 81). To some extent this is due to the costs involved in making an issue (Merret and Sykes, 1965) and the desire to avoid external scrutiny. But the main reason is that a new issue, by increasing the supply of a company's shares, is likely to push down the share price and inflict a capital loss on the firm's existing shareholders. (This is of course excepting the rights issue, which, in fact, is the most common form.)

This consideration is irrelevant in the Modigliani–Miller world where the outcome of a new issue depends only on whether the return on the investment to be financed by the new issue was greater or less than the current interest rate. If it was greater, a new issue would lead to a capital gain for existing shareholders, since the valuation of the company would increase by more than the proceeds of the new issue. If it was less, a capital loss would ensue. In general, therefore, the existing shareholders' view of the new issue would depend on the use to which its proceeds were put.

In practice, in an imperfect capital market, in order to sell a new issue an incentive is required, this being provided by an increase in the expected rate of return on the firm's shares above what it would otherwise have been (Wood, 1975, pp. 54–56). This may again be achieved by a reduction in the share price (again excepting the rights issues). In some circumstances, it may be in the interests of both the firm's owners, and its managers, to raise funds in this way. For example, if there are special opportunities for growth, a new issue may be the only appropriate way to obtain funds. For, with a given gearing limit, only a proportion of investment could be financed by increased borrowing. Increasing retentions by enough to finance the remainder would require a reduction in the payout ratio, which may not be considered desirable (see Chapter 7).

The above considerations apply only to a limited extent to issues made in exchange for the shares of other companies in the course of growth by acquisition. The costs involved in arranging the issue are likely to be lower, and there is likely to be less uncertainty involved in the outcome of the issue. It may be easier to persuade investors to undertake what is, in effect, a change in the name of a company, than to persuade them to purchase additional shares for cash. The latter would require a rearrangement of the investors' existing portfolio, where existing shares may have to be sold to obtain the requisite cash.

How do the costs of equity capital vary with size? The initial costs incurred on raising capital (costs of the prospectus, advertising, accountants' reports, and so on) are a small component of total costs. Several studies of quoted companies have shown that costs fall considerably with size of issue (Prais, 1976, p. 108), ranging from 10–15 per cent of the sum raised to some 3–5 per cent. If these costs are capitalised, the variations reduce to a difference of only about 1 per cent when expressed in terms of annual running costs. However, substantial differences emerge in earnings-yield (taking it as a proxy for the cost of servicing equity funds of different size). A number of studies have shown that earnings-yields decline with size (see Davenport, 1971). The differential in yields between large and small companies has persisted over time, even though it has narrowed somewhat.

It has been suggested that part of the explanation for the easier terms at which capital is supplied to large firms lies in the development of financial institutions, such as the pension funds and insurance companies (Prais, 1976; Utton, 1982 and Kumar, 1983). Because of greater marketability of shares, lower investigation costs, and the institutions' desire to invest in substantial holdings, there may be a tendency to prefer large rather than small firms, but as a Department of Industry (1979) survey showed, there was no particular tendency at the end of 1975 for institutional shareholdings to be concentrated in the largest of the companies. The institutions then held roughly similar proportions of the top three size groups, covering about 800 companies. These were 42.3 per cent of the total issue of the largest size group (companies with the market value of shares of over £130 million), 47.3 per cent of the middle group (with a market value between £40 and £130 million) and 46.6 per cent of the bottom group (with a market value between £4 and £40 million). (Size groups are based on the market value of share issues on 1 July 1975.) However, in the smallest size group, containing a large number of firms (over 1700) but representing only some 6 per cent of the total value of quoted UK ordinary shares, the institutional holdings were certainly underrepresented. Whilst this may indeed reflect a possible reluctance by the financial institutions to hold the shares of smaller companies, another important factor could be that among smaller companies family-controlled shareholdings, which seldom come onto the market, are likely to be prevalent.

6.2 Financing patterns: empirical evidence

6.2.1 Variables used

In addition to the two indicators, growth by retentions and growth by external finance, which were described in Chapter 2, for each firm a number of other indicators were calculated for analysing the financing behaviour. A brief description of each of these is given below. (Precise definitions are given in Appendix A1.)[4]

Growth by equity: total (A). This is defined as a firm's issue of ordinary shares as a proportion of its opening net assets. This is then averaged over a number of years for each of the three periods, 1960–1965, 1966–1971 and 1972–1976, giving average annual growth rates. (All the following variables are similarly defined as a proportion of opening net assets, and similarly averaged.)

Growth by equity: in exchange (A_1). This consists of ordinary shares issued in exchange for subsidiaries.

Growth by equity: cash (A_2). This consists of the issue of equity minus the shares issued in exchange for subsidiaries.

Growth by gearing issues: total (B). This is obtained by taking the issue of preference shares, and the issue of long-term loans. (It is important to note the exclusion of short-term loans. As noted in Chapter 2, in the third period there was a sharp increase in these.)

Growth by gearing issue: in exchange (B_1). This includes preference shares and long-term loans issued in exchange for subsidiaries.

Growth by gearing issue: cash (B_2). This is obtained by deducting growth by gearing issue in exchange from total growth by gearing issues.

Apart from these variables which focus on components of growth by external funds, the following two variables were also constructed which measure the role of retentions in financing investment and acquisitions.

Growth by acquisition financed by retentions (C). Issue of shares and loans in exchange for subsidiaries were obtained by adding variables A_1 and B_1. To these were added the minority interests and long-term liabilities of subsidiaries. The variable was then obtained by deducting this sum from total growth by acquisition.

Growth by internal investment financed by retentions (D). This variable includes that proportion of expenditure on net investment in fixed assets and working capital which was financed by internal funds. It is obtained by deducting from the total expenditure on the two items, the total external finance raised for cash (i.e. variables A_2 and B_2). (Note that in the construction of this variable we have had to include working capital as part of internal investment. This is because we cannot distinguish between retentions used for working capital from those used for new investment. Working capital is excluded in other chapters in defining new investment.)

6.2.2 Correlation analysis

Tables 6.1 and 6.2 give matrices of correlations between four of the above variables $(A, B, C$ and $D)$ and size, growth and profitability, for the last two time periods for all the companies in the population. (The full set of variables were not available for the first period.) Consider the period 1966–1971. As Table 6.1 indicates, there was virtually no systematic relationship between opening size, and growth financed by equity and by gearing issue. This is an important result in view of the earlier discussion on the financial economies associated with size. The relationship between profitability and equity growth may also seem unexpected. The value of the correlation coefficient (0.11) indicates that less than 2 per cent of the variation in growth by equity is associated with the variation in profitability $(R^2 = 0.0121)$. It may be thought that, *ceteris paribus*, the higher the profitability, the more favourable the capital market would have been, and the more willing the firms would be to raise equity funds. That this does not appear to have been the case may be due, in part, to equity financing of acquisitions by share-for-share exchange. In such a situation profitability would be a less relevant consideration (see Section 6.6 for further discussion). That profitability is also uncorrelated with growth by gearing may be more readily explicable, since profit variability may be a more important variable in the decisions regarding gearing. Note also that com-

94

Table 6.1 *Matrix of correlation between variables used in the analysis of financing behaviour, 1966–1971*

	S	G	PA	A	I	P	E	R	A_R	I_R
Opening size S	1.00	-0.08	-0.11	-0.04	-0.15	-0.31	-0.03	-0.01	-0.09	-0.10
Growth G	-0.08	1.00	0.71	0.88	0.40	0.32	0.88	0.68	0.24	0.14
Growth of physical assets PA	-0.11	0.71	1.00	0.68	0.31	0.58	0.59	0.59	0.09	-0.04
Acquisition A	-0.04	0.88	0.68	1.00	0.17	0.19	0.89	0.63	0.43	-0.26
Investment I	-0.15	0.40	0.31	0.17	1.00	0.37	0.23	0.23	0.78	0.28
Profitability P	-0.31	0.32	0.58	0.19	0.37	1.00	0.11	0.00	0.29	0.37
Growth by equity E	-0.03	0.88	0.59	0.89	0.23	0.11	1.00	0.49	0.17	-0.12
Growth by gearing R	-0.01	0.68	0.59	0.63	0.23	0.00	0.49	1.00	0.15	-0.13
Acquisitions financed by retentions A_R	-0.09	0.24	0.09	0.43	0.78	0.29	0.17	0.15	1.00	-0.42
Investment financed by retentions I_R	-0.10	0.14	-0.04	-0.26	0.28	0.37	-0.12	-0.13	-0.42	1.0

Notes: Number of firms 1021. Correlation coefficient above an absolute value of 0.07 is significantly different from 0 at the 5 per cent level.

Table 6.2 *Matrix of correlation between variables used in the analysis of financing behaviour, 1972–1976*

	S	G	PA	A	I	P	E	R	A_R	I_R
Opening size S	1.00	-0.20	-0.11	-0.06	-0.12	-0.28	-0.05	0.06	-0.12	-0.22
Growth G	-0.20	1.00	0.56	0.53	0.46	0.56	0.63	0.48	-0.03	0.57
Growth of physical assets PA	-0.11	0.56	1.00	0.53	0.34	0.21	0.50	0.39	0.17	0.12
Acquisition A	-0.06	0.53	0.53	1.00	0.10	-0.02	0.79	0.56	0.50	-0.32
Investment I	-0.12	0.46	0.34	0.10	1.00	0.28	0.12	0.17	0.09	0.39
Profitability P	-0.28	0.56	0.21	-0.02	0.28	1.00	0.02	-0.05	-0.03	0.65
Growth by equity E	-0.05	0.63	0.50	0.79	0.12	0.02	1.00	0.43	0.11	-0.05
Growth by gearing R	0.06	0.48	0.39	0.56	0.17	-0.05	0.43	1.00	0.10	-0.11
Acquisitions financed by retentions A_R	-0.12	-0.03	0.17	0.50	0.09	-0.03	0.11	0.10	1.00	-0.43
Investment financed by retentions I_R	-0.22	0.57	0.12	-0.32	0.39	0.65	-0.05	-0.11	-0.43	1.00

Notes: Number of firms 824. Correlation coefficient above an absolute value of 0.07 is significantly different from 0 at the 5 per cent level.

panies which had above average equity growth, also had above average growth by gearing issue – a consequence of these two variables being highly correlated with growth of net assets. This suggests that firms which had the opportunities for growth were willing to obtain funds from external sources, without preference for borrowing or for equity shares (this needs to be qualified – see below). It is also noticeable that both equity and gearing growth are more highly correlated with acquisition activity, than with new investment. This strengthens the general view that on average external financing was used more in the process of acquisition than for internal growth.

There is a rather high negative correlation between acquisitions financed by retentions, and investment financed by retentions. To the extent that internal funds were used for acquisitions, this indicates a trade-off between the two forms of growth. This supplements the results in Chapter 4 which showed a positive association between acquisitions and investment in a cross section. In the discussion in that chapter it was noted that there may be a trade-off between these two activities for financial reasons. The empirical results, however, found a positive relationship. The present result indicates that where access to external finance is limited (or typically where share exchange for acquisitions may not be possible) then high acquisition activity may be at the expense of new investment. ('Investment' here includes both new fixed investment and current assets.)

The results for 1972–1976 (Table 6.2) provide a somewhat different picture. Whilst opening size is still negatively correlated with equity growth, there is a slight positive relationship between size and growth by gearing issues. Total growth is again highly correlated with gearing and equity issues, but in addition there is a stronger relationship between growth, and investment financed by retentions. However, the correlation between growth and acquisition activity is lower than in the earlier period, whilst that between growth and investment is slightly greater.

The earlier result that there was some trade-off between investment financed by retentions, and acquisitions similarly financed, continues to hold. Moreover, there is a negative relationship between acquisition expenditure in total and investment by retentions. But there is again no evidence of substitution between overall investment (financed from all sources) and acquisition expenditure.

Thus there are three main conclusions to be drawn from the two tables: small firms did not seem to be deterred by the fixed costs of making new equity or gearing issues; firms which had a high reliance on equity issues did not have above average profitability; and, there was a negative relationship between acquisitions financed by retentions and investment similarly financed.

6.2.3 Disaggregate analysis

This section extends the first two of the above issues by examining the association between size, growth and profitability, and source of finance for firms in individual industries. The aim is to consider whether the differences in technology and market environment, as well as the entry barriers, which characterise different industries, exert any strong influence on the firms' financing pattern. For example, it might be thought that, other things equal, firms operating in capital intensive industries would rely on internal funds more than others.[5]

Consider first Table 6.3. For 1960–1965, as the first column indicates, growth

Table 6.3 *The correlation between growth by internal funds, and size, growth and profitability*

Industry	1960–1965			1966–1971			1972–1976		
	size	Internal funds and growth	profitability	size	Internal funds and growth	profitability	size	Internal funds and growth	profitability
21 Food	-0.05	0.37	0.79	-0.23	0.59	0.43	-0.25	0.70	0.86
23 Drink	-0.17	0.31	0.81	-0.20	0.39	0.70	-0.27	0.94	0.49
26 Chemicals	-0.28	0.81	0.85	0.01	0.70	0.94	-0.27	0.76	0.84
31 Metal manf.	-0.36	0.69	0.87	-0.12	0.53	0.72	-0.38	0.86	0.81
33 Non-elec. eng.	-0.28	0.59	0.86	-0.24	0.39	0.85	-0.38	0.69	0.77
36 Elec. eng.	-0.21	0.50	0.90	-0.09	0.28	0.78	-0.01	0.95	0.82
38 Vehicles	-0.25	0.70	0.82	-0.30	0.71	0.82	-0.45	0.92	0.67
39 Metal goods	-0.25	0.56	0.92	-0.18	0.50	0.66	-0.29	0.67	0.70
41 Textiles	-0.06	0.59	0.88	-0.01	0.86	0.16	-0.35	0.86	0.82
44 Clothing etc.	-0.27	0.62	0.87	-0.42	0.87	0.86	-0.69	0.50	0.89
46 Bricks etc.	-0.09	0.55	0.80	-0.34	0.56	0.04	-0.26	0.89	0.75
47 Timber etc.	-0.42	0.72	0.89	-0.49	0.72	0.75	0.09	0.79	0.81
48 Paper etc.	-0.13	0.43	0.74	-0.19	0.52	0.82	-0.15	0.92	0.70
49 Other manf.	-0.33	0.81	0.91	-0.18	0.32	0.76	-0.40	0.87	0.72
All manufacturing	-0.21	0.60	0.86	-0.14	0.53	0.60	-0.39	0.78	0.77
50 Construction	0.07	0.50	0.85	-0.03	0.60	0.71	-0.40	0.69	0.78
70 Transport	-0.21	0.66	0.89	-0.30	0.42	0.73	-0.58	0.71	0.92
81 Wholesale	-0.12	0.71	0.82	-0.21	0.68	0.84	-0.27	0.62	0.70
82 Retail	-0.14	0.39	0.82	-0.23	0.69	0.80	-0.28	0.66	0.84
88 Misc.	0.13	0.57	0.79	-0.40	0.38	0.80	-0.40	0.60	0.79
All non-manufacturing	-0.06	0.52	0.81	-0.21	0.45	0.77	-0.37	0.65	0.82
All industries	-0.18	0.55	0.55	-0.16	0.52	0.63	-0.38	0.72	0.76

Notes: Number of firms is as in Table 4.1. Size is measured by net assets.

financed by retentions was negatively correlated with opening size across firms in all but two industries. The influence of size was not strong in absolute terms but, because of the large number of firms being analysed, it was generally statistically significant. There was, however, no tendency for firms in capital intensive industries (such as Chemicals, Engineering and Vehicles) to exhibit any stronger negative relationship than firms in other industries. The second column indicates the correlation between growth of net assets, and retentions. Not surprisingly, there is a significantly positive relationship but its magnitude is again not high – on average the correlation is around 0.6 ($R^2 = 0.36$), indicating that only about a third of the variance in total growth can be associated with retentions. Whilst firms in some industries, notably Chemicals, Metal goods and Vehicles, do have stronger correlations, in general growth rates exhibit a high degree of variation independent of the availability of internal funds. The third column shows the correlation between profitability and retentions. Here there is a consistently strong and significantly positive relationship.

The second and third parts of Table 6.3 provide similar information for 1966–1971 and 1972–1976. Whilst the results for the last period are similar to those for the first one – there is a mild negative relationship between size and retentions, and a strong positive one between the latter variable and growth, and profitability – the second period is somewhat different. The direction of the association between variables is the same but the magnitudes are generally lower (in absolute terms). For example, the correlation with growth is around 0.5, and that with profitability around 0.6. It is plausible to argue that to a considerable extent this may be due to the reliance of firms during the second period on above average acquisition activity, and the different forms of financing which go with it.

Table 6.4 presents the relationship between growth by external funds and the other variables. In all three periods, there was no marked tendency for smaller firms to rely less on the capital market than larger firms. Note, however, that since the growth of smaller firms was slightly greater, this suggests that as a proportion of total growth, they may have relied marginally less on external funds than did larger firms. For growth, there is a high correlation for firms across all industries. This is far from being the case for profitability. In general, the relationship between external financing and profitability is weak, and in a number of industries there is a clear negative relationship. At the simplest level, this may reflect the fact that higher profitability, acting as a proxy for the high availability of internal funds, is associated with limited recourse to the capital market. This effect, thereby, outweighing the consideration where profitability is regarded as a proxy for the efficiency with which funds are used (see below for further discussion).

6.3 Financing patterns: growth by external funds

This section examines further whether there is any systematic relationship between growth by external funds, and some of the other aspects of firm growth and performance studied earlier. The following are some of the questions on which evidence is provided below. Do firms which grow faster than average by external funds also grow faster than average by internal funds? Do these firms have significantly greater reliance on acquisitions compared to new investment? Does the contribution of the two main components of growth by external funds – equity and

Table 6.4 *The correlation between growth by external funds, and size, growth and profitability*

Industry	1960–1965			1966–1971			1972–1976		
	size	External funds and growth	profitability	size	External funds and growth	profitability	size	External funds and growth	profitability
21 Food	-0.04	0.94	-0.13	-0.01	0.99	-0.19	-0.25	0.42	-0.43
23 Drink	0.30	0.93	0.23	0.19	0.98	0.21	0.19	0.60	0.10
26 Chemicals	-0.07	0.68	0.13	-0.12	0.80	0.05	0.01	0.50	-0.16
31 Metal manf.	-0.08	0.91	0.24	-0.07	0.98	-0.01	-0.04	0.24	-0.15
33 Non-elec. eng.	-0.14	0.92	0.07	-0.01	0.93	0.01	-0.13	0.88	0.14
36 Elec. eng.	-0.03	0.91	-0.04	0.36	0.92	-0.21	0.21	0.13	-0.26
38 Vehicles	-0.09	0.91	0.22	-0.34	0.89	0.18	-0.23	0.66	0.04
39 Metal goods	0.06	0.91	0.12	0.11	0.94	0.02	0.12	0.76	-0.02
41 Textiles	0.01	0.92	0.18	0.15	0.51	0.10	0.11	0.51	0.04
44 Clothing etc.	0.10	0.88	0.07	-0.30	0.97	0.53	-0.26	0.89	0.02
46 Bricks etc.	0.01	0.95	0.19	-0.05	0.97	0.41	0.19	0.56	0.16
47 Timber etc.	0.02	0.84	0.23	0.06	0.75	0.09	0.08	0.67	-0.13
48 Paper etc.	0.22	0.89	-0.10	-0.14	0.71	-0.17	0.28	0.20	-0.17
49 Other manf.	0.01	0.92	0.41	-0.10	0.90	0.06	0.00	0.72	0.34
All manufacturing	-0.01	0.90	0.18	0.02	0.91	0.02	0.02	0.69	0.03
50 Construction	-0.18	0.82	-0.13	-0.21	0.96	0.23	0.03	0.77	0.01
70 Transport	-0.23	0.98	0.40	0.22	0.91	-0.07	-0.05	0.68	0.02
81 Wholesale	-0.07	0.93	0.19	0.21	0.76	0.04	0.03	0.68	0.0
82 Retail	-0.17	0.96	-0.08	-0.05	0.84	0.05	0.01	0.75	-0.03
88 Misc.	-0.06	0.93	-0.02	-0.23	0.99	0.50	0.16	0.76	-0.05
All non-manufacturing	-0.13	0.96	0.25	-0.05	0.95	0.23	0.03	0.72	0.01
All industries	-0.15	0.92	0.07	-0.02	0.92	0.08	0.02	0.70	0.03

Notes: Number of firms is as in Table 4.1

gearing issues – vary as growth increases? In order to examine these questions firms were classified first by their growth due to external funds, and second by their total growth. Using this classification, further information was also obtained supplementing the information provided by the correlation between external growth on the one hand, and size, growth and profitability on the other.

Consider, first, classification by external funds. The results in Tables 6.5 and 6.6 give a very considerable amount of information. We discuss below only the more salient features. In the period 1960–1965, 724 firms, that is nearly two-fifths, raised no external finance at all. The average growth of net assets of these firms financed by retentions, was 5.8 per cent. This is less than two-thirds of the average growth rate of 9.2 per cent for the whole population. In terms of physical assets, they also had lower growth, although the difference was somewhat less. These companies had however the *highest* average profitability in the population. It is difficult to provide any causal explanation of the factors influencing these firms' aversion to the capital market: high profitability may have provided sufficient internal funds, but if the firms had had more opportunities for growth, external funds might have been necessary. (At the same time, if there is a trade-off between growth and profitability, profitability may in turn have been lower.) A particular feature to note about these firms is that their average size is only marginally less than the overall average.

For the next two groups, the average opening size increases sharply, but both groups have lower profitability. (Somewhat perversely, the growth of net assets of the first group is slightly greater than that of the second group.) The proportion of growth due to acquisition is considerably higher for these groups compared to the first one, but it is still less than the overall average. As between gearing and equity issues, the preponderant form is equity, although in both cases there is a high degree of variation around the average. (Note that the growth due to gearing and equity issues seems to be slightly less than growth by external funds. The difference is accounted for by changes in the interest of minority shareholders. See Appendix A1.)

When the next two groups are examined, those between 5.0 and 7.5 per cent, and between 7.5 and 10.0 per cent, it appears that there is a non-linear pattern. For example, the size of these companies is considerably smaller than the two preceding groups. Indeed, for the group 7.5–10.0 per cent, the average size is just over half that of the average of the total sample of firms (it was £3.6 million compared to £5.9 million for the average). Secondly, the profitability is a little higher. The pattern regarding equity and gearing issues is, however, similar, with equity growth being almost twice as important as that due to gearing issues.

For the firms which relied most heavily on external funds, three features are prominent (Row 6, Table 6.5). First, these firms were somewhat smaller than the average; second, the very high growth of net assets (27.9 per cent) was achieved mainly by external finance – retentions were not significantly above average; and third, growth by acquisition accounted for more than half the total growth. Note also that, in general, equity growth was more than double that due to gearing except for the last group, where it was almost three times as great.

The period 1966–1971 provides some noticeable contrasts. The following are the main features:

(i) A small proportion (327 firms, or less than a third) undertook no external financing at all.

Table 6.5 Analysis by growth by external funds: characteristics and performance

Growth by external funds	Profitability m	Profitability s	External financing m	External financing s	Equity m	Equity s	Gearing issues m	Gearing issues s	Retentions m	Retentions s	Net investment m	Net investment s	Acqui-sitions m	Acqui-sitions s	Physical assets m	Physical assets s	Net assets m	Net assets s	Opening size m	Opening size s	No of firms
1960–1965																					
< 0.0	19.3	8.6	-0.4	0.9	0.0	0.0	-0.4	0.9	6.1	4.2	3.2	3.6	0.8	2.2	9.9	7.3	5.8	4.3	5.8	12.9	724
0.0 < ≤ 2.5	15.8	9.2	0.9	0.8	0.6	1.0	0.2	0.8	4.6	4.2	3.0	3.6	1.5	2.8	10.3	7.1	5.5	4.3	8.8	29.1	361
2.5 < ≤ 5.0	15.6	6.6	3.7	0.7	2.3	2.0	1.1	1.9	5.0	3.7	4.4	3.7	2.2	3.1	12.6	9.0	8.7	3.8	12.5	52.5	200
5.0 < ≤ 7.5	16.5	8.3	6.2	0.7	4.0	2.4	1.8	2.5	5.1	4.4	5.6	4.2	3.4	4.3	15.7	8.9	11.3	4.5	6.3	15.3	127
7.5 < ≤ 10.0	16.3	7.5	8.7	0.7	5.1	3.0	2.9	3.0	5.3	3.9	6.6	4.8	5.1	5.0	16.8	7.4	14.0	4.1	3.6	5.8	98
> 10.0	17.8	8.3	21.1	16.1	14.2	14.5	5.3	5.4	6.8	5.1	11.9	10.5	5.6	17.8	32.5	23.5	27.9	17.9	4.7	9.9	237
All firms	16.3	8.8	4.2	9.3	2.9	7.3	1.1	3.0	4.9	4.4	4.5	6.0	3.4	8.7	13.5	13.8	9.2	11.1	5.9	24.0	1747
1966–1971																					
< 0.0	16.5	9.9	-0.5	1.2	1.0	0.4	-0.4	1.1	3.8	4.8	2.1	4.9	0.4	2.0	1.2	7.0	3.3	5.2	4.8	13.5	327
0.0 < ≤ 2.5	16.7	8.3	0.9	0.8	0.5	0.8	0.4	0.9	4.1	4.0	2.9	3.7	1.2	2.5	8.2	5.9	5.0	4.1	13.7	41.2	232
2.5 < ≤ 5.0	16.4	11.2	3.8	0.7	1.4	1.7	2.2	2.1	4.9	11.9	4.2	4.0	2.0	8.6	11.4	17.5	8.7	11.9	20.0	41.2	139
5.0 < ≤ 7.5	15.6	8.5	6.1	0.7	2.2	2.3	3.4	2.4	4.4	4.8	5.1	5.2	2.8	3.3	11.8	6.0	10.5	5.0	24.1	115.8	86
7.5 < ≤ 10.0	15.8	6.5	8.7	0.7	4.0	3.0	4.0	3.1	4.8	4.1	5.8	4.8	5.8	5.2	15.5	8.3	13.9	3.9	27.3	55.3	62
> 10.0	17.8	11.3	25.5	23.8	15.4	17.9	7.8	7.7	5.3	6.1	7.4	7.6	21.3	26.5	33.1	37.0	30.8	26.2	11.0	27.6	175
All firms	16.6	9.7	6.0	13.5	3.4	9.3	2.1	4.6	4.4	6.3	4.0	5.5	4.9	13.9	13.0	19.9	10.4	15.7	12.9	46.4	1021
1972–1976																					
< 0.0	19.6	12.2	-1.0	3.8	0.1	0.3	-0.5	1.2	14.9	9.1	4.0	6.0	0.8	3.2	15.8	8.2	13.9	10.5	8.5	17.9	289
0.0 < ≤ 2.5	21.0	8.9	0.9	0.7	0.7	1.0	0.1	0.9	16.1	7.5	5.0	6.3	1.4	2.5	17.8	8.3	17.1	7.5	30.2	78.8	227
2.5 < ≤ 5.0	19.8	10.6	3.7	0.7	2.3	1.7	0.7	1.4	14.8	10.7	5.3	6.1	3.4	8.0	21.0	18.9	18.4	10.7	38.0	80.0	115
5.0 < ≤ 7.5	21.3	8.0	6.1	0.7	3.8	2.4	1.7	2.4	16.9	8.7	6.5	7.0	4.5	4.9	21.3	17.3	22.9	8.7	51.4	193.9	76
7.5 < ≤ 10.0	14.7	11.7	8.8	0.6	4.7	2.0	3.5	3.1	11.1	13.8	7.0	10.2	6.3	7.3	22.8	13.0	19.9	13.9	28.1	41.8	29
> 10.0	20.4	13.2	22.5	16.5	13.7	12.7	7.2	8.1	15.4	10.9	8.1	10.3	19.2	18.0	37.2	19.4	37.9	19.4	23.9	66.1	88
All firms	20.1	11.0	3.7	9.1	2.5	5.9	1.0	3.8	15.3	9.4	5.2	7.1	3.8	9.1	20.1	14.3	19.0	13.2	25.0	83.0	824

Notes: m = mean growth of variable % per annum except profitability which is % per annum. Opening size is £ million.
s = standard deviation.

Table 6.6 *Analysis by growth by external funds: equity and gearing issues*

Growth by external funds	Equity for cash		Equity for exchange		Gearing issue for cash		Gearing issue for exchange		Acquisition by retentions		Investment by retentions		External funds for cash	
	m	s	m	s	m	s	m	s	m	s	m	s	m	s
1966–1971														
≤ 0.0	0.0	0.0	0.0	0.0	-0.4	1.1	0.0	0.0	0.5	2.1	3.8	5.0	-0.4	1.1
≤ 2.5	0.2	0.6	0.2	0.5	0.3	0.9	0.1	0.3	0.8	2.4	3.6	3.9	0.5	0.9
≤ 5.0	0.6	1.3	0.7	1.3	2.0	2.1	0.2	0.7	0.9	8.7	4.2	10.5	2.6	2.0
≤ 7.5	1.1	1.8	1.2	1.8	3.1	2.5	0.3	0.8	0.9	2.8	3.6	4.8	4.2	2.5
≤ 10.0	1.8	2.6	2.2	2.8	2.8	3.1	1.1	1.8	1.7	4.5	2.9	4.8	4.6	3.6
> 10.0	3.2	5.0	12.2	17.6	3.2	4.6	4.6	8.5	2.2	7.8	1.7	8.2	6.4	6.8
All firms	0.9	2.6	2.5	8.6	1.2	2.9	0.9	3.9	1.0	5.1	3.4	6.5	2.1	4.1
1972–1976														
≤ 0.0	0.1	0.3	0.0	0.0	-0.5	1.2	0.0	0.0	1.3	4.2	14.4	9.3	-0.4	1.2
≤ 2.5	0.5	0.8	0.2	0.6	0.1	0.9	0.0	0.0	1.0	2.6	15.3	7.6	0.6	1.0
≤ 5.0	1.5	1.6	0.8	1.3	0.6	1.3	0.1	0.5	1.8	7.8	12.8	1.8	2.1	1.6
≤ 7.5	2.3	2.3	1.5	2.2	1.6	2.5	0.1	0.6	2.3	4.3	14.5	8.8	3.9	2.5
≤ 10.0	2.6	2.7	2.1	2.6	2.5	3.5	1.0	1.7	2.6	6.9	8.8	13.3	5.1	3.4
> 10.0	3.8	4.5	9.9	12.8	3.2	5.5	3.9	7.1	3.8	7.4	10.8	12.0	7.1	6.3
All firms	1.1	2.2	1.5	5.2	0.5	2.6	0.5	2.6	1.7	5.1	13.8	10.6	1.6	3.5

Notes: See Table 6.5. Number of firms is as in Table 6.5.

(ii) This time, these firms were the smallest in terms of opening size (the average size being a third of all firms). Whilst their growth was also the lowest, their profitability was the same as that of the average. At the other extreme, the firms which had the highest growth by external funds were, again, somewhat smaller than the average. But this time they were still more than twice the size of firms which had not had recourse to the capital market at all.

(iii) Generally in this period growth by gearing issues was greater than in the earlier period. Except for the group relying most heavily on external funds, it was not much less than, and in some cases it was more than, growth by equity. As noted earlier, issues of gearing for the acquisition of ordinary shares of another company may have been used to restructure a company's capital. Since this period saw a high rate of acquisition activity, this to some extent may explain the results.

(iv) Despite the higher growth rates, the retentions were lower than in the earlier period, but there was again no systematic relationship between profitability and external finance.

(v) The dominant feature of this period is the very high average growth by acquisition – exceeding growth by new fixed investment – and it was accompanied by above average external funds.

One main characteristic of the period 1972–1976 is the heavy reliance on retentions, which accounted on average for more than 80 per cent of the growth of net assets. As noted in Chapter 2, a high proportion of growth in assets in this period was due to the increase in current assets including stocks. Since stock appreciation is included in profits and retentions, this result is to be expected.

Table 6.6 provides additional information on equity and gearing issues, as well as on the financing of investment and acquisitions by retentions. (The information should be considered in conjunction with that given in Table 6.5. Note that in Table 6.6 comparable data were not available for the period 1960–1965.) For the period 1966–1971, the following two results stand out:

(i) Issues of equity for cash were only slightly less than those in exchange for subsidiaries, for the majority of firms. But for the group with the greatest reliance on external funds, issues of equity for cash were only about a quarter of the issues in exchange. More surprising is the evidence that the gearing issues for cash exceeded those in exchange, for all groups except the last one. Since equity by exchange also exceeded gearing by exchange, it shows that, for the majority, acquisitions were undertaken with share-for-share exchange rather than with loan-for-loan exchange. Superficially at least, this suggests that the earlier argument that gearing issues for exchange may have been extensively used to alter companies' capital structure does not seem to be generally valid.

(ii) Acquisitions by retentions accounted for a very small proportion of acquisitions (Tables 6.5 and 6.6). But external funds for cash were far from negligible – for example, for the group with external funds between 5.0 and 7.5 per cent, the average funds for cash were 4.2 per cent out of a group mean of 6.1 per cent. Similarly, for the next group funds for cash were 4.6 per cent out of the group mean of 8.7 per cent. To the extent that these funds were used for investment, the earlier impression that new investment (fixed and current) was largely financed by retentions needs to be modified.

The period 1972–1976 presents a similar picture with regard to the first of the

Table 6.7 *Analysis by growth of net assets*

Growth	Profitability m	s	External financing m	s	Equity m	s	Gearing issues m	s	Retentions m	s	Net investment m	s	Acqui-sitions m	s	Physical assets m	s	Net assets m	s	Opening size m	s	No of firms
1960–1965																					
< 0.0	3.3	0.5	-0.6	0.2	0.1	0.1	-0.5	0.1	-2.0	0.2	-1.0	0.3	0.2	0.3	2.5	0.6	-2.6	0.2	3.7	15.7	125
< | < 2.5	10.3	5.0	-0.1	1.2	0.1	0.8	0.0	–	1.5	0.1	1.3	2.4	0.8	3.0	6.1	6.3	1.4	0.7	4.0	12.9	225
< | < 5.0	14.3	5.1	0.3	1.2	0.3	1.0	0.1	0.9	3.5	1.3	2.3	2.6	0.8	2.2	8.4	6.3	3.8	0.7	7.3	28.4	319
< | < 10.0	17.8	6.3	1.9	2.5	1.2	2.0	0.6	1.7	5.5	2.5	4.0	3.1	1.5	2.8	11.8	7.3	7.3	0.1	8.7	35.1	516
< | < 15.0	20.1	8.3	5.0	3.8	3.2	3.1	1.5	2.8	7.1	3.5	5.8	3.7	3.0	3.8	14.9	3.8	12.1	1.4	4.2	8.5	268
< | < 20.0	22.9	10.3	8.7	5.1	5.4	4.3	2.8	3.4	8.5	4.8	7.6	5.0	6.3	6.5	21.4	9.5	17.3	1.5	4.2	9.7	122
> 20.0	22.1	10.3	23.6	18.5	16.4	16.4	5.3	5.9	9.7	6.2	14.2	11.1	18.3	19.8	37.9	25.2	33.3	18.6	3.1	7.4	172
All firms	16.3	8.8	4.2	9.3	2.9	7.3	1.1	3.0	4.9	4.4	4.5	6.0	3.4	8.7	13.5	13.8	9.2	11.1	5.9	24.0	1747
1966–1971																					
< 0.0	5.5	12.0	-0.8	2.5	0.20	0.9	-0.6	2.1	-2.8	8.0	-1.6	4.4	-0.9	10.6	2.1	7.6	-3.6	7.5	8.8	25.1	81
< | < 2.5	11.6	5.5	0.001	0.9	0.20	0.5	-0.1	0.8	1.3	1.1	0.8	3.3	0.5	1.9	4.9	5.9	1.3	0.7	7.0	12.6	133
< | < 5.0	15.4	6.4	0.7	1.5	0.5	1.1	0.2	1.1	3.1	1.5	2.1	2.9	1.0	2.1	6.2	4.4	3.7	0.7	15.5	46.6	166
< | < 10.0	18.0	7.8	2.6	3.2	0.9	2.0	1.5	2.2	4.8	3.3	3.9	3.3	1.7	3.1	9.7	5.1	7.4	1.4	16.8	69.8	289
< | < 15.0	19.5	8.8	6.0	4.1	2.6	3.0	2.8	3.1	6.2	3.9	5.5	3.6	4.0	4.0	15.4	16.7	12.2	1.4	17.1	43.7	162
< | < 20.0	20.2	8.6	9.7	4.7	4.8	4.0	4.0	3.8	7.5	4.8	7.0	5.9	7.0	6.4	18.8	8.0	17.1	1.4	9.3	15.4	58
> 20.0	22.0	12.4	28.5	26.9	17.7	19.9	8.2	8.7	9.3	11.7	9.8	8.5	25.0	29.5	38.1	41.1	37.8	28.5	6.1	13.6	132
All firms	16.6	9.7	6.0	13.5	3.4	9.3	2.1	4.6	4.4	6.3	4.0	5.5	4.9	13.9	13.0	19.9	10.4	15.7	12.9	46.4	1021
1972–1976																					
< 0.0	-4.8	18.0	-2.8	13.8	1.7	3.1	-1.3	3.5	-6.0	9.3	-4.3	14.3	4.2	17.6	6.4	8.8	-8.8	13.4	17.0	23.2	24
< | < 2.5	7.4	8.4	-0.7	2.9	0.4	0.9	-0.5	2.4	2.0	2.9	0.6	5.3	2.7	3.9	11.0	7.1	1.2	0.6	9.6	7.7	10
< | < 5.0	8.5	5.4	-0.3	1.5	0.3	1.2	-0.4	0.4	4.1	1.4	1.7	2.7	1.6	3.6	21.9	45.8	3.8	0.7	11.6	13.9	18
< | < 10.0	13.4	6.5	0.7	2.5	0.5	1.1	0.2	2.0	7.3	2.5	2.8	4.4	1.2	2.5	13.0	6.8	8.0	1.4	36.0	78.0	96
< | < 15.0	16.6	5.0	1.2	2.5	0.9	1.4	0.1	1.7	11.2	2.7	3.2	4.6	1.3	2.9	15.1	7.3	12.4	1.5	29.3	61.0	185
< | < 20.0	21.4	7.6	2.1	3.6	1.4	2.3	0.5	1.7	15.3	3.9	4.1	5.1	2.4	4.5	18.9	7.5	17.4	1.4	36.0	147.6	168
> 20.0	26.2	10.2	7.7	12.6	4.9	8.7	2.3	5.3	22.7	8.6	8.7	7.4	6.9	12.4	27.0	15.4	30.4	12.5	15.2	44.6	323
All firms	20.1	11.0	3.7	9.1	2.5	5.9	1.0	3.8	15.3	9.4	5.2	7.1	3.8	9.1	20.1	14.3	19.0	13.2	25.0	82.7	824

Notes: See Table 6.5.

105

above results. Equity issues for cash were larger than those in exchange, except for the group relying most heavily on external funds. Gearing issues for cash were on average similar to those in exchange for subsidiaries. Even for the above group there was a smaller difference between these issues for cash and for exchange (note again that gearing issues in exchange were considerably smaller in this period). The main difference is in the financing of acquisitions – a considerable proportion of these were financed by retentions. For example, for the first four groups, on average almost half the growth due to acquisition was financed by internal funds.

Finally, Table 6.7 presents the average values of variables examined earlier according to growth of net assets. This supplements and extends the above results. Three main points are of some interest. First, in all time periods reliance on external financing increased as growth increased. Second, retentions also increased concomitantly, though this does not mean that those having an above average reliance on external funds also had an above average reliance on retentions. Third, issues of equity exceeded considerably the gearing issues, especially in the case of the fastest growing firms.

6.4 The gearing and retention ratios

The previous analysis has focused on the rate of change of assets associated with alternative forms of financing. This section examines the *average* values of gearing and retention ratios for firms in different size classes. The results for the average of the ratios for the two recent periods are shown in Table 6.8.[6] As this table shows, there is an almost uniform increase in the average gearing ratio as firm size increases. In the period 1966–1971, the average gearing of the largest firms was more than twice that of the smallest. This reflects to a considerable extent the fact that, owing to their relatively more stable performance, given industry environment and so on, large firms are both willing, and able, to undertake higher gearing. It is noticeable that in the last period there was a decline in this ratio across all size classes, but that it was much more pronounced for the smallest firms. Firms with assets greater than £32 millions had a gearing ratio which was now more than three times as high as that for the smallest firms.[7]

There has been some discussion of the reasons why firms in this period might have shunned long-term debt. Pepper *et al.* (1978) claimed that the government had 'crowded out' private firms from the long-term debt market, which were forced to increase their short-term borrowing from banks, and from other sources, such as rights issues. Others have suggested that the reason lies more in the uncertainty regarding the inflation rate and the interest rate (Flemming *et al.*, 1976). This seems more plausible since there is very little direct evidence to suggest that any form of 'crowding out' did, in fact, occur.

It is noticeable that the retention ratio does not vary significantly with size. (The results for £8–16 million are influenced by a small number of extreme observations as indicated by the standard deviation.) Following the discussion in Section 6.1, one might have expected larger, more managerially dominated, firms to have higher retention ratios. The result that this is not so, simply reinforces the fact that specific managerial preferences are only one element in the firms' financial decisions. Over time there is an increase in this ratio, but again there is no systematic relationship with size.

Table 6.8 *Gearing and retention ratios*

A 1966–1971

Opening size	Gearing ratio		Retention ratio		Growth		
	m	S.D.	m	S.D.	m	S.D.	n
≤ 2m	12.1	11.6	43.3	71.9	11.5	16.7	380
≤ 4m	16.7	13.0	42.0	55.5	9.4	14.8	242
≤ 8m	18.3	14.9	46.0	85.8	10.5	20.4	164
≤ 16m	19.5	14.2	41.3	98.1	10.0	10.3	89
≤ 32m	17.6	11.6	49.9	59.4	8.6	9.6	70
> 32m	25.8	11.2	40.4	32.7	9.7	10.4	76
All firms	16.2	13.3	41.6	76.3	10.4	15.7	1021

B 1972–1976

Opening size	m	S.D.	m	S.D.	m	S.D.	n
≤ 2m	6.6	8.7	66.8	37.5	24.6	14.1	143
≤ 4m	10.1	9.5	67.2	144.9	20.6	14.1	203
≤ 8m	13.8	16.5	63.7	108.8	17.1	13.5	176
≤ 16m	15,4	10.3	59.9	178.1	17.2	11.5	118
≤ 32m	15.1	9.6	67.4	17.2	16.1	8.1	68
> 32m	21.6	11.2	64.2	43.0	15.6	10.7	116
All firms	13.1	12.4	65.4	169.8	19.0	13.2	824

Notes: m denotes annual average of the variable for the period, for firms in each size class. S.D. denotes standard deviation, and n the number of firms (same for the three variables). Opening size is measured in terms of net assets.

6.5 Impact of external financing on subsequent growth and profitability

6.5.1 The capital market and efficiency

The findings that acquisitions, which did not on average lead to any improvement in profitability, were externally financed, and that on average there was no relationship between profitability and issue of equity, call into question the 'capital market discipline' argument. The main proposition is that the process of raising finance through the market leads to a more efficient use of funds, and higher profitability, than do retentions (Baumol, 1965). Empirical evidence is provided by Baumol *et al.* (1970), Whittington (1972) and McFetridge (1978). The first two of these studies relate to a period in the 1950s. The exercise below provides some related evidence for the recent periods. In addition, the direct effect of external finance on firms' subsequent growth is examined.

The mechanism affecting profitability is supposed to operate in two ways. First, the return on the *new funds* raised should be regarded as satisfactory by the market; otherwise the interest and dividends will be paid at the expense of the existing shareholders. Second, raising external funds will generally require optimistic plans and forecasts concerning the *overall* profitability of the firm. The basic premise is that there is considerable uncertainty regarding the probable return on investment, and that this uncertainty will be lessened if the firm can produce an encouraging forecast about its overall profitability, rather than merely about the profitability of the new investment which is being financed (Whittington, 1972, p. 153).

To the extent that profitability is positively correlated with growth of assets, the above mechanism would generate an expectation of higher growth as well. Between two otherwise similar firms, that is, having similar profit and growth rates in the period in which external financing is observed, the firm raising external funds would be expected to have the higher future profitability and growth. (Note that the second argument implies that it is the *fact* of recourse to the capital market, rather than the amount of funds raised, which improves future profitability.) But to the extent that, after a point, growth is at the expense of profitability, the above mechanism would suggest a *lower* growth rate. The argument would be that market discipline would require firms to undertake growth only up to the point where there was a positive return. Thus a firm which would otherwise have pursued the goal of growth maximisation would be restrained (cf. Mueller, 1969, who argued that 'mature' firms with limited investment opportunities, rely on retentions to invest at the expense of their shareholders).

6.5.2 Empirical evidence

The empirical evidence tries to assess whether the consequence of the capital market's discipline is that firms which have been subject to it, do indeed have higher future profitability, and higher growth, than otherwise similar firms which rely more heavily on internal funds. The sample consists of a total of 832 firms which continued in independent existence between 1960–1971, and 694 firms which continued between 1966–1976. Consider first the effect on growth: a cross-sectional model of the following form was estimated:

$$G_{i,t} = \alpha + \beta E_{i,t-1} + \epsilon_{i,t} \tag{6.1}$$

where G is total growth, E is growth due to external funds, i refers to ith company, ϵ is the error term, t refers to the period 1972–1976 (or 1966–1971) and $t-1$ refers to the period 1966–1971 (or 1960–1965). (This equation was based on Whittington, 1972.) An alternative equation was

$$G_{i,t} = \alpha + \beta D_{i,t-1} + \epsilon_{i,t} \tag{6.2}$$

where D is a dummy variable which equals 1 when E exceeds 0.01, and is otherwise zero.

The results of fitting these equations across all manufacturing firms are given in equations (1) and (2) of Table 6.9. The first impression is that, contrary to the expectation, the raising of external funds has some positive impact: the value of the coefficient b (0.39), implies that 10 per cent higher than average externally financed growth in one period was associated with 3.9 percentage points higher than average subsequent total growth. However, the amount of variation in

Table 6.9 *Impact of external financing on growth, 1960–1971*

	Equation number	E	D	P	$\bar{R}^2$
Manufacturing firms	(1)	0.39* (0.07)			0.05
	(2)		0.025* (0.01)		0.01
	(3)			0.17* (0.07)	0.01
	(4)	0.39* (0.07)		0.16* (0.06)	0.06
	(5)		0.03* (0.01)	0.19* (0.07)	0.02
Non-manufacturing firms	(6)	0.04 (0.04)			0.01
	(7)		-0.01 (0.01)		0.001
	(8)			0.22* (0.08)	0.04
	(9)	0.03 (0.04)		0.22* (0.08)	0.04
	(10)		-0.001 (0.01)	0.22* (0.08)	0.4

Notes: Standard errors are given in brackets.
* denotes significantly different from 0 at the 5 per cent level.
Number of firms: manufacturing 635, non-manufacturing 197.

subsequent growth explained by externally financed growth is small. In the equation with the dummy variable, the value of 0.025 implies that firms which raised external finance in 1960–1965 had growth in 1966–1971 which was on average only 0.025 percentage points above that of internally financed firms. This suggests that the event of going to the market is not important for subsequent growth.

Since past profitability has a considerable impact on future growth, this was next taken into account. Equation (3) shows the impact of past profitability alone: the equation tested was

$$G_{i,t} = \alpha + \beta P_{i,t-1} + \epsilon_{i,t} \tag{6.3}$$

where P denotes profitability. The results of incorporating this are given in equations (4) and (5). The effect of external financing continues to be similar to that obtained earlier. Equations (6) to (10) provide similar estimates for the sample of firms in non-manufacturing industries which continued over the period 1960–1971. These results are much weaker – the effect of external financing is quantitatively much smaller, and it is not statistically significant. For the next period, 1966–1976, this result occurs for all firms – whether or not they operated in the manufacturing industries. As Table 6.10 indicates, the discipline of the stock market in

Table 6.10 *Impact of external financing on growth, 1966–1976*

	Equation number	E	D	P	$\bar{R}2$
Manufacturing firms	(1)	0.02 (0.03)			0.001
	(2)		−0.001 (0.01)		0.001
	(3)			0.46* (0.06)	0.12
	(4)	0.01 (0.03)		0.46* (0.06)	0.12
	(5)		0.001 (0.01)	0.46* (0.06)	0.12
Non-manufacturing firms	(6)	0.03 (0.07)			0.002
	(7)		0.03 (0.02)		0.01
	(8)			0.69* (0.11)	0.19
	(9)	0.07 (0.06)		0.72* (0.11)	0.19
	(10)		0.03 (0.02)	0.68* (0.11)	0.19

Notes: Standard errors are given in brackets.
* denotes significantly different from 0 at the 5 per cent level.
Number of firms: manufacturing 510, non-manufacturing 184.

the sense noted above, tended to have an insignificant impact on the future rate of growth. The event of going to the market provides a similarly negative conclusion.

Next consider whether these results are mirrored in the impact of external finance on future profitability. The equation tested was as in (6.1), but this time the dependent variable was profitability in the period 1966–1971 (or 1972–1976). The results for the first period are given in Table 6.11. These present a sharp contrast to the results for growth. Superficially it appears that external financing had a negative impact on subsequent profitability; whilst it is true that the coefficient on the finance variable is quantitatively small, it is nevertheless statistically significant for manufacturing firms, and whilst the degree of variability explained by this variable alone is negligible, the result is the converse of what might be expected on the basis of the usual arguments. As Table 6.12 indicates, the results are ameliorated for the second period. The coefficient still has a negative sign, but its magnitude is very small and it is statistically insignificant. Further, the variability in profitability explained by external financing is also negligible. In all, for this latter period the conclusion would have to be that recourse to the stock market exerts no particular economic 'discipline'.

Table 6.11 *Impact of external financing on future profitability, 1960–1971*

	Equation number	E	D	P	$\bar{R}^2$
Manufacturing firms	(1)	-0.09* (0.04)			0.01
	(2)		-0.02* (0.007)		0.02
	(3)			0.61* (0.03)	0.33
	(4)	-0.11 (0.06)		0.62* (0.03)	0.34
	(5)		-0.01 (0.006)	0.61* (0.03)	0.34
Non-manufacturing firms	(6)	-0.04 (0.04)			0.01
	(7)		-0.03* (0.01)		0.03
	(8)			0.66* (0.05)	0.44
	(9)	-0.06* (0.03)		0.67* (0.05)	0.45
	(10)		-0.02 (0.01)	0.65* (0.05)	0.45

Notes: Standard errors are given in brackets.
* denotes significantly different from 0 at the 5 per cent level.
Number of firms: manufacturing 635, non-manufacturing 197.

One explanation for these two sets of results may be that, in testing the market discipline hypothesis, it is postulated that the main difference between firms relates to the degree of their recourse to the capital market. In particular it is implicit that the firms have similar objective functions. It may be argued, however, that firms which rely more on external funds on average, have different objectives from those relying mainly on retentions. If this is the case, then to some extent the empirical results may be explicable. For, assume that, on average, more firms relying on external funds have an objective such as growth maximisation. This would lead to the expectation that for these firms, growth in the firms' operations would be higher than for other firms. In view of the possible trade-off (after a certain point) between growth and profitability, it might be expected that profitability would thereby be adversely affected. Thus comparing the performance of these firms, with those relying on internal funds, one may expect to find the sort of result obtained above.

This argument is tentative since it relies not only on the assumption of a non-neoclassical maximand for one set of firms, but also on the premise that it is growth maximisers who mainly have recourse to the market. In view of the findings of Section 6.3, the latter would not be too unrealistic (see in particular Table 6.5).[8]

Table 6.12 *Impact of external financing on future profitability, 1966–1976*

	Equation number	E	D	P	$\bar{R}2$
Manufacturing firms	(1)	-0.003 (0.03)			0.001
	(2)		-0.014 (0.01)		0.005
	(3)			0.74* (0.04)	0.38
	(4)	-0.02 (0.02)		0.74* (0.04)	0.39
	(5)		-0.01 (0.03)	0.74* (0.05)	0.39
Non–manufacturing firms	(6)	0.04 (0.05)			0.003
	(7)		-0.02 (0.02)		0.005
	(8)			0.86* (0.07)	0.47
	(9)	-0.09* (0.04)		0.90* (0.07)	0.48
	(10)		-0.03* (0.01)	0.87* (0.07)	0.48

Notes: Standard errors are given in brackets.
* denotes significantly different from 0 at the 5 per cent level.
Number of firms: manufacturing 510, non–manufacturing 184.

The factors which may have led to this outcome are likely to be complex. As noted above, the growth of institutional investors in this period is said to have led to inefficiency in the allocative mechanism of the market. Others have noted that whilst the institutions are likely to operate in a manner very different from that of the individual investors, this need not necessarily imply a weakening of the market mechanism (see Wilson, 1980). In either case, there is little existing evidence which suggests the way the changes in the structure of the stock market may have affected its operations.

6.6 Summary

The main issues examined in this chapter, and the results which were obtained, are as follows:

(i) It is generally argued that the high fixed costs of making new equity issues deter firms from entering the capital market. Yet the small firms in this study achieved an above average rate of growth by equity issues, and by external funds generally. Whilst not suggesting that the oft-voiced concern for improving the allocation of capital to small firms is always misplaced (see, for example, Blume,

1980), the results do indicate that small size is not necessarily a major hindrance to recourse to the capital market.

(ii) The weak relationship between growth by equity and profitability might seem to suggest that the capital market does not allocate funds efficiently. If it did so, it might be expected that firms raising new equity would be able to obtain an above average return on investment. However, there are a number of reasons why the inference that the capital market is inefficient may not be the proper one to draw from these results. First, the requirement for economic efficiency is that funds should be given to those firms which can use them best in the future – whereas the profitability observed for this result is a mixture of past and future profitability at the time of raising new equity. Second, the profitability here relates to the return on average assets, whereas the requirement for efficient allocation of resources is related to the profitability on the purchase of new assets.[9] The investigation into the effect of past recourse to the capital market on future profitability, did overcome the first objection. It suggested that, as far as the general recourse to the capital market is concerned, there does not appear to be any significant impact on profitability, and so perhaps the efficiency with which funds are utilised.

(iii) The results suggest that the constraints which profitability imposed upon growth by acquisition were much weaker than was the case for new investment. Typically, firms undertaking acquisition, almost regardless of their profitability, were able to raise substantial external finance. It has been suggested that because of imperfections in the capital market and the role of uncertainty, there are two reasons why this might be so. First, the company's uncertainty over the result of an issue may be much lower in a share-for-share exchange than in an issue-for-cash. Second, as noted in Chapter 4, the uncertainty attaching to the future earnings from expansion may be smaller when it is undertaken by acquisition than when it consists of new investment.

(iv) There was found to be a negative correlation between acquisitions financed by retentions and new investment similarly financed. This suggests that in cases where access to external finance may have been limited then, in a cross-sectional framework, there may be a trade-off between expenditure on acquisitions and on new investment. But there was again no evidence of a trade-off between total expenditure on new investment and total expenditure on acquisition.

(v) In the period 1972–1976, equity issues for cash were larger than equity issues in exchange for subsidiaries. The exception to this was the set of firms relying most heavily on external funds. For this set, equity issues for cash were just over a third of the equity issues in exchange.

(vi) The gearing issues for cash were in general greater than the gearing issues in exchange for subsidiaries. The exception was again the firms relying most heavily on external funds.

(vii) The gearing ratio of firms increased almost uniformly with an increase in size. In the case of the retention ratio there was no relationship with firm size, and over time there was an increase in this ratio for firms in all size classes.

7

Investment, acquisition and dividend behaviour

In Chapter 4 the cross-sectional relationship between acquisitions and investment was examined, whilst in the last chapter we examined the link between these activities and the different ways of financing them. These chapters analysed variables averaged over a number of years. An important question arises as to the behaviour of these activities over a shorter time period. The purpose of this chapter is to examine them using data on an annual basis. Further, a number of other factors which impinge on them directly, such as dividend disbursals, are examined. Apart from studying each of these activities separately, they are also examined using a simultaneous model. The aim of this chapter is therefore threefold. First, to enquire into some determinants of investment and acquisition expenditure as well as of dividend disbursals and external finance. This extends and supplements the analysis in Chapters 4 and 6. Second, to study whether these provide a stable explanation over different years. Third, and more important, to determine whether these decisions are mutually determined – and hence should be investigated in the context of a simultaneous equation model as advocated, for example, by Dhrymes and Kurz (1967) – or whether, as Fama (1974) argued, single equation models of each of these decisions are adequate. (Fama only considered dividend and investment behaviour.) In the Modigliani–Miller framework, with a perfect capital market, optimal investment decisions by a firm are independent of financing decisions. A corollary of this is that investment decisions should not be determined by dividend behaviour. The investigation below examines empirically the extent to which the dividend and investment expenditure are interrelated. This is carried out, however, in the context of the earlier results – where a link was shown between investment and acquisition expenditure, and between external funds and acquisitions.

Two earlier studies, which tested econometrically an explicit link between the above variables, were made by Dhrymes and Kurz (1967) and Mueller (1967). These studies, however, did not include acquisition as an endogenous variable. Furthermore, their analysis related to the firms operating in the US in the period before 1960. Such an investigation has not been undertaken for firms in any other advanced economy. The approach employed below is based on a simultaneous equation model which is tested over a series of cross sections. The sample used consists of 664 firms for which data were available for the period 1968–1976. The structural form of this model is estimated over the period 1970–1976 in order to enquire into the stability of its structure in different macro-economic environments.

The rest of the chapter is arranged as follows. In Section 7.1 the formulation of the model is considered, whilst Section 7.2 discusses the sample and the estimation procedure. Sections 7.3 and 7.4 provide the main results using OLS and simultaneous equation techniques. Section 7.5 provides a further analysis of acquisition expenditure and finance decisions, using some specialised statistical techniques. The last section summarises the conclusions and draws out their implications.

7.1 The structure of the model

7.1.1 General structure
The general structure of the econometric model which is used to investigate the above issues is as follows:

$$I_1 = g_1(I_2, A, D, EF, \mathbf{X}) \tag{7.1}$$

$$I_2 = g_2(I_1, A, D, EF, \mathbf{X}) \tag{7.2}$$

$$A = g_3(I_1, I_2, D, EF, \mathbf{X}) \tag{7.3}$$

$$D = g_4(I_1, I_2, A, EF, \mathbf{X}) \tag{7.4}$$

$$EF = g_5(I_1, I_2, A, D, \mathbf{X}) \tag{7.5}$$

where
I_1 = investment in new fixed assets; this is gross investment, that is, it includes both net and replacement investment;

I_2 = investment in current assets and stocks (net of increase in current liabilities and short-term debt);

A = total expenditure on acquisitions;

D = dividends paid on ordinary shares;

EF = (net) external finance obtained from issue of ordinary and preference shares, and long-term loans;

These variables are measured on an annual basis. $\mathbf{X}$ is a vector of predetermined variables, and $g_i = 1, 2, \ldots, 5$ denotes a general function.

The predetermined variables include sales, profits, depreciation, gearing and so on, and will be discussed presently.

In addition to the structural model, there is a constraint on a firm's behaviour implied by the flow-of-funds identity:

$$A + I_1 + I_2 = EF + P - D + Dep \tag{7.6}$$

Here Dep denotes depreciation provisions and P denotes profits (net of depreciation, interest payments and tax). (Other variables are as above.)

Using this constraint, it is possible to express one endogenous variable as a function of other variables, and so eliminate that variable from the system of equations above. In order to focus on the four decision variables which have been considered in earlier chapters, the variable I_2 was eliminated. So the model finally estimated consisted of four equations. The first equation and equations 7.3–7.5.[1] The next section discusses the variables which were included in each of these equations.

7.1.2 The choice of variables

The investment equation. One main framework for analysing investment expenditure is that in which a firm maximises the present value of its future income stream subject to a production function. This determines the 'optimal' capital stock; the rate of investment is determined by adjustment costs, which relate to the planning, ordering and supply of investment goods (cf. Junankar, 1973 and Nickell, 1978). The maximisation problem itself depends on expectations of future demand as well as on relative prices (of factors, and of products). In addition, it is likely that in a world of uncertainty, and imperfect capital markets, profits and depreciation funds would be important in financing investment (see e.g. Meyer and Kuh, 1957, Eisner, 1978). Profits would indicate not only the availability of funds, but would also act as a proxy for future returns. This is so to the extent that the firm views present profits as a result of past investment, and it may use them as a measure of returns expected from similar investments. If depreciation provisions reflected accurately the deterioration of the capital stock caused by production activity, then depreciation provisions would denote that part of investment which is undertaken for replacement purposes. As noted earlier, however, depreciation provision, especially in the period under consideration, is unlikely to reflect accurately the consumption of capital stock, and so it would provide resources for net investment, and other purposes (see Chapter 5, and Meeks, 1974).

In addition to the variables reflecting expectations and the availability of funds, this equation includes the other three jointly determined variables: viz., acquisitions, dividends and external finance. The earlier chapters noted the reasons why acquisitions and external finance are likely to be important for investment. Dividend disbursals are included to investigate whether they represent competing demands on the resources available to the firm. It may be argued that investment would be affected by dividend policies; it may have to be curtailed because of the inability of the firm simultaneously to make a 'satisfactory' dividend payment (see e.g. Sargent Florence, 1961). This is, of course, contrary to the Modigliani-Miller view of the world where investment decisions should not be affected by dividend decisions.

The acquisition equation. The causal factors influencing acquisition expenditures have also been discussed extensively. In a detailed survey Hughes *et al.* (1980) distinguish three categories of determinants of acquisitions. First, 'real' motives based on demand and cost conditions – to bring about an increase in profits by either increasing the market power of the firm, or reducing its costs, or both. Second, speculative motives based on valuation discrepancies in expected earnings. The basic proposition is that at any given time there will be differences in individual expectations about the future income stream of a firm and thus about its present value, and that these differences may provide a spur to acquisition (see Gort, 1969). Third, managerial motives due to managerial efforts to make personal gains by, for example, emphasising growth or sales maximisation, the gains in such a case not being shared by both sets of shareholders.[2]

From this general formulation three variables would seem to be directly relevant. First, if economies of scale are an important factor determining acquisition activity, there should be a tendency for small firms, other things being equal, to spend more on acquisition (relative to their size) than larger ones. This suggests that a variable reflecting the size of firm should be included. Second, for vertical or conglomerate acquisitions, the risk-spreading factors are likely to be important. This suggests that variations in profit levels are likely to explain at least part of the variance in acquisition expenditure. To standardise for size differences among firms, the coefficient of variation is included, rather than the raw variance in profits. Third, there are several hypotheses about differences in leverage ratios among firms which may lead to differences in risk. These hypotheses can be related to hypotheses concerning the determinant of acquisition by assuming that the differences in risks, resulting from differences in leverage ratios, can lead to acquisition. Firms which have either relatively high, or relatively low, leverage ratios will undertake acquisition more than firms with 'normal' leverage ratios. A variable to take into account the effect of liquidity was also included. This was done following a number of earlier studies which suggest that firms with above average liquidity, *ceteris paribus*, may have above average acquisition expenditures (see Levine and Aaronovitch, 1981).

In addition to these variables, the availability of external finance is likely to exercise an influence. For a sizeable proportion of firms acquisitions are directly accompanied by recourse to the capital market often in the form of share-for-share exchange. With regard to the two other endogenous variables, consider first the effect of dividends: the relationship with acquisition expenditure and dividend disbursals may not be clear cut. There may be a trade-off, or a complementarity, between the two. The first, because of competing demands for funds for acquisition and dividends. The second, to the extent that higher dividends have a positive effect on share valuation, firms may find it easier to raise external funds for acquisition. It has been already noted that there is likely to be a complex relationship between investment and acquisition expenditures, and there is no reason to expect a simple trade-off between the two.

The dividend equation. There are a number of explanations which have been offered to explain the level of dividend disbursals (see, for example, Feldstein and Green, 1983). These explanations are based on factors such as the investors' preference for current income, the informational content of dividends, and the residual theory of dividends (that is, dividends will be distributed only after internal investment opportunities have been exhausted). One explanation which has received wide acceptance is that dividends are used to convey information to the market on the inherent profitability of the disbursing firm.[3] If this is so then it is likely that the policy of firms would be to maintain a steady dividend per share and to change it only when the directors of the firm perceive that a 'permanent' change in the economic environment has occurred (King, 1977, p. 168). A constant dividend per share does not, of course, imply that the dividend-profit ratio would remain constant.

In addition to the effect of past dividends, current dividend disbursal depends upon current profits. For the reasons mentioned earlier investment and acquisition plans may also have an influence on dividends. Dhrymes and Kurz (1967) have argued that external finance is another explanatory variable, the rationale being that it will enable the firm to make its planned dividends even when the rate of profit is low and investment programmes are extensive.[4]

The external finance equation. The external finance variable includes both equity issues and long-term borrowing. We have already considered the influence which other endogenous variables would exercise on the decision to raise external finance;

there is likely to be a positive relationship with two of these variables, investment and acquisition expenditures. But the relationship with dividends is not likely to be unambiguous. This is for reasons similar to those for the acquisition-dividend relationship (*viz.*, higher dividends may facilitate the raising of funds *via* a positive influence on expectations and share valuation. But they would also decrease the availability of internal funds). There are a number of other variables which would also exercise an influence: profits and depreciation provisions are the two obvious ones. Further, it may be argued that the recourse to external finance is likely to depend negatively on the rate of interest. Apart from the cost factor, this may be due to the reluctance of firms to borrow long term when the rate is high and there is considerable uncertainty as to its behaviour, as was the case in the period under consideration (see Chapter 2 above). But the costs involved are likely to vary considerably for firms in different size classes. Across firms, the lower the cost, the less unwilling they may be to borrow in this way. In order to examine whether the firms' capital structure has any influence on the total external finance raised (as suggested, for example, by Blume, 1980), a gearing variable was also included in this equation.

7.1.3 Estimated equations

The precise form of the estimated equations is noted below. The variables are for each company's financial year, unless otherwise stated, and are denoted by the following symbols:

I_t = expenditure on gross fixed investment
A_t = expenditure on acquisitions
D_t = dividends paid on ordinary shares
D_{t-1} = lagged dividends (by one year)
EF_t = issue of equity shares and debentures *plus* long-term borrowing
S_t = sales (in current prices)
S_{t-3} = lagged sales (by three years)
K_t = net assets
P_t = net profits (net of depreciation)
P_{t-1} = net profits lagged
$Debt$ = net long-term debt outstanding, in nominal terms
Dep = depreciation provision
R_t = interest payments on long-term debt. (This is not likely to be a satisfactory measure of the interest rate measuring the cost of capital, but it is the only one readily available.)
L_t = net current position of the firm. This is defined as the excess of cash, short-term securities, stock and accounts receivable over accounts payable and other short-term liabilities.
S^* = $(S_t - S_{t-3})/S_{t-3}$. (This is a proxy variable for expectations of changes in future output.)
G_t = gearing ratio
P_{var} = variability of profits

The estimated equations using the above symbols are as follows:

$$I = g_1(P_{t-1}, Dep, S^*, A, D, EF) \qquad (7.7)$$

$$A = g_2(K_{t-1}, P_{var}, G, L, I, D, EF) \qquad\qquad (7.8)$$

$$D = g_3(D_{t-1}, P, I, A, EF) \qquad\qquad (7.9)$$

$$EF = g_4(R, G, P, I, A, D) \qquad\qquad (7.10)$$

(All variables are for year t (I denotes I_t, A denotes A_t, and so on). $g_{i,i=1\ldots4}$ denotes functional form, which was assumed to be linear.)

In the empirical estimation of the model, apart from the variables S^*, G_t and P_{var}, the other variables were deflated by the opening net assets, K_{t-1}.[5] This was done to reduce heteroscedasticity in the error term and make it correspond more closely to the assumptions of the estimation technique used. This procedure is commonly employed in econometric studies of firm behaviour, where it is assumed that the variance of the error term is unlikely to be constant across firms of different sizes. The simplicity of the procedure is its main attraction. It should be noted, however, that one may be able to improve upon it by taking into account the precise form of heteroscedasticity (see Glejser, 1969). Nevertheless, the procedure adopted here is likely to be sufficiently reliable.[6]

One further question relates to the composition of the external finance variable. Above it has been defined as the issue of loans and equity in total – that is, for both cash, and for issues in exchange for subsidiaries. The main rationale for this is to consider the recourse to the capital market for all funds – and not just those raised for cash. There are, however, some theoretical and empirical grounds for considering only the funds raised for cash. On *a priori* grounds it may be argued that the recourse to the capital market which is entailed in the share-for-share exchange in the course of acquisition is of a quite different nature from the raising of new funds. Essentially, the former may be regarded as involving much less uncertainty as to the outcome than the latter. Indeed, in many cases the exchange issue may be regarded as dealing with a captive market and, therefore, by-passing the scrutiny, and costs, of raising new funds. From an econometric point of view, the presence of external finance (in total) and acquisition expenditure as explanatory variables may lead to some problems of multicollinearity (these variables are highly correlated), so that the estimates of the coefficients may be difficult to disentangle. For both these reasons, it may be more appropriate to consider only the issue of new funds in analysing external finance behaviour.

In view of these considerations, empirical analysis using each of the two variables, external finance in total and external finance for cash, was undertaken in turn. Whilst this involved some multiplicity of results, it does seem to have been justified since it led to interesting insights into the firms' decision process. Accordingly, two sets of estimates of the above model are reported: Section 7.3 reports estimates using total external finance, whilst the following section reports results using only external finance for cash.

7.2 The sample and the estimation procedure

The sample consists of 664 firms for which continuous data were available for the period 1968–1976. Although the model is estimated for the period 1970–1976, data for 1968 and 1969 were required for variables using lagged values. The source of data is, as before, the DI Databank – the sample is based on firms in all

Table 7.1 *Characteristics of the sample of firms used in the simultaneous model*

Size and average profitability

Opening size class	No. of firms	Profitability mean	S.D.
$\leq$ 2m	14	11.6	6.8
$\leq$ 4m	106	12.3	7.4
$\leq$ 8m	142	10.9	9.0
$\leq$ 16m	128	9.5	6.6
$\leq$ 32m	109	11.0	8.9
> 32m	165	9.4	6.9
Total	664	10.4	7.8

Distribution of firms by industry

Industry	No. of firms	Industry	No. of firms
21 Food	19	44 Clothing etc.	18
23 Drink	36	46 Bricks etc.	36
26 Chemicals	32	47 Timber etc.	19
31 Metal manf.	28	48 Paper etc.	45
33 Non-elec. eng.	65	49 Other manf.	22
36 Elec. eng.	39	50 Construction	30
38 Vehicles	29	81 Wholesale	53
39 Metal goods	53	82 Retail	55
41 Textiles	55	88 Misc.	30

Note: Profitability is for 1970.

industries considered in earlier chapters. To reflect the sample of firms in different industries, it would have been appropriate to allow the coefficients on the variables to differ across industries (say by using slope dummies). Unfortunately, the econometric package used for simultaneous testing of the model did not allow this option to be used. The option of estimating the model for each industry separately would have been too cumbersome. Therefore, the model had to be estimated for the sample as a whole. Table 7.1 provides the size distribution of firms and the average profitability at the start of the estimation period (1970), as well as the industrial distribution of the firms. As can be seen, the sample represents a reasonable cross section across industries and size classes. This is important, since it indicates that there was no particular bias in favour of any particular size class, or any particular industry.

7.2.1 Estimation procedure

The model is estimated using one of the standard simultaneous model estimation techniques; in particular, the three stage least squares (3SLS). These techniques are quite sensitive to the specification of the model, and require quite stringent assumptions regarding the error structure in the model. (The model was estimated for some years using 2SLS, but 3SLS was found to be more appropriate.)[7] If the investment, acquisition, dividend and finance decisions are jointly determined, then estimation of equations explaining any of these variables using OLS would lead to biased estimates of the structural parameters, except in the case of a recursive system. If, however, these decisions are determined in some sequential manner (or independently), then OLS would be quite appropriate. One general method for determining the correct specification is to test whether the coefficients on the endogenous variables are significantly different from zero in the simultaneous model. This is undertaken presently. However, since in the existing literature each of the decision variables is often modelled using OLS, it would be appropriate initially to present OLS estimates for these equations – albeit at the risk of having a specification error. If the decisions are not simultaneous, the estimates given by the OLS procedure should be similar to those given by the simultaneous equation method. On a more positive note, as Maddala points out, even though OLS will yield inconsistent estimates, it may be useful because it is more robust against specification errors. He argues, 'it is fruitful to report OLS estimates of the structural equations (even if they are not consistent) along with those from the other methods that give consistent estimates' (1977, p. 231).

7.3 Empirical results using total external finance

7.3.1 Single equation estimates

Consider first the estimates for the investment equation (Table 7.2). For all years except 1975, lagged profits, as expected, exercise a significantly positive influence. (In this and subsequent equations t-ratios above an absolute value of 1.96 denote that the coefficient is significantly different from 0 at the 5 per cent level.) Similarly, the depreciation provision has a positive impact; the coefficient is significantly different from 0 for all seven cross sections. The 'expectations' or 'accelerator' variable, S^*, however, is generally insignificant, and for the first three cross sections it has the wrong sign. The acquisition variable has a positive sign for five of the seven years, although it is significant for only two of these years. In view of the results in Chapters 4 and 5, this mildly positive relationship is to be expected. The most interesting result in this equation relates to the dividend variable. Its coefficient is generally negative; that is, there is some adverse effect of dividend disbursals on investment. So firms which had above average dividend disbursals, *ceteris paribus*, had below average investment expenditure. (Note that all these variables are normalised by firms' total assets.) Finally, the external finance variable has an almost uniformly positive influence, although it is significant for only two cross sections. The explanatory power of the equation, as measured by $\bar{R}^2$ (significant in the first six years according to the F test), is very reasonable in view of the cross-sectional framework of the investigation.

It is noticeable that the equation provides varying degrees of explanation across the years, and that the values of the coefficients also vary considerably across the period. In general the fit is more reasonable for earlier years. To some extent this

Table 7.2 *OLS estimates of gross investment equation*

Year	P_{t-1}	Dep	S^*	A	D	EF	$\bar{R}^2$	F
1970	0.30 (3.26)	1.04 (8.69)	-0.01 (-1.22)	0.09 (1.79)	-0.15 (-0.94)	0.02 (0.44)	0.26	20.77
1971	0.40 (5.41)	1.21 (10.93)	-0.01 (-0.51)	-0.11 (-3.31)	-0.20 (-1.32)	0.11 (2.55)	0.33	28.6
1972	0.47 (6.84)	1.01 (8.66)	-0.03 (-5.71)	0.02 (0.46)	-0.36 (-2.61)	0.06 (1.53)	0.31	26.8
1973	0.24 (3.66)	1.37 (10.01)	0.02 (3.44)	0.15 (3.64)	-0.07 (-0.30)	0.30 (6.71)	0.42	43.1
1974	0.28 (4.91)	1.10 (8.53)	0.001 (0.01)	0.16 (7.53)	-0.04 (-0.21)	-0.004 (-0.05)	0.49	57.0
1975	-0.02 (-0.33)	2.32 (21.23)	0.01 (0.72)	0.17 (1.47)	0.20 (0.76)	0.05 (0.72)	0.59	83.3
1976	0.35 (4.46)	1.31 (7.15)	0.03 (1.32)	-0.40 (-3.60)	-0.47 (-1.39)	0.05 (0.41)	0.14	9.47

Notes: t-ratios are given in brackets.
For definitions of variables see text.

may reflect the macro-economic developments in this period. This point is considered below.

The acquisition equation (Table 7.3) shows that the first variable, P_{var} (intended to capture the likely attempts by a firm to reduce the variability of its income stream), has generally a positive but statistically insignificant coefficient. The second variable, gearing ratio, indicates that firms with relatively low gearing tended to have above average acquisitions (although for the first two years there is a direct relationship). The coefficient on the liquidity variable, L_t, has an almost uniformly negative sign. One reason for this may be the tendency of firms with relatively low liquidity to acquire, in the expectation of actually increasing liquidity. If one considers that in general the financing of acquisition itself is not a drain on the firm's liquid resources, this explanation does not appear implausible (cf. Mueller, 1967).

The three endogenous variables give a mixed picture in terms of their influence on acquisitions. Investment itself has a positive influence in five out of seven cross sections – although it is by no means similar across the years. Dividends generally have a positive influence – if one assumes that because of market imperfections and tax regimes, dividends are preferred to retentions, and that this tends to be reflected in share valuation of the firms concerned, then a positive association would be expected. This would be because a firm relying on share-for-share exchange for acquisition (or in a minority of cases raising cash for it) would have an incentive to have as high a valuation as possible – which may be achieved by above average dividend disbursal. Finally, the external finance variable is uniformly pos-

Table 7.3 *OLS estimates of acquisition equation*

Year	P_{var}	G	L	I	D	EF	$\bar{R}^2$	F
1970	0.003 (0.55)	0.02 (0.63)	-0.05 (-2.73)	0.05 (0.89)	0.22 (1.80)	0.93 (26.33)	0.70	138.8
1971	0.0004 (0.40)	0.02 (0.43)	-0.003 (-1.31)	-0.29 (-3.84)	0.38 (1.98)	1.21 (10.10)	0.97	120.4
1972	0.001 (1.33)	-0.07 (-1.54)	-0.10 (-4.70)	0.01 (0.13)	0.07 (0.40)	0.90 (39.90)	0.85	330.4
1973	0.001 (0.12)	-0.10 (-1.80)	-0.003 (-0.15)	0.14 (2.40)	0.15 (0.56)	0.96 (31.90)	0.77	192.2
1974	0.001 (0.75)	-0.02 (-0.23)	-0.03 (-2.42)	1.26 (13.51)	-0.84 (-1.86)	0.82 (4.39)	0.38	44.4
1975	-0.003 (-2.61)	-0.004 (-0.18)	-0.01 (-1.52)	0.02 (1.33)	0.004 (0.04)	0.14 (4.78)	0.09	5.0
1976	-0.002 (-0.76)	-0.03 (-1.16)	-0.06 (-5.02)	-0.12 (-3.37)	0.23 (3.32)	0.58 (9.61)	0.25	19.9

Note: t-ratios are given in brackets.

itive and highly significant. The overall fit of the equation is quite good, except for the last two years. For 1975 the variation in acquisition expenditures explained by the equation is rather small, with an uncharacteristically low value for the external finance variable. One explanation for this may in fact be the significantly below average acquisition activity in the last two years. If a large proportion of firms do not undertake acquisitions, then the discontinuity in the dependent variable may render standard regression techniques unsatisfactory.[8]

This is a rather important point which has not been generally considered in the literature on econometric modelling of firms' activities. The problem arises when the *endogenous* variable is discontinuous across the sample. Here for example, when the overall acquisition activity is low, it is very likely that a proportion of firms would have zero acquisition expenditure and others a significant amount. Estimation of an equation such as this using ordinary regression methods may lead to inconsistent results. We adopt another estimation procedure in Section 7.5, which takes into account the discontinuity in both the finance and acquisition variables. (Note that this problem is less acute when we are averaging over a number of years, as in the earlier chapters. There, the distribution was relatively more continuous.)

In the dividend equation (Table 7.4), lagged dividends exert a significantly positive influence across all years. The value of the coefficient on lagged dividends is generally between 0.7 and 0.9 (cf. King, 1977). Current profits also exert a positive influence in all cases, and although it is highly significant, the magnitude of the effect is quite small. There is generally a negative relationship between investment and dividends – again suggesting, at least, the presence of some trade-off between

123

Table 7.4 *OLS estimates of dividend equation*

Year	D_{t-1}	P_t	I	A	EF	$\bar{R}^2$	F
1970	0.70 (26.31)	0.15 (12.83)	−0.01 (−1.23)	0.002 (0.20)	0.01 (1.40)	0.85	401.2
1971	0.77 (8.02)	0.14 (11.53)	−0.02 (−2.21)	0.01 (1.73)	−0.01 (−1.02)	0.88	303.4
1972	0.78 (27.91)	0.08 (0.74)	−0.01 (−0.93)	−0.003 (−0.42)	0.01 (1.71)	0.83	305.1
1973	0.55 (32.90)	0.04 (4.51)	−0.02 (−3.20)	0.01 (1.31)	0.005 (1.01)	0.82	332.6
1974	0.80 (35.01)	0.03 (5.11)	−0.01 (−2.39)	0.01 (2.42)	0.02 (1.57)	0.83	351.8
1975	0.84 (36.64)	0.03 (5.67)	0.001 (0.21)	0.02 (1.55)	0.41 (6.34)	0.83	350.1
1976	0.88 (35.46)	0.001 (2.37)	−0.01 (−3.07)	−0.01 (−1.56)	0.03 (3.49)	0.81	285.1

Note: t-ratios are given in brackets.

the two variables. This mirrors the results obtained for dividends in the investment equation discussed above. Similarly, the generally positive coefficient on dividends in the acquisition equation is reflected in this equation, where acquisitions have a positive sign in five out of seven years. The external finance variable has also a positive influence. The equation as a whole performs quite well for all years and a very high degree of variation in the dividends is accounted for by the explanatory variables.

The last equation, for external finance, yields good results for the first four years, but it is somewhat unsatisfactory for the rest of the period (Table 7.5). Considering individual variables, the gearing ratio is generally positively associated with external finance, whilst profits also have a positive influence. Of the endogenous variables, acquisition has a consistently positive, and significant, influence – but the magnitude of this varies quite considerably, for example, from a value of 0.83 in 1972 to 0.08 in 1974. Both the dividend and investment variables generally have a positive influence on the amount of external finance raised.[9]

There are two caveats to the above results. First, as noted in Section 7.1 above, it may be argued that for the external finance variable one should consider only the new funds raised by the firm; in so far as the variable used is correlated with acquisition expenditure, the influence of these two variables would be difficult to disentangle. Second, if there is a simultaneity in the decision making process, it would render OLS estimates biased and inconsistent. We next consider the estimation of

Table 7.5 *OLS estimates of external finance equation*

Year	G	P	I	A	D	$\bar{R}^2$	F
1970	0.05	-0.09	0.09	0.70	0.20	0.70	137.3
	(1.50)	(-1.23)	(1.81)	(26.67)	(1.14)		
1971	-0.01	0.08	0.17	0.79	-0.32	0.97	136.5
	(-0.10)	(0.81)	(2.99)	(10.24)	(-1.46)		
1972	0.11	0.02	0.07	0.83	0.29	0.85	330.2
	(2.35)	(0.36)	(1.07)	(38.13)	(1.43)		
1973	0.13	-0.14	0.28	0.73	0.22	0.80	179.3
	(2.32)	(-1.73)	(5.61)	(29.79)	(0.86)		
1974	0.03	0.11	-0.05	0.08	0.03	0.11	7.0
	(1.18)	(3.45)	(-1.58)	(5.42)	(0.19)		
1975	0.14	0.04	0.05	0.38	0.65	0.14	9.6
	(3.83)	(0.01)	(1.94)	(4.36)	(3.31)		
1976	0.02	0.04	0.03	0.34	0.21	0.22	16.7
	(0.75)	(2.44)	(1.13)	(9.10)	(1.51)		

Note: t-ratios are given in brackets.

the model as a whole using the simultaneous equation technique, and to take into account the first caveat, we present in Section 7.4 the results based on the narrower definition of external finance.

7.3.2 Simultaneous equation estimates

Consider first the investment equation (see Table 7.6). Lagged profits exert a positive influence, which is statistically significant for the first five years. For the last two years there is weak negative effect. The depreciation variable is also generally positive and statistically significant. The accelerator variable again has the wrong sign with a greater magnitude (in absolute terms) than in the OLS. More interestingly, there does not appear to be any significant change in the coefficient on the acquisition variable. It varies considerably across the cross sections and whilst it is significant for four out of seven years, it is by no means a sharp improvement over the OLS estimates. The dividend variable has a negative influence on investment expenditures, but it is nowhere statistically significant. The last variable, external finance, has a negative sign for six out of seven years, although it is significant for only three of these years. The same variable was positive for almost all years in the OLS, although its influence was again not generally significant.

This equation, in contrast to the one estimated using OLS, suggests that there is no systematic evidence for the interdependence of dividend and investment activities of firms, although there is some evidence for the codetermination of the activities regarding investment and acquisitions, and investment and external finance.[10]

Table 7.6 *3SLS estimates of gross investment equation*

Year	P_{t-1}	Dep	S^*	A	D	EF
1970	0.58	0.65	−0.17	0.73	−0.60	0.45
	(2.23)	(1.82)	(−2.33)	(1.27)	(−1.27)	(0.62)
1971	0.80	1.58	−0.51	−2.03	−0.84	−1.97
	(2.89)	(4.64)	(−2.33)	(−2.41)	(−1.56)	(−2.28)
1972	0.36	0.90	−0.04	0.49	0.49	−0.35
	(4.96)	(7.31)	(−6.40)	(3.68)	(3.68)	(−2.51)
1973	0.26	0.78	0.01	1.60	−0.64	−1.34
	(4.32)	(5.01)	(1.54)	(5.35)	(−1.73)	(−4.35)
1974	0.39	4.12	0.05	−0.70	−0.62	−3.06
	(3.97)	(3.73)	(1.10)	(−2.51)	(−1.47)	(−1.31)
1975	−0.06	2.43	0.04	−0.28	0.43	−0.24
	(−0.91)	(17.66)	(0.96)	(−0.29)	(1.19)	(−0.58)
1976	−1.25	2.49	−0.25	1.36	−0.45	−1.29
	(−0.53)	(0.54)	(−0.59)	(2.31)	(−0.13)	(−0.91)

Note: t-ratios are given in brackets.

The other three equations tend to reinforce this impression. Consider first the exogenous variables in the acquisition equation: the P_{var} variable and the liquidity variables, are generally similar to their estimates using OLS (Table 7.7). However, the gearing ratio now exerts a positive influence on acquisition expenditures in four out of seven years, and a significant but negative influence for two years. Of the endogenous variables, investment has a positive effect on acquisition in four years, and for two years this effect is significant. In contrast to the investment equation, however, the dividend variable has a generally positive influence but, as before, it is not significant. The variable which is most significant is the external finance variable – though as explained earlier this may reflect to a large extent the characteristic mode of financing acquisition, rather than indicate simultaneity of two separate decisions (i.e., that concerning acquisition, and that concerning the financing of such acquisition).

Of the other two equations, the dividend equation yields fairly satisfactory results, but for the external finance equation there is not much improvement (Tables 7.8 and 7.9). There are again some notable differences compared to the OLS results. Consider first the dividend equation. The effect of lagged dividends and profitability is generally positive and significant, the coefficients being quite similar to those obtained using OLS. Regarding the endogenous variables, there is some change for investment; in general the effect is still negative but the significance is much lower. The main change occurs in the acquisition variable: the coeffi-

Table 7.7 *3SLS estimates of acquisition equation*

Year	P_{var}	G	L	I	D	EF
1970	0.001	−0.09	−0.001	−1.31	0.15	1.48
	(0.04)	(−2.44)	(−0.08)	(−2.24)	(0.82)	(14.07)
1971	−0.02	0.02	−0.003	−0.13	0.20	1.25
	(−1.12)	(0.36)	(−0.09)	(−1.17)	(0.99)	(9.33)
1972	0.001	−0.06	−0.04	0.16	0.16	0.99
	(0.62)	(−1.42)	(−2.13)	(1.41)	(0.83)	(22.40)
1973	0.001	0.03	−0.01	0.29	0.31	0.85
	(0.51)	(0.78)	(−2.31)	(3.45)	(1.00)	(13.82)
1974	0.002	0.11	0.03	1.91	−1.12	−4.00
	(1.04)	(0.91)	(0.01)	(8.46)	(−1.54)	(−2.86)
1975	−0.001	−0.05	−0.01	−0.01	−0.16	0.47
	(−1.01)	(−2.04)	(−1.63)	(−0.66)	(−1.35)	(5.41)
1976	−0.001	0.04	−0.04	0.09	0.13	2.09
	(−0.02)	(0.77)	(−0.25)	(1.02)	(0.42)	(5.48)

Note: t-ratios are given in brackets.

cient is greater and it is significant in four of the cross sections. The external finance variable is also better determined, although now it is negative in three of the cross sections.

With regard to the external finance equation, the gearing and profitability variables are similar to the OLS. Similarly, the investment and acquisition coefficients are again positive, although the investment coefficient is lower. The most pronounced change occurs in the dividend variable, which generally has a negative impact, although it is not significant.

The overall picture which emerges from this part of the investigation is the following: for investment, the important explanatory variables appear to be lagged profits, depreciation provisions and acquisition expenditures, whilst for acquisitions, the main variables are investment, external finance and firms' gearing positions. For dividends, lagged dividends and profits exercise an important influence, although investment also has some effect, whilst for external finance, acquisitions and profits seem to exert the main influence. The power of these explanatory variables, however, varies quite considerably from year to year.

Within the framework of the model, there is certainly some simultaneity between investment and acquisitions on the one hand, and financing activities on the other. However, whilst within this framework investment affects dividends significantly in an adverse manner, there is only weak evidence that the converse holds – that investment is affected by dividends. Nevertheless, there is some inter-

Table 7.8 *3SLS estimates of dividend equation*

Year	D_{t-1}	P	I	A	EF
1970	0.67	0.15	0.05	0.20	−0.29
	(21.74)	(10.41)	(1.60)	(4.80)	(−3.73)
1971	0.75	0.14	−0.01	0.001	0.003
	(29.53)	(11.02)	(−0.81)	(0.016)	(0.06)
1972	0.74	0.12	−0.01	0.06	−0.08
	(23.06)	(5.91)	(−0.39)	(2.21)	(−2.82)
1973	0.79	0.13	−0.08	0.07	2.14
	(21.39)	(4.34)	(−1.34)	(2.19)	(3.12)
1974	0.74	0.07	−0.05	0.03	(−0.25)
	(23.53)	(4.34)	(−1.76)	(1.92)	(−3.36)
1975	0.83	0.04	0.01	−0.08	0.03
	(31.45)	(6.43)	(1.85)	(−1.15)	(1.10)
1976	0.88	0.002	−0.04	0.14	0.23
	(27.70)	(0.42)	(−5.07)	(3.62)	(2.75)

Note: *t*-ratios are given in brackets.

relationship between the two activities. In general, for the model as a whole, the coefficients are somewhat better determined in the simultaneous framework, and the investigation does tend to suggest that in modelling these decision variables one should take into account other endogenous variables.

It is notable, however, that for both the OLS and the 3SLS the equations perform better and the coefficients are more stable in the earlier part of the period. To what extent does this reflect the macroeconomic developments in this period? The period 1970–1973 was relatively stable. Both the inflation and unemployment rates were low. The inflation rate (retail price index) in 1970 was 6.4 per cent rising to 9.2 per cent in 1973, whilst the unemployment rate (excluding school leavers) averaged around 3 per cent. However, from 1974 onwards there was increasing instability. Although the unemployment rate in 1974 remained at 2.6 per cent, inflation rose to 16.1 per cent, increasing to 24.2 per cent in 1975. Unemployment also began to rise in 1975 and in 1976 reached 5.3 per cent (although inflation in that year came down to 11.5 per cent). The GDP growth in 1974 and 1975 was − 1.5 per cent and − 1.6 per cent respectively. The uncertainty engendered by these developments may account for the relative instability of the explanatory variables in the investment equation. This explanation may also apply to the pattern observed in other equations. (This explanation is tentative since there is of course a complex inter-relationship between the firms' activities and the performance of the economy.)

Table 7.9 *3SLS estimates of external finance equation*

Year	G	P	I	A	D
1970	0.58	0.01	0.21	0.68	-0.12
	(2.28)	(0.31)	(2.25)	(13.31)	(-0.90)
1971	-0.01	0.01	0.11	0.80	-0.16
	(-0.31)	(0.90)	(1.20)	(9.39)	(-1.00)
1972	0.08	0.23	-0.28	0.90	0.41
	(1.92)	(2.02)	(-2.11)	(17.41)	(1.85)
1973	0.034	0.33	0.31	0.73	-0.18
	(1.43)	(1.45)	(1.43)	(14.51)	(-1.62)
1974	0.03	0.09	0.12	-0.80	-1.71
	(1.40)	(1.78)	(1.15)	(-0.80)	(-1.71)
1975	0.11	0.04	0.05	1.24	0.20
	(2.73)	(1.09)	(1.26)	(2.23)	(0.86)
1976	-0.02	-0.001	-0.05	0.45	-0.06
	(-0.75)	(-0.16)	(-1.16)	(7.42)	(0.38)

Note: t-ratios are given in brackets.

7.4 External finance for cash

We next consider whether the above results are modified by using the external finance variable, which includes only the new funds raised by the firm. Thus it excludes both the issue of shares and the issue of loans in exchange for subsidiaries during the course of acquisition. It may be argued that it is the raising of new funds, which involves the firm appealing to the capital market and which may involve some simultaneity with other decision variables. Since, in the system of equations being considered, external finance is an explanatory variable in the first three equations, the effect of using the new variable would be reflected not only in the finance equation itself, but also in the other equations. In addition to meeting the objections which may be raised against the results obtained in the previous section, the use of this variable is likely to provide results which are interesting in their own right.[11]

The model was reestimated using OLS and 3SLS. The detailed results for this are included in Appendix A3. Here the results for 3SLS are summarised together with the earlier results for OLS and 3SLS (see Table 7.10).

In the investment equation the profit and depreciation variables yield similar results, but there is a noticeable change in the acquisition variable. There is a decrease in the magnitude of the coefficient, but it is more often positive and significant. This tends to confirm that there is some codetermination of investment and acquisition expenditure. The dividend variable does not display any systematic

Table 7.10 *Summary of the OLS and 3SLS results*

	Gross investment equation						Acquisition equation						Dividend equation					External finance equation				
	P_{t-1}	Dep	S^*	A	D	EF	P_{var}	G	L	I	D	EF	D_{t-1}	P_t	I	A	EF	G	P	I	A	D
I OLS (external funds, total)																						
+	6	7	4	5	1	6	5	3	1	5	5	7	7	7	1	5	6	6	5	5	7	6
-	1	0	3	2	6	1	2	5	6	2	2	0	0	0	6	2	1	1	2	2	0	1
sig +	6	7	1	2	0	2	0	0	1	2	1	7	7	6	0	1	2	3	2	2	7	1
sig -	0	0	1	2	1	0	1	0	3	2	1	0	0	0	4	0	0	0	0	0	0	0
II 3SLS (external funds, total)																						
+	5	7	3	4	2	1	4	4	1	4	2	6	7	6	2	6	4	5	6	5	6	2
-	2	0	4	3	5	6	3	3	6	3	5	1	0	1	5	1	3	2	1	2	1	5
sig +	5	5	0	3	1	0	0	0	0	2	0	6	7	6	0	3	1	2	1	1	6	0
sig -	0	0	3	1	0	3	0	2	2	1	0	1	0	0	1	0	3	0	0	1	0	0
III 3SLS (external funds, cash)																						
+	6	7	3	6	3	4	3	5	2	4	3	6	7	7	2	5	5	5	2	4	5	4
-	1	0	4	1	4	3	4	2	5	3	4	1	0	0	5	2	2	2	5	3	2	3
sig +	5	5	2	4	1	2	3	2	0	4	1	5	7	7	0	4	3	2	0	3	5	2
sig -	0	0	1	1	0	1	0	1	1	1	2	1	0	0	3	1	2	0	2	2	0	1

Note: The numbers refer to the number of years in which the coefficient was positive, negative and significant.

pattern and, as before, it is significant in only one case, for which the sign is opposite to that expected. However, the external finance variable improves considerably – it is positive in four cross sections and significant in two.

In the acquisition equation, the profit variability indicator is now significantly positive in three cross sections. The effect of the gearing and liquidity variables is similar to that obtained earlier, except that gearing has a significantly positive impact in two cross sections. In the case of endogenous variables, investment has a stronger association with acquisition – statistically the impact is significant in five years, with an indication of some substitutability between the two in one of these years. The dividend variable has a negative impact in four of the cross sections. Interestingly, the external finance variable has again a highly significant impact, which is positive in all years except one. Overall, this equation provides a slightly better fit than it does in the case of total external finance.

As before, the effect of past dividends and current profits is positive for all years in the dividend equation. On the other hand, there is stronger evidence of some trade-off between investment and dividends – the coefficient is significantly negative in three years. The acquisition variable presents a rather mixed picture (see Table 7.10). The coefficient is significant in five cross sections, but it has a negative sign for one of these. The influence of external finance is greater, and now there is greater evidence suggesting that dividend and finance decisions are codetermined. (The variable is significant in five cross sections, and positive in three.) Finally, in the external finance equation itself, the acquisition variable generally has the expected sign and it is significant in a number of cases. The dividend variable has a significant influence in three cases, in two of which it is positive. With regard to investment there is also some improvement.

In a number of cases there is a distinct instability in the estimates. As noted earlier, this may be partly due to the discontinuities in the acquisition and external finance variables. In view of this, we next consider an exercise which was carried out using an appropriate statistical technique to handle this problem.

7.5 The application of Tobit and Logit techniques

In the estimation of the four equations discussed in the previous two sections, there were two distinct methodological considerations. First, the problem of simultaneity for all, or some, of the decision variables; second, for two of the equations (external finance and acquisition), the problem of discontinuity in the dependant variables. The solution would have been to take account of both these points in the same step, that is, to employ simultaneous equation estimation techniques which can also handle the problem of discontinuity. Instead, the procedure adopted was sequential: first to consider the simultaneity and, second, if it appeared that the discontinuity might have some effect, to apply appropriate techniques to overcome that. In this section we undertake the latter.

The methodology we employ has not been used before for explaining the finance-acquisition behaviour of firms. The general characterisation of the techniques is that they focus on statistical models in which the endogenous variables take discontinuous values. (For a survey of the literature in this area see Amemiya, 1981.) There are two types of questions which can be investigated using these techniques. First, which variables explain *whether or not* a firm will raise external

Table 7.11 Tobit and Logit analysis: acquisition equation

	Tobit analysis						Logit analysis					
	P_{var}	G	L	I	D	EF	P_{var}	G	L	I	D	EF
1970	0.01 (1.78)	0.48 (3.54)	-0.31 (-5.59)	0.45 (2.78)	1.94 (3.65)	0.23 (0.85)	0.02 (1.21)	2.78 (3.72)	-1.07 (-3.23)	1.45 (1.54)	0.97 (0.32)	2.46 (1.54)
1971	0.001 (0.02)	1.71 (4.83)	0.79 (-6.70)	0.25 (0.65)	4.41 (3.27)	-2.73 (-3.38)	-0.01 (-0.61)	3.57 (4.76)	-0.67 (-2.29)	2.07 (2.39)	1.58 (0.56)	-3.42 (-2.04)
1972	-0.02 (-1.16)	0.35 (2.32)	-0.33 (-5.56)	0.45 (3.09)	1.43 (2.84)	0.48 (2.81)	-0.20 (-1.83)	2.89 (3.92)	-0.75 (-2.50)	1.39 (1.78)	-0.16 (-0.06)	1.80 (1.92)
1973	-0.001 (-0.08)	0.48 (3.17)	0.11 (2.96)	0.37 (3.39)	2.92 (3.85)	0.72 (2.89)	-0.07 (-0.88)	2.86 (3.64)	-0.75 (-2.97)	0.10 (0.16)	2.96 (0.77)	2.13 (1.52)
1974	0.01 (1.35)	0.40 (2.18)	-0.32 (-2.33)	-0.31 (1.86)	3.41 (2.50)	0.45 (1.13)	-0.01 (-0.59)	3.31 (4.23)	-0.53 (-1.90)	1.09 (1.34)	-6.44 (-1.40)	3.61 (1.50)
1975	0.02 (1.81)	0.55 (3.81)	-0.35 (-4.31)	1.21 (2.01)	2.20 (1.46)	0.70 (1.01)	-0.01 (-0.67)	1.24 (1.61)	-0.69 (-2.17)	1.34 (1.46)	-4.23 (-0.90)	2.34 (1.64)
1976	0.03 (1.98)	0.44 (2.61)	-0.34 (-7.10)	0.46 (1.97)	2.43 (1.95)	0.42 (1.76)	-0.03 (-0.78)	2.35 (2.01)	-1.03 (-2.69)	0.98 (1.74)	2.12 (0.13)	1.45 (3.10)

Note: t-ratios are given in brackets.

finance, or undertake acquisition activity. This is investigated using the Logit model and the results are discussed presently. Second, the question of *how much* finance is raised, or of *how much* of the expenditure is on acquisition, is not tackled by this model but by the Tobit model. This is a multi-response model where the dependent variable, although discontinuous, can take on a number of values. The two models, Logit and Tobit, are complementary, the former determining the influence of the right-hand side variables on whether or not either of the two activities is undertaken, and the latter determining the actual magnitude of the endogenous variable.

Both these models were run for acquisition and external finance equations. Consider first the acquisition equation (see Table 7.11). In both the Logit and the Tobit analysis, the significance of the independent variables shows a remarkable improvement; for example, both the gearing and liquidity variables are significant across most cross sections, whereas in earlier estimation procedures this was seldom the case. With regard to the other variables, the coefficient on investment in the Tobit model is generally less than that in the Logit model. Although, because of the differing techniques, the two results are not directly comparable, this does suggest that, of the firms undertaking some acquisition (regardless of the actual amount), there are likely to be some who have considerably above average investment. (The relationship is not systematic since the standard error of the estimate is quite high, and the coefficient is insignificant.) But once we take into account the actual expenditure on acquisition, the positive relationship with investment becomes more systematic (and statistically significant) although the actual magnitude is considerably reduced.

With the dividend variable, the result is the opposite of this: if we just compare the firms with some acquisition (Logit model) to those with no acquisition, we find a weak positive relationship for the first few years. But when we consider the actual magnitude of acquisition the relationship is much stronger and uniformly positive. For both these models the goodness of fit, as evaluated by the standard likelihood ratio test, was quite impressive. Although it is not possible to compare precisely this measure of fit with that obtained from $\bar{R}^2$ in the earlier results, it emerges quite strongly that these models performed better than those using OLS.

As regards the external finance equation, using these models to take into account the specific nature of the variables also improved the results quite dramatically (see Appendix A3, Table A3.1). For example, the acquisition variable was significant more often and was much better determined than in the OLS equations. The investment variable was also more stable across years. Further, for 1975, the discontinuity which was noticed earlier was much less marked. The goodness of fit of this equation also improved quite considerably.

7.6 Summary

The object of this chapter was to investigate the importance of some determinants of investment and acquisition expenditure and the dividend and external finance variables. Unlike in the earlier chapters where three of these variables were averaged over a number of years, here the variables were considered on an annual basis, over the years 1970–1976. The investigation was further concerned with ascertaining the stability of the explanatory variables over different time periods, and with examining the degree of simultaneity between the endogenous variables.

The explanatory variables which were of importance have been summarised above. The following main conclusions emerged.

(i) The coefficients were more stable, and the equations provided a better fit in the first three to four years, compared to the rest of the period. This, it was argued, may have reflected the increasingly unstable macro-environment over the last two–three years. Despite this, however, the OLS estimates and the exercise with the simultaneous estimation provided a number of significant results which extend the conclusions of earlier chapters. For example, it was shown that within any given year there was a noticeable simultaneity in investment and acquisition decisions. On the whole, this relationship was again positive.

(ii) The results provided some weak support for the hypothesis that investment expenditure may affect dividends adversely, but little for the view that investment may itself be affected by dividends. This emerged from two sets of equations: those using external finance in total and those using only finance raised for cash. This tends to support the corollary to the Modigliani-Miller theorem noted earlier. But at the same time there was also some evidence that financing decisions (especially the raising of new funds) are interrelated with investment.

(iii) Another interesting result was the rather strong dependence between acquisitions and dividends. In particular, acquisition activity had a strong effect on dividend disbursals. This does tend to suggest that, other things being equal, firms relying on acquisitions tended to have a policy of greater disbursal – in order perhaps to have a positive impact on share valuation. It was also noticeable that, even within the simultaneous framework, the impact of lagged dividends is very substantial. To the extent that within this framework, the other decision variables are taken into account, the effect of lagged dividends might have been expected to be less pronounced.

(iv) Regarding external finance, it emerged that the raising of new funds is rather more sensitive to profitability than emerged in Chapter 6. Further external finance in total was strongly related to acquisition expenditure.

(v) Finally, on a methodological note, this investigation has shown that, in modelling firm activities involving discontinuous variables, results using OLS can be improved significantly by using procedures which take this into account. This further revealed that a firm's capital structure, and its liquidity position, exercise a significant influence on its acquisition expenditure.

Chapters 3 to 7 have examined the growth and performance of firms without considering explicitly the role of foreign markets. In the next two chapters we extend that analysis by taking into account how the reliance on overseas markets is related to the other characteristics of firms. This is done initially by examining the export activities of the firms, and then by undertaking an investigation into their overseas production activities.

8

Exports, acquisitions and firm size

The previous chapters have examined firms' growth without distinguishing between their domestic and overseas operations. An important set of questions relates to whether there is any systematic difference in the characteristics and performance of firms which rely mainly on the domestic markets and those which also serve foreign markets. This chapter examines firms which serve foreign markets by exporting home-produced goods, whilst the next chapter considers firms undertaking production abroad.

The importance of exports to an economy such as that of the UK hardly needs emphasising. They may also be crucial from the point of view of the individual firms. For many products, economies of scale may be achieved only by relying on demand from foreign markets. Even in the case of products where there is a large enough domestic market at a given time, a firm may wish to export if the market is not expanding as fast as the firm intends to grow. In this case exports would be an alternative to acquisition or to product diversification in the domestic market.

This chapter examines two specific issues which follow from the investigations in the previous chapters. The first concerns the relationship between size, total growth and exports; the second, the relationship between acquisition growth and exports. There is little existing empirical evidence on either of these issues for the UK or for any other advanced country. This limited evidence is noted below, and the issues are elaborated and examined empirically. Section 8.1 discusses the likely relationship between a firm's exports, acquisitions and size, whilst Section 8.2 provides empirical evidence for this. Section 8.3 presents the results of an investigation into the relationship between acquisition activity and export behaviour. The last section provides a summary and some implications.

8.1 The effect of acquisitions and firm size on exports

At the firm level, there are two related ways of analysing the relationship between acquisitions and exports. First, one can regard them both as policy variables requiring strategic decisions by the firm's management. These decisions may in turn be based on motives of profit or growth maximisation, or simply on satisficing. Analysing these motives, and the likely constraints involved, one may examine whether there is any complementarity or trade-off between these two activities. Second, one may regard acquisition as leading to a change in a firm's environment, and a change in the opportunities which are open to it; one can then examine how far these changes influence exports. The two approaches are not mutually exclusive. For example, a firm may decide to increase its exports and it may regard the acquisition of another firm as entailing the desired changes in its resources or opportunities.

8.1.1 Acquisitions and exports

Regarding the first approach, consider a firm trying to decide on a feasible method for achieving a given growth rate. As noted in Chapter 1, the scope for growth would lie in one or more of the following activities: the undertaking of new investment and increasing its market share; the acquisition of an existing firm; increasing export sales and/or production abroad; and diversification. Obviously, these activities are not mutually exclusive. For example, acquisitions may play an important role in diversification, or new investment may provide capacity to increase export sales.

If the firm has underutilised productive capacity, but perceives a demand constraint in the domestic market (in the sense that the market is static or not growing fast enough), one alternative to increasing its domestic market share would be to seek out foreign markets. Of course, even if there is no demand constraint the firm may want to sell in overseas markets because they may be more profitable. These are in any case the only alternatives to product diversification. If there is no excess capacity, exporting will entail new investment. The alternative may be the acquisition of existing firms, which would bring in new capacity and markets. Even in the case of underutilised capacity, acquisitions may be regarded as facilitating the use of existing capacity (if, for example, the acquired firm has complementary technology or other assets). In this context, it has been suggested that acquisitions by replacing investment would have an adverse impact on the proportion of output exported. The argument is that the management would be 'distracted by the excitement of merging, and by its subsequent problems, from undertaking internal growth, for example, by promoting exports' (Newbould and Luffman, 1978, p. 50). Even if, in the long run, acquisition may be considered to alleviate managerial constraints considerably, in the short run it may be true that managerial factors do exercise an adverse effect. This argument is essentially based on the impact of acquisitions on new investment – an impact which the earlier extensive investigation has shown need not always be adverse. But in some cases it has been suggested that there may be an adverse impact on exports, for reasons to be noted presently, independent of the influence on investment (cf. Cowling et al., 1980). Therefore it is important to examine the relationship between acquisitions and exports more directly.

8.1.2 Firm size and exports

Acquisitions may also be expected to influence exports by their effect on the size of the firms, and by the changes they entail in the structure of industry. Consider first the relationship between firm size and the level of exports, and firm size and the export rate (i.e., exports as a proportion of sales). Acquisitions are of course a very quick way of increasing a firm's size and size is positively correlated with exports (see Section 8.2). The United Kingdom's exports, as those of other advanced countries, depend to a considerable extent on a relatively small number of large firms (Hughes and Kumar, 1984). A number of case studies which have inquired in depth into the individual firm's motives for acquisitions have also noted the emphasis placed on size for exporting activities.[1] The advantages of size have also been extensively discussed in the context of industrial policy in the UK. For example, the UK government in the late sixties established the Industrial Reorganisation Corporation to restructure industry in an attempt to make it more efficient. In turn, the Corporation played a significant role in promoting acquisitions and mergers. One of the reasons put forward for this was that large size was important for exports and that without state encouragement firms would not become large enough, soon enough (cf. McClelland, 1972). This emphasis has continued into the present (see Monopolies and Mergers Commission, 1978).

The following are some of the reasons for expecting size to have a positive influence on the export level and on the export rate:

(i) Production economies of scale, increasing cost and price competitiveness.

(ii) Economies in marketing and research and development. Given the high fixed costs of information, and the high risk associated with selling in international markets, larger firms may be able to obtain better information and adapt products more easily to foreign tastes.

(iii) High fixed costs of entry. Larger firms may find it easier to enter into new markets, and to be able to compete successfully with the established suppliers (cf. Auquier, 1980). If the variable costs of distribution, transportation and taxes are greater for exports than for domestic activities, the larger firm may be better able to absorb these higher costs.

As opposed to the above considerations, which are internal to the firm, one may consider the relevance of external factors. For example, it may be argued that in a concentrated industry, firms may be able to come to some domestic market share agreement. Other things being equal, they may then be more willing to venture into foreign markets than if the structure were competitive, and if there were greater uncertainty regarding the domestic market position (see Caves, 1979). Another consideration would be the relationship between structure and innovation activity, independent of firm size. If firms in concentrated industries had higher rates of innovation activity, they might compete better internationally. (The empirical evidence on any structure–innovation relationship is, however, inconclusive – see Scherer, 1980.)

It is plausible to argue, however, that larger size allows domestic firms to undertake production abroad and that this can have an adverse effect on their exports from the domestic economy. The argument is based on the proposition that there is a threshold size for foreign direct investment. In the short run, firms may exceed it after merger (cf. Singh, 1975). Over time, larger size would also be attained by internal growth, and a similar argument might then apply to the effect on exports.

There has, however, been some discussion which tends to indicate that the setting up of foreign production may be a support, and not a substitute, for exports. Hirsch's (1976) theoretical analysis showed that if foreign investment was carried out by a single product firm, a decision by such a firm to invest abroad would be certainly a decision to refrain from exporting. This would be the case, assuming the firm was taking its decision on the basis of minimising the costs attached to producing in the domestic market and exporting, or producing in the foreign market. If costs were lower for the second possibility, exports would be adversely affected.

However, as Hirsch concluded 'once intermediate production and more goods are considered, it is no longer possible to state on a priori grounds whether international direct investment is export enhancing or export replacing' (1976, p. 265). There are two reasons for this. First, by establishing production abroad, the costs of marketing products which the firm was previously exporting are reduced and could become equal to those of its competitors. In such a situation, the list of exportables may be increased. So, even if production abroad results in the elimination of certain exports, it may turn other goods into exportables. These could not be exported before the investment because of their high marketing-cost differential. (Hirsch does not consider why this should be so. It could be because of marketing overheads – since transport costs would still be the same.) Second, goods which prior to overseas production were not exported, may be turned into exportables by the establishment abroad of a manufacturing affiliate which imports parts or semi-finished goods from the home economy, while finishing operations are performed by the affiliate. However, contrary to Hirsch's assumption, this need not be an automatic outcome since, presumably, a firm would only do this if there were benefits from vertical integration. Overall, however, this type of analysis does suggest that the net effect on exports of a foreign production decision is uncertain, and that large size may not be correlated with lower exports simply because it is correlated with high foreign direct investment. (For a detailed empirical investigation which suggested some positive relationship between exports and foreign investment see Reddaway, 1968.)

Finally, it is worth noting the relationship between exports and domestic demand pressure, and the way size of firms and their acquisitions may be related to it. The domestic demand pressure hypothesis maintains that high levels of domestic demand, or substantial increases in its rate of change, are negatively related to exports in the short run (see Winters, 1981). This is owing to a price effect and a supply constraint effect. Consider first the price effect. The proposition is that, owing to competition, and assuming an upward sloping marginal cost curve of the firm, costs and prices would rise in periods of domestic demand expansion. If the demand for exports is sufficiently elastic, their value may be reduced. However, it is generally accepted that, at least in oligopolistic industries, the pricing policy of the firm has to be explained not in terms of marginal costs, but by the full-cost pricing principle (see Coutts, Godley and Nordhaus, 1978). In such a case an upward shift in the firm's demand curve would leave prices unchanged, with production increasing up to the full capacity of plants. Acquisitions, by influencing the structure of industries, may affect the firm's price response to a change in domestic demand (see Holmes, 1978). Thus there may be a smaller impact on exports through prices because of the change in structure. Even if the pricing factor is not important in practice, the commitment of large firms to exports may have a similar effect. Consider next the supply constraint effect. Here the proposition is that if firms are running close to full capacity, with prices unchanged, other allocative mechanisms will come into operation in order to match an increase in excess demand to the given capacity: either goods and resources which would otherwise be used to supply export markets will be diverted to domestic sales, or queues will form and excess demand will result in lengthening delivery dates and waiting times. In this case, the commitment to export is important. If one assumes that some firms regard exporting as part of a long-term strategy of expansion, there is no reason to expect exports to worsen as a result of domestic supply constraints, even though domestic sales may become more profitable in the short run. This would be because firms may be unwilling to risk losing their established customers and damaging their reputation, in the overseas markets (cf. Cooper *et al*., 1970, and Hague *et al*., 1974). It is generally assumed that larger firms are more likely to regard exports as a permanent part of their activities than are smaller firms. If the larger firms do have a different (that is, a more stable) strategy towards exports than the smaller firms, one may expect the supply constraint to affect export deliveries less for these firms.

8.2 Size and exports: empirical evidence

Table 8.1 shows the mean export rate for each industry and the sample standard deviation of that rate inside each industry, calculated over all the firms in the sample.[2] The average export rate for each industry is computed as follows:

$$\text{export rate} = \frac{1}{n} \sum_{i=1}^{n} (E_i/S_i) \tag{8.1}$$

where n is the number of firms in the industry, E_i denotes exports of firm i, and S_i its total sales. The very high variation in mean export rates across industries is not unexpected: the export rates range from a minimum of 0.046 for Food, to a maximum of 0.225 for Vehicles. These variations can be due to a large number of factors: e.g. the nature of products, transport costs, the international division of labour, cross-country differences in tastes, factor endowment and efficiency. Similarly, when the standard deviation of the rates inside each industry is examined, it can be seen that these too exhibit a high degree of variability.

Table 8.1 also presents Pearson's correlation coefficient between three pairs of variables. In column (3) the correlation between E_i and S_i is shown and this yields highly positive coefficients which are nearly all statistically significant. Note that the correlation could be spurious, since E_i is a part of S_i, so that for given values of $S_i - E_i$, drawings of E_i's from a random distribution would produce S_i positively correlated with E_i (given that $S_i - E_i$ is never negative). However, column (4) shows a similar (although lower) positive correlation between E_i and $S_i - E_i$. Here any spurious effect would be negative since, for a given value of S_i, drawings of E_i's would generate a variable $S_i - E_i$ negatively correlated with the latter (the higher the E_i, the lower the $S_i - E_i$).

As noted above, apart from the mere size effect (*ceteris paribus*, the larger the size, the more the exports), there may be some causal economic explanations for these results. Exporting is likely to enable firms to reap economies of scale in production by relaxing the constraint of market size. But entry to the foreign market may also raise the quantity sold at home through a reduction in average unit cost, and so a positive correlation would be expected between domestic sales and exports. Even if the production economies were unimportant, other factors such as high fixed-cost elements in information, and marketing costs, would still lead to an expectation that larger firms would tend to have higher exports than would smaller ones.

As column (5) shows, however, there is a negative correlation between size (measured by sales *minus* exports) and export rate in all industries but three (Drink,

Table 8.1 *Size and exports in manufacturing industries*

Industry	n	(1) Export ratio	(2) S.D.	(3) E_i and S_i	(4) E_i and $(S_i - E_i)$	(5) $E_i/S_i - E_i$ and $S_i - E_i$
21 Food	19	0.046	0.052	0.57	0.54	−0.22
23 Drink	38	0.051	0.109	0.64	0.53	0.07
26 Chemicals	33	0.169	0.144	0.91	0.86	−0.16
31 Metal manf.	28	0.129	0.111	0.98	0.97	−0.04
33 Non-elec. eng.	71	0.202	0.130	0.64	0.49	−0.15
36 Elec. eng.	39	0.214	0.139	0.95	0.91	−0.12
38 Vehicles	17	0.225	0.120	0.98	0.98	0.34
39 Metal goods	48	0.141	0.108	0.87	0.84	−0.09
41 Textiles	55	0.169	0.121	0.96	0.93	−0.002
44 Clothing etc.	19	0.102	0.093	0.96	0.96	−0.20
46 Bricks etc.	35	0.108	0.121	0.64	0.61	−0.26
47 Timber etc.	20	0.060	0.063	0.92	0.90	0.05
48 Paper etc.	46	0.093	0.148	0.62	0.59	−0.07
49 Other manf.	26	0.174	0.094	0.98	0.98	−0.18
All manufacturing	512	0.143	0.131	0.77	0.70	−0.08

Notes: n = Number of firms; E_i = exports of firm i in 1976; S_i = Sales of firm i in 1976.
Columns (3) to (5) indicate the correlations.

Vehicles and Timber). Although none of the correlations is statistically significant, it is still an important, and rather surprising, result. It indicates that whilst large firms place greater reliance on foreign markets than do smaller firms, this is only in absolute terms and not in relation to their total activity. There are, however, some deficiencies in the available data which should be borne in mind when interpreting these results. The data on sales are for firms' world-wide sales which do not distinguish between domestic and foreign operations; this may lower the export rate for larger firms since these are more likely to have foreign operations than smaller firms. In addition, the degree of vertical integration may vary between firms: suppose, for example, larger firms are more likely to own and operate retail outlets in the domestic economy than are smaller firms, and that in these outlets products manufactured by other firms are also sold. In such a case, if one examined a firm's total sales, its export rate would be lower than if exports had been considered as a proportion of the sales of only the firm's own products.[3] Finally, a consideration operating in the opposite direction would be if relatively more of smaller firms' products were exported indirectly (i.e. where the producing firm itself is not involved in exporting at all).

Unfortunately, there is no evidence on the magnitude of the bias which is likely to be imparted by the last two of these considerations. The bias due to the first consideration is investigated in the following chapter, when the firms' export rates are adjusted for their overseas activities. It may be argued that, despite the possibility of bias, and despite the earlier *a priori* arguments, there may still be some underlying negative relationship between size and export rate. Paradoxically, this may be so if exports are undertaken essentially to achieve economies of scale: the larger the domestic sales, the higher the probability of reaping the benefits of large-scale production without incurring the extra costs associated with exports. There is one empirical study for the UK and some studies for other advanced countries which obtain similar results. For the UK, evidence is provided by Hannah and Kay (1977) who, using discrete size classes, found a negative relationship between firm size and export rate for 1976 for large quoted firms. Similar conclusions are reached for Japanese firms: it was found that larger Japanese firms are significantly more likely to export than smaller ones and that, among firms that are exporting, smaller firms are likely to exhibit a higher export rate (see Rapp, 1976). A similar result emerges from a study of Belgian exporters (Glejser *et al.*, 1980).

In view of the discussion in Section 8.1, and of the low level of significance of the results, it is also possible that there may be some non-linear relationship between size and export rate. Further, the above evidence pertains to a single year. If there are any cyclical factors which affect differentially the firms in different size classes, their export performance may also be affected. For example, it was noted earlier that the pressure of domestic demand may affect firms differentially. In particular, smaller firms may decrease their exports relative to larger firms. We have taken these two factors into account by dividing the firms into a number of discrete size classes and comparing the export rates between them averaged over a number of years.

Table 8.2 presents the results for the years 1968–1972. The size classes are based on firms' total sales in 1968, and the export rate for each firm is calculated as an arithmetic average of its export rate for the five years. This is then averaged for firms in each of the five size classes. Consider first the aggregate of industries: the mean export rate of firms which had sales less than £5m in 1968 was 13.1 per cent, for firms with sales between £5m and £20m it was 12.8 per cent, and so on. But clearly the decline in export rate is not monotonic with size. For the firms with initial sales in the range £40m–£80m, the export rate is greater than for any other size class. For the lowest size class, however, the pattern exhibited by the first three size classes continues, with the very largest companies having the lowest export rates.

It is likely that the non-linear pattern hides a considerable diversity of experience in different industries. To allow for this, each of the industries was examined separately. Consider, for example, Non-electrical engineering. The pattern here is similar to that obtained for the aggregate; the export rate declines monotonically for the first three size classes, it rises for the next size class, but falls again for the largest firms. However, for the largest firms it is considerably greater than that for the third size class. A similar picture is obtained for Chemicals and Paper.

For other industries, however, there is an absence of any systematic pattern. For Vehicles, the pattern is reversed with the largest firms having the highest export rates; in Electrical engineering, the second and the fourth size classes have the highest rates, whilst in Textiles the smallest firms do so. It is clear, therefore, that the negative correlation in Table 8.1 tells only part of the story: there is a considerable variation in the export behaviour of firms in different size classes, and in different industries. Looking at this evidence, a more appropriate conclusion would be that there is no systematic relationship between firms' size and export rates.

Table 8.2 *Export rate by opening size class*

Opening size	21 Food n	Food mean	Food S.D.	23 Drink n	Drink mean	Drink S.D.	26 Chemicals n	Chemicals mean	Chemicals S.D.	31 Metal manf. n	Metal manf. mean	Metal manf. S.D.	33 Non-elec. eng. n	Non-elec. eng. mean	Non-elec. eng. S.D.
1 < 5,000	4	0.76	0.56	17	1.5	15.2	12	17.5	11.6	10	10.6	14.6	32	26.7	17.1
2 < 20,000	9	2.2	2.3	15	1.1	4.3	18	12.8	9.4	22	13.0	10.8	51	21.7	15.4
3 < 40,000	4	4.1	2.3	5	10.5	10.4	4	6.1	6.0	4	10.1	3.2	15	13.6	5.9
4 < 80,000	7	3.2	2.5	–	–	–	3	13.5	12.0	3	8.4	1.5	9	23.0	11.4
5 > 80,000	4	2.7	3.1	7	5.1	8.9	8	10.1	6.0	3	11.5	5.0	2	17.4	1.2
All firms	28	2.6	2.4	44	4.6	10.7	45	13.0	9.7	42	11.7	10.5	109	22.1	15.0

Opening size	36 Elec. eng. n	Elec. eng. mean	Elec. eng. S.D.	38 Vehicles n	Vehicles mean	Vehicles S.D.	39 Metal goods n	Metal goods mean	Metal goods S.D.	41 Textiles n	Textiles mean	Textiles S.D.	44 Clothing etc. n	Clothing etc. mean	Clothing etc. S.D.
1 < 5,000	17	14.0	12.5	7	8.6	8.1	34	14.1	13.8	26	15.0	12.7	11	9.1	9.1
2 < 20,000	15	22.3	20.5	11	14.1	5.4	25	11.1	9.7	30	10.1	8.6	17	9.2	8.0
3 < 40,000	7	14.5	8.5	2	26.1	27.3	5	11.4	10.4	9	14.2	6.9	1	10.5	–
4 < 80,000	5	20.9	5.9	4	23.2	7.4	2	17.7	0.6	–	–	–	1	0.9	–
5 > 80,000	7	15.3	6.5	4	28.9	6.4	4	18.0	13.0	4	13.4	4.3	1	10.2	–
All firms	51	17.3	14.1	28	17.0	10.9	70	13.2	11.9	69	12.7	10.1	31	9.0	8.0

Opening size	46 Bricks etc. n	Bricks etc. mean	Bricks etc. S.D.	47 Timber etc. n	Timber etc. mean	Timber etc. S.D.	48 Paper etc. n	Paper etc. mean	Paper etc. S.D.	49 Other manf. n	Other manf. mean	Other manf. S.D.	All industries n	All industries mean	All industries S.D.
1 < 5,000	15	6.4	10.0	14	3.1	4.4	23	11.8	20.0	16	12.4	9.2	247	13.1	9.2
2 < 20,000	12	11.3	10.0	13	1.8	2.0	21	7.7	9.5	16	19.9	13.3	282	12.8	8.4
3 < 40,000	6	3.7	3.1	1	1.9	–	3	5.0	4.6	2	13.2	2.9	68	11.0	10.1
4 < 80,000	3	2.5	1.5	1	9.4	–	5	6.2	6.6	1	14.6	–	47	13.8	15.2
5 > 80,000	3	2.3	2.0	–	–	–	5	5.1	2.4	1	7.8	–	56	10.9	12.1
All firms	39	6.9	8.9	29	2.7	3.6	57	8.8	14.2	36	15.7	11.3	700	12.7	12.8

Notes: Opening size is £'000 and is measured by sales in 1968; n denotes number of firms; mean refers to the average export rate (each firm's export rate is averaged over 1968–1972); S.D. denotes the Standard deviation. All firms, exporting and non-exporting, are included.

Table 8.3 *Export growth of manufacturing firms*

Opening size class	26 Chemicals			31 Metal manf.		
	n	mean	S.D.	n	mean	S.D.
≤ 5m	10	11.46	11.42	6	7.72	20.06
≤ 20m	15	9.23	18.96	18	10.09	10.13
≤ 40m	3	6.79	9.23	4	2.59	8.95
≤ 80m	3	9.10	6.93	3	6.39	11.76
> 80m	8	10.97	7.10	3	11.51	8.58
All firms	39	9.90	15.49	34	8.65	12.77

Opening size class	33 Non-elec. eng.			36 Elec. eng.		
	n	mean	S.D.	n	mean	S.D.
≤ 5m	24	14.05	15.42	15	20.07	26.49
≤ 20m	42	6.81	20.89	13	10.67	11.53
≤ 40m	14	10.22	10.55	7	6.14	8.49
≤ 80m	9	9.24	9.44	5	9.57	2.57
> 80m	2	6.61	7.12	7	9.49	4.37
All firms	91	9.60	17.18	47	12.91	17.36

Note: Firms with no exports in 1968 are excluded.

Before leaving Table 8.2, note that the variation in export rates generally tends to be lower for firms in the larger size classes. Although for the aggregate of industries, the variation is higher, an examination of the individual industries points the other way. It is also worth noting that our sample includes all firms, and not just exporting ones. It seems likely that, other things being equal, the smaller size class of firms would contain a relatively higher proportion of non-exporting firms. In this case, the variation would be expected to be greater in the smaller size classes.

Whilst the export rate gives an indication of the reliance of firms on overseas markets in a given period, a measurement of export growth indicates how that reliance is changing over time. To the extent that smaller firms were more dynamic and growing faster, the expectation would be that their growth in exports would also be higher than that of the larger firms. Table 8.3 provides some evidence for this. Growth in exports was calculated as the geometric average over the years 1968–1972. (To measure the growth in exports, firms which had no exports in the opening year were excluded.) The results are for a sample of 211 firms in four manufacturing industries, for the period 1968–1972. Apart from Metal goods, the growth in exports of the smallest firms was indeed considerably greater than the export growth of firms in other size classes. But again there is no monotonic relationship between firm size and export growth. Some of the lowest growth was recorded by the firms in the medium size range. Note also that these results cannot be taken to mean that the proportion of smallest firms' exports to their total sales was also rising over this period. This would be the case only if the growth in sales of these firms were the same or less than that of others. As the evidence in Chapter 3 suggested, this was not so. So it is unlikely that there has been any significant change in the relative export rate of firms in different size classes.

8.3 Acquisitions and exports

As noted earlier, there are obvious differences in the nature of acquisition and exporting activities. Acquisition, like new investment, entails a significant outlay of resources, and can involve a considerable change in organisation and production. Exporting, on the other hand, involving as it does in the main the marketing of products, may be less taxing for the firm's organisation. Yet both these activities can provide an avenue for growth for the firm and may compete for scarce resources. As Newbould and Luffman (1978) argued, therefore, it is not too implausible to suggest that there may be some trade-off between the two activities.

This section provides some preliminary empirical evidence about the relationship between the two activities. First consider some descriptive results for the two five-year periods 1968–1972 and 1972–1976. (All the variables are as described in Chapter 2.) For the period 1968–1972, total growth in exports was highly correlated with growth by acquisition, the coefficient being statistically significant at the one per cent level (Table 8.4). However, to the extent that before merger both acquiring and acquired firms may be engaged in exporting, it is to be expected that high acquisition growth would be associated with high export growth. What is of more interest in such a situation is the growth in exports *relative* to growth in sales (this is considered presently). The average of the export rate, however, was not related to acquisition growth. There is also no evidence that firms with a high proportion of exports tended to have higher profitability. Other things being equal, one might expect that exporting firms would tend to be more efficient – and that this may be reflected in higher profitability (see Saunders, 1978). A noticeable characteristic, however, is the positive relationship between profitability and export growth. To the extent that export growth is highly correlated with total growth, as also are growth and profitability, this result may be expected. However, there is also a causal relationship involved here. It is not unlikely that high profitability in domestic operations may make firms both more willing and able to expand faster in the foreign markets which, initially at least, may be riskier, and may entail high overhead costs (Saunders, 1978).

For the second period, the size–export rate and size–export growth relationship is reversed, and now the latter is significantly negative. Further, the correlation between export growth and acquisition, as well as that between export growth and new investment, is now lower. But, whilst export growth is positively correlated with acquisition, this does not imply any causal relationship between the two. To determine whether there were any differences in the export activity of those firms which had engaged in heavy acquisition and those which had made fewer acquisitions, the following two exercises were undertaken.

In the first exercise, for the period 1968–1976, acquisitions and exports of a larger sample of firms were examined. Since we were interested in the change in

Table 8.4 *Correlation between export rate, export growth and other variables*

	1 Size	2 Growth	3 Growth by new investment	4 Growth by acquisition	5 Profitability	6 Export rate
1968–1972						
Export rate	–0.01	–0.05	–0.06	–0.05	–0.04	1.0
Export growth	0.03	0.23**	0.18**	0.27**	0.07	0.03
1972–1976						
Export rate	0.04	–0.08	–0.04	–0.06	–0.04	1.0
Export growth	–0.10*	0.66**	0.02	0.10*	0.11**	–0.13

Notes: For correlations between export rate and other variables, the number of firms is 700 and 585, for the two periods respectively. For export growth the numbers are 556 and 485 respectively (for export growth, firms with no exports in 1968 were excluded).

The variables 2–6 and export growth are averages over each of two five year periods.

**, * denote statistical significance at the 1 per cent and 5 per cent level, respectively.

exports over the period, only those companies which had some exports at the beginning of the period were included in the exercise; this gave a sample of 454 manufacturing firms. The firms were divided into three groups based on their average acquisition growth during the period. Group 1 included those 207 firms which had undertaken 'moderate' acquisition growth over the period 1968–1976. This was defined as growth by acquisition greater than 1 per cent but less than 10 per cent. Group 2 included 181 firms with acquisition growth less than 1 per cent (negligible) and Group 3 66 firms with acquisition growth greater than 10 per cent (high).

The results of the comparison of the three groups are given in Table 8.5. First compare the size, export activity and investment of non-acquirers and acquirers (Groups 2 and 3 respectively). The acquirers were larger at the beginning, with average sales of £38 million: the mean difference, however, was not statistically significant. Although the level of exports of the acquirers was also higher, exports as a proportion of sales were slightly lower than those for the non-acquirers (rows 2 and 3). The average growth in exports and sales over the whole period was, however, significantly greater for the acquirers; whilst they had an export growth of 42.4 per cent, the non-acquirers had only 18.3 per cent. The sales growth of the acquirers was also greater – more than four times that of non-acquirers. The net result of this was that the export growth as a proportion of sales growth of acquirers, whilst still being considerably higher than that of non-acquirers, was not as high as that suggested by export growth alone. (Note that the export growth/

Table 8.5 *Exports and acquisitions*

Variable	Group	Mean	Std. Error	Difference	t-ratio	Group	Mean	Std. Error	Difference	t-ratio	Group	Mean	Std. Error	Difference	t-ratio
1 Size 1968	3	38M	16M			1	65M	11M			3	38M	16M		
	2	30M	5M	8M	0.47	2	30M	5M	25M**	2.86	1	65M	11M	−27M	−1.44
2 Exports 1968	3	5.0M	2.8M			1	6.0M	1.3M			3	5.0M	2.8M		
	2	3.4M	0.7M	1.6M	0.54	2	3.4M	7.3M	2.6M	1.67	1	6.0M	1.0M	−1.0M	−0.32
3 Exports/sales 1968	3	0.12	0.01			1	0.12	0.009			3	0.117	0.012		
	2	0.13	0.009	−0.01	−0.89	2	0.13	0.009	−0.01	−0.57	1	0.123	0.009	−0.006	−0.41
4 Export growth	3	42.4%	4.09			1	24.8%	0.78			3	42.4%	4.09		
Average 1968–1976	2	18.3%	0.41	24.1%**	3.18	2	18.3%	0.41	6.5%*	2.33	1	24.8%	0.79	17.6%**	4.11
5 Sales growth	3	31.1%	3.34			1	12.1%	0.10			3	31.1%	3.34		
Average 1968–1976	2	7.1%	0.07	24.0%*	2.10	2	7.1%	0.07	5.0%***	6.18	1	12.1%	0.10	19.0	1.87
6 Export growth	3	5.62	2.07			1	2.97	0.68			3	5.62	2.07		
/Sales growth	2	3.60	1.67	2.02	0.76	2	3.60	1.67	−0.63	−0.36	1	2.97	0.40	2.65	1.52
7 Investment growth	3	4.85%	0.006			1	3.5%	0.002			3	4.85	0.006		
Average 1968–1976	2	3.36%	0.003	1.49%*	2.50	2	3.4%	0.003	0.1%	0.31	1	3.50%	0.002	1.34%*	2.12
8 Acquisition growth	3	21.6%	0.02			1	3.8%	0.002			3	21.6%	0.02		
Average 1968–1976	2	0.001%	0.001	21.6%**	9.54	2	0.0%	0.001	3.8%***	19.77	1	3.8%	0.002	17.8%**	7.82
				Difference=Group3-Group2					Difference=Group1-Group2					Difference=Group3-Group1	

Note: *, ** denote significantly different from 0 at 5 and 1 per cent respectively.

sales growth ratio is computed for each firm separately, and is not a ratio of the average of export growth to average of sales growth across firms.) It is still an interesting result, which does not suggest that acquisitions were in general associated with declining exports. In this, the finding differs from the major empirical study by Newbould and Luffman which had concluded that acquisition activity had tended to displace exports – mainly, it was suggested, by diverting managerial resources which could have been used in undertaking new investment and promoting exports. (It is also worth noting that the expenditure on net investment is greater for the acquirers, the difference being statistically significant at the 5 per cent level. Cf. Chapter 4.)

Next, we compare firms engaging in moderate acquisition activity with the non-acquirers. Moderate acquirers were significantly larger than the non-acquirers and also had higher exports at the beginning of the period, but their export rate was marginally lower. As for the growth in exports (row 4) the moderate acquirers' average annual growth of 24.8 per cent was appreciably greater than that of the non-acquirers, the difference being significant at the 5 per cent level. However, the sales growth of the former group was almost twice as high, with the result that over the period 1968–1976 the export growth as a proportion of sales growth of non-acquirers was greater than that of the moderate acquirers. The interesting point is that whilst the growth in the sales and exports of both the moderate acquirers and the high acquirers is greater than that of non-acquirers, it is only the high acquirers whose export growth as a proportion of sales growth is greater. It may be argued that the high acquirers are generally more dynamic firms who have the experience of acquiring and assimilating firms, without running into managerial and other constraints (cf. Chapter 5). The evidence provided by Reid (1968) is of some relevance here. After an intensive empirical study he concluded that active acquirers in most cases had developed both an expertise and an organisational structure which permitted them to pursue acquisition growth more efficiently than others who had been active only sporadically. So the moderate acquirers may not only have been less willing to engage in excessive acquisition activity, but they may also have found it difficult to benefit fully from the acquisitions which they did undertake.

Finally, consider the relative performance of high acquirers and moderate acquirers. Moderate acquirers were larger, and had greater exports and a higher export rate than high acquirers. But both the export growth and the sales growth of moderate acquirers were less than that of high acquirers, as was the growth in exports as a proportion of sales growth. The variation in this proportion between the high acquirers was, however, very considerable, with the result that the difference was statistically insignificant.

Superficially, at least, this exercise suggests that, if anything, high acquisition growth was associated with high export and sales growth over the period 1968–1976, although export growth as a proportion of sales growth was higher for only the most intensive acquirers. It could be argued that, as this period saw sharp variation in the level of acquisition activity as well as in the macro-economic and market environment, a shorter time period may be more appropriate. To take account of this, the period was divided into two sub-periods, 1968–1972 and 1972–1976, and a similar analysis was undertaken for these two sub-periods separately. The results obtained for the entire period were somewhat modified, but the conclusion that acquisition growth was not associated with any general decline in export activity was maintained.[4]

It is clear that the above results do not necessarily indicate the direction of causality. Both the high acquisition activity and the increase in exports may be a response to some exogenous change. For example, consider the increasing import penetration of the domestic economy. In such a situation both may reflect some defensive strategy in the face of increasing competition, and the latter, in addition, greater international division of labour (cf. Aaronovitch and Sawyer, 1975a, Ch. 11). The results for individual industries suggested that this is unlikely to be the complete explanation. For, assuming firms in a given industry do not face radically different environments in terms of competition from imports, if some firms then do undertake acquisitions in that industry, it may be argued that the changes in their performance are at least partly attributable to acquisitions, But this argument is admittedly tentative, and a second exercise was undertaken which offers some more evidence on this issue.

A sample of 311 manufacturing firms which continued in independent existence over the period 1965–1976 was selected, and divided into two sub-groups according to the firms' acquisition growth in the period 1965–1970. (Again firms which had no exports in 1968 were excluded; note that 1968 was the first year for which data on exports were available.) Growth by acquisition was averaged over the period 1965–1970: firms with 5 per cent or more of acquisition growth (Group 1) were compared with those which grew by less than 1 per cent in this way (Group 2). A comparison was then undertaken of the export and sales growth of the two groups over the period 1971–1976. The rationale of this exercise was that by examining export growth in a period following a period of low or high acquisition activity, one may be able to infer the impact of acquisition on exports. The results are shown in Table 8.6. The acquirers at the beginning of the period were considerably smaller than the non-acquirers, but their growth was rapid and already by 1968 their sales were greater than the average for the non-acquirers (not shown here). In 1968, whilst the level of exports of the acquirers was substantially greater than that of the non-acquirers, their export rate was similar. More importantly, the export growth of the acquirers was only marginally greater than that of the non-acquirers over the 1968–1971 period.

Consider next the growth in exports of the two groups over the period 1971–1976. The export growth of the acquirers was almost twice that of the non-acquirers (row 4). However, the variation within the acquirers' group was significantly greater than that for the non-acquirers (the computed F-statistic for difference in variance amongst the two groups was 26.82); thus the difference in average export growth amongst the two groups was not statistically significant. The sales growth of acquirers was also considerably greater than that of the non-acquirers, even though the difference was somewhat smaller than in the case of export growth (export/sales growth of the two groups was 3.49 per cent and 2.75 per cent respectively). Note that for the period 1971–1976, the acquisitions by both the earlier categories of acquirers and non-acquirers were similar; for the acquirers there was a very considerable decline from the earlier period; for the non-acquirers there was an increase. The similarity of acquisition activity of this period suggests that, at a

Table 8.6 *Acquisitions and subsequent exports*

	Variable	Group	No. of firms	Mean	Standard error	Mean difference	t-ratio
1	Size 1965	1	49	12.9m	4m		
		2	262	19.8m	4.8m	−6.9m	−1.09
2	Exports 1968	1		6.4m	3.7m		
		2		4.2m	1.0m	2.2m	0.58
3	Exports/Sales 1968	1		0.12	0.020		
		2		0.11	0.018	0.01	0.60
4	Exports/Growth 1971–1976	1		35.3%	1.71		
		2		17.5%	0.14	17.8%	1.34
5	Sales/Growth 1971–1976	1		14.5%	0.40		
		2		8.9%	0.09	5.6%	1.07
6	Acquisition growth 1965–1970	1		8.5%	0.55		
		2		0.06%	0.04	8.44%*	15.41
7	Acquisition growth 1971–1976	1		1.73%	0.34		
		2		1.39%	0.34	0.34%	0.71
8	Profitability 1971–1976	1		8.8%	0.55		
		2		8.5%	0.26	0.3%	0.49

Notes: Mean difference=Group 1−Group 2.
Group 1 includes firms with high acquisition activity, 1965–1970.
Group 2 includes firms with negligible acquisition activity, 1965–1970.

minimum, export growth in this period is unlikely to have been hindered by the earlier acquisition activity.[5]

8.4 Summary and conclusions
There are two main results established in this chapter.

(i) It was found that there was a strong positive relationship between the size of firms and their exports. There was some negative relationship between size and export rate, but it was statistically insignificant and not stable over different time periods. Hannah and Kay (1977) suggested that an important explanation for the lack of any positive relationship between firm size and export rate may be that large firms are more likely to own foreign subsidiaries, and supply through them, rather than by direct exports. Theoretical analysis as well as some empirical work for the UK suggests that there need not be any simple negative relationship between the presence of foreign subsidiaries and exports. Part of the explanation may in fact lie in the data used in the analysis. In particular, the total sales of firms, which are used as the deflator, are likely to include a much higher proportion of overseas sales for large firms than for small ones. In the next chapter we examine the extent to which taking this into account alters the size–export rate relationship.

To anticipate the results, it still appears that, with this taken into account, there is no tendency for larger firms to have higher export rates. From a policy perspective this seems an important result. It appears to call into question the considerable emphasis in the UK's industrial policy (starting with the Industrial Reorganisation Corporation in the late 1960s) on encouraging the formation of large firms which are thought to be better able to compete internationally. This result must however be regarded as rather tentative, since it is based on data on export performance in broad industrial groups. It is obvious that within a group such as Electrical engineering or Chemicals, technical factors might dictate a very high minimum efficient size for certain products – products which could not even be produced by small or medium-sized firms. Thus, whilst the average performance across a broad industrial group may be similar, the composition of products is likely to be different, and more research needs to be undertaken before one can conclude that the policy of encouraging large firms in order to improve international competitiveness had been misplaced.

(ii) It has been suggested that acquisitions may have deflected firms' managements from undertaking new investment and that this may have had an adverse effect on exports. The earlier chapters showed that in general there was no evidence of a negative relationship between the former two activities. Here a direct investigation was undertaken of the relationship between acquisition and exports. It was found that there was some non-linear association between the two variables. There was no indication, however, of a negative relationship between them. This result received further support when the effect of acquisitions on subsequent exports was examined.

This result is open to a number of interpretations. The most obvious one seems to be that it reinforces the earlier findings that there is likely to be considerable variation in firms' ability and willingness to undertake acquisitions. There will be, for instance, dynamic firms, by no means necessarily the largest, who may attain above-average acquisition growth as well as have an edge in exploiting foreign markets by exports. Another interpretation could be that acquisitions have a directly beneficial effect on exports owing to the kind of factors noted in Section 8.1. Whatever the interpretation, at a minimum these results suggest that acquisitions are not associated with any deteriorating export performance and, to this extent, from a policy perspective one should not count this as yet another cost of merger. The overall effect of mergers on firm performance and industrial structure, and the policy to be adopted towards them, is further discussed in Chapter 10.

9

Overseas production and firm growth

The last chapter examined two main issues relating to the way firms may supply overseas markets by exporting: the relationship between firm size and export rate and export growth, and the relationship between acquisitions and exports. This chapter examines the alternative method of supplying foreign markets – by locating production overseas. There has been an increasing reliance by UK firms, as by those in other advanced countries, on foreign production and, for an understanding of firm growth and performance, it is important to examine the implications of this. In particular, the chapter examines the following questions which arise from our earlier investigations: To what extent is the relationship between firm size and export rate altered when firms' overseas production is taken into account? What is the relationship between firm size and overseas operations? In what ways do firms with overseas activities differ from those with only domestic operations? Is there any systematic effect of overseas activities on growth and profitability of firms?

Although there is a considerable general literature on overseas production, there is only a limited amount of evidence on these questions. In particular, there have been very few studies which have examined these questions for UK firms. Furthermore, most studies (for the UK and for other countries) have examined only the largest firms (typically the largest 30–50 firms in any given economy). There has been no recent investigation into the comparative performance of firms with only domestic production and those with some overseas production as well.

The discussion below is arranged as follows. Section 9.1 notes some theoretical approaches which have been used in studying the behaviour of firms with overseas production and considers the existing empirical evidence on their performance relative to performance of firms producing only in the domestic economy. Section 9.2 describes the additional data collected for this investigation and provides new empirical evidence on the overseas activities of a large sample of firms. (The term 'overseas activities' or 'overseas operations' denotes only production overseas. It does *not* include exports from the domestic economy.) Section 9.3 then examines the relationship between firm size, overseas operations and exports, whilst Section 9.4 considers the difference between national and international firms, and the effect of firms' overseas operations on their growth and profitability. The last section provides a summary of the results and some extensions to them.

9.1 Basic approaches and existing studies

There have been a number of different approaches to explaining firms' overseas activities. (For a survey, see Dunning, 1981 and Caves, 1982.) One main approach, formalised by Hymer (1970), suggested that international firms operated in imperfect markets, where it was necessary to acquire and sustain certain advantages, such as superior technology, innovatory capacity, capable management and so on (see below). (Throughout this chapter, the term 'international' or 'multinational' (MNE) denotes firms with some overseas production activities. These are compared with 'domestic' or 'national' firms which have no overseas production.) An extension of this approach has been made by Dunning (1981), called the 'eclectic approach'. The principal proposition of this approach is that a firm will undertake overseas operations if the following three conditions are satisfied. First, that the firm possesses (or can acquire, on more favourable terms) assets which its competitors do not possess (that is, the firm has 'ownership' advantages). Second that it is more beneficial to the firm to make use of them itself rather than to sell or lease them (that is, for it to internalise its advantages). Third, that it is profitable for the firm to exploit these assets either in conjunction with at least some inputs (including natural resources) outside the home country, or where there are some barriers to exports.

Hymer and Dunning (as well as other theorists) place considerable emphasis on the technological advantages which the MNEs are believed to have acquired *vis à vis* local competitors within imperfectly competitive environments (see Hood and Young, 1979, Ch. 2). New products and processes are the most tangible component of this, but there are other aspects which are considered to be important. In particular the ability to differentiate products may be significant where technology is standardised. Product differentiation in turn is a reflection of more general marketing skills. Another source of technological advantage is considered to lie in the superior organisational skills and management techniques of MNEs. The advantage may arise from better trained or educated, or more experienced, managers.

Another source of advantage to MNEs derives from an oligopolistic market structure and behaviour. It is argued that large size is an important attribute for successful innovation, given the high costs of research and development and the economies of scale available. Further, the profitable exploitation of technology is thought to require some degree of monopoly. In addition, large firms are more able to protect themselves by the patent system, given the high costs of taking out patents internationally. The main feature of industrial organisation in this approach is that of firm economies of scale. These include advantages derived from the centralisation of R and D, marketing, finance and other management functions.

There have also been a number of other attempts to develop oligopoly models of the MNEs. These are based on the proposition that oligopolists follow each other into new foreign markets as a defensive strategy (see e.g. Knickerbocker, 1973). Once one firm establishes manufacturing facilities, the others follow suit in order to negate any advantage that the former might gain in the particular market. This approach thus differs from those noted above by shifting the focus from the supposed ownership advantages possessed by MNEs (and their superior performance) to the exigencies of the competitive process.

There are, however, no recent studies which have examined empirically the comparative characteristics and performance of domestic and multinational firms. Earlier studies by Vernon (1971), Vaupel (1971), Horst (1972) and Parker (1978) did provide some direct evidence. Vernon used a sample of 187 large U.S. multinationals and came to the conclusion that these firms were considerably more profitable than either the largest 500 firms or all US firms taken together. (In this study, a multinational was a company which had six or more overseas subsidiaries.) This was a striking result, and a large amount of theoretical analysis in the 1970s treated this as a 'stylized' fact and tried to provide explanations for it. Vernon also found that the MNEs made extensive use of skilled technical manpower and had high expenditure on research and development (1971, pp. 5–13). Vaupel (1971) also examined a sample of US firms and found that there was a strong positive relationship between the degree of multinationality and firm size, profitability, and research and development expenditures. Parker (1978) undertook a comparison of large European multinationals and domestic firms. He found that about one half of all multinational firms were considered to be research-intensive compared to only about 15 per cent of others with lower foreign involvement.

The general conclusions of the earlier studies were questioned by the results obtained by Horst (1972). He found that for a large sample of US firms once the inter-industry differences are taken into account, the only influence of any separate significance is firm size. That is, apart from industry and size, there were no consistent differences among the multinational firms and the total sample of manufacturing firms regarding the profitability, capital intensity, research and development and product diversity. The positive influence of firm size on the propensity of a firm in any industry to invest abroad was found to be very pronounced. Horst also examined the differences in the overseas investment propensities of firms of given size, but in different industries. His main conclusion was that industries with high research and development expenditures tended to have firms with above average overseas operations.

Two recent studies, adopting rather different methodologies, also tend to suggest that multinationality does not necessarily indicate superior performance. Buckley and Dunning (1978) examined the relationship between firm size, multinationality and growth for the world's largest companies. They hypothesised that multinationality would exercise a positive influence on growth. The statistical tests showed that such an influence did exist for the period 1967–1972 for all firms and for just US firms, but not for any firms for the longer period 1962–1972.[1]

Siddharthan and Lall (1982) also examined the extent to which multinationality may affect firm growth. Drawing on the industrial organisational approach they argue that greater multinationality will be positively associated with growth for the sort of reasons noted above (possession of monopolistic advantages, innovatory capacity, product differentiation etc.). Against this, however, they suggest the possibility that managerial constraints increase with the degree of multinationality: physical distance, linguistic and cultural differences, legal barriers, etc., may increase the costs of assimilating new management above those borne by a similar-sized purely domestic firm. (In addition, in the period they consider (1976–1979), there were a number of other factors which would lead to an expectation of a negative relationship between multinationality and growth for US firms. These include the deterioration of the US dollar and a marked instability in the international economy.) Their empirical analysis showed that, for a sample of the largest 74 US manufacturing firms during the period 1976–1979, multinationality exercised a uniformly negative effect on growth. The authors conclude that perhaps multinationality does set a separate managerial constraint on growth – but they note that in view of the results obtained by Buckley and Dunning, they would ascribe the findings to the peculiarities of the period studied.

Nevertheless, the last three studies tend to question the superiority of the multi-national firms. But their conclusions are still based on only the very largest firms in the world, or the largest firms in the US. There has been no study for any other country, which has used a wide range of firm size and a measure of the degree of multinationality to compare the characteristics and the performance of national and multinational firms.

9.2 The sample of firms and the data

In the previous chapters we have examined the UK quoted firms whose accounts are included in the Department of Industry's databank. To focus on the same set of firms, data on the overseas operations of a sample of these firms were obtained. In theory there is a drawback in this, since these firms are supposed to operate mainly in the UK (oil companies, for example, most of whose operations are overseas, are excluded). In practice, however, as the data below show, there were a considerable number in the sample which had very substantial overseas operations. Indeed of the 43 UK multinationals identified in a directory of the world's largest multinationals, 35 were in this sample (see Stopford *et al*., 1981).

An attempt was made to obtain information on the degree of multinationality of the firms which had continued in independent existence over the period 1972–1976. In other words, the starting population was that of the 824 firms which has been studied in the earlier chapters (see Table 9.1 for the industrial composition of these firms). It turned out to be possible to obtain information on 691 of them, giving us a good cross-section of firms both in terms of size and industrial composition, and in terms of their degree of overseas operations. In theory there are a number of indicators available to measure the overseas operations of the sample firms. These include the proportion of employees and assets overseas, the proportion of sales and profits originating overseas and the number of overseas subsidiaries; in practice the only accessible and reliable indicator was the proportion of sales originating overseas. (Note that this is the variable which has been generally used in the empirical literature on the degree of overseas operations; see e.g. Buckley and Pearce, 1977.) We attempted to obtain a measure of this variable for the two years, 1972 and 1976. (1972 was the first year for which data on this variable were available on a consistent basis. 1976 was the last year for which information was available on the other variables which are used in the analysis below.)

The initial source of the information was 'Extel Cards' and companies' annual reports. For about 65 per cent of the companies it was relatively straightforward to obtain their overseas sales as a proportion of total sales where overseas sales *exclude* exports – that is, they include only sales of goods produced abroad. As a check on this, we also considered the number of operating subsidiaries overseas (excluding sales subsidiaries). If the proportion of overseas sales seemed out of step with this (the simplest case being where the reports indicated overseas sales, but no overseas subsidiaries), further investigation was carried out.

For these companies, the main difficulty was that, even when a company report referred to 'overseas sales', there was uncertainty as to the proportion of these which were simply exports from the UK. To these companies, and to the rest for

154

which there was no information on overseas sales at all, but which *did* have overseas subsidiaries, a small questionnaire was sent. The main question was the following: 'What was the proportion of your overseas sales in the years 1972/3 and 1976/7? (where overseas sales includes all goods produced and sold abroad, but excludes finished goods imported from the parent company for resale)' (cf. Buckley and Dunning, 1978).

The response from the companies was reasonably satisfactory, with about 35 per cent of the companies responding with the requested information. In all, from company reports and from the survey, we were able to obtain this information for 691 of the original 824 firms. Of these, 19 had no overseas operations in 1972, but had some in 1976. In order to examine only those firms which had overseas operations in both years, we have excluded them from the analysis, leaving us with the sample of 672 firms which is studied below. We also tried to obtain a broad geographical distribution for overseas sales. Two categories were distinguished: sales of goods produced in mainland Europe, and of those produced in the rest of the world. Unfortunately this information was only available for about a third of the firms (see Table 9.3). In view of this limited sample, in the analysis we have only considered overseas sales as a whole.

9.2.1 The description of firms' overseas operations

Information on companies by proportion of sales of goods produced overseas in 1976 is provided in Table 9.1. Of the 672 companies which are examined, 359, or just over one half, had no overseas operations whilst 313 did have some. This proportion, however, varies very considerably across the two main sectors (manufacturing and non-manufacturing) as well as within them. In manufacturing, 235 of the 482 companies, or almost 49 per cent, had no overseas sales, whereas in non-manufacturing 124 out of 190, or 65 per cent, were in this category.

In manufacturing, the 'more technology intensive' (MTI) industries such as Chemicals, Engineering and Vehicles had a very high proportion of firms with overseas operations.[2] Furthermore, the proportion of firms having more than 5 per cent overseas sales was particularly marked for these firms. On the other hand, 'less technology intensive' (LTI) industries, such as Food, Drink, Textiles, Clothing and Paper, had a much lower proportion of firms with overseas operations. The distribution of firms in this sample thus broadly agrees with the generally accepted views of the industrial distribution of the overseas operations of UK firms. (See Caves, 1974 for a general discussion of this and Dunning, 1979, for evidence for the UK.) According to these views, other things being equal (such as the size distribution of firms and the growth of demand), the more technology intensive the industry, the more scope there is for product differentiation and the greater the propensity of firms to engage in overseas production. It is interesting to note, however, that in some LTI industries, such as Textiles and Paper, although the number of international firms is small, there are a number which have quite a substantial share of operations overseas.

Table 9.2 provides additional information on the overseas operations of the international firms. For firms in each industry, it provides the average value of overseas sales as a proportion of total sales for the years 1972 and 1976, and the change in this proportion over the four-year period. Once the firms which have no overseas

Table 9.1 *Distribution of firms by proportion of sales originating in overseas subsidiaries*

Industry	0 No	0–5 No	5–15 No	>15 No	Total no	No in pop.
21 Food	7	3	2	5	17	20
23 Drink	27	1	2	3	33	39
26 Chemicals	12	2	4	15	33	40
31 Metal manufacture	17	3	3	7	30	33
33 Non-electrical eng.	16	3	6	35	60	77
36 Electrical eng.	11	5	8	10	34	44
38 Vehicles	8	4	3	7	22	26
39 Metal goods	18	3	7	21	49	59
41 Textiles	28	3	5	16	48	60
44 Clothing etc.	15	0	1	2	18	27
46 Bricks etc.	18	4	6	12	40	44
47 Timber etc.	15	1	2	1	19	22
48 Paper etc.	27	2	3	8	40	52
49 Other manf.	10	1	3	6	20	26
All manufacturing	235	26	65	156	482	587
50 Construction	22	2	5	4	33	50
70 Transport	5	1	3	2	11	13
81 Wholesale	33	5	5	6	49	62
82 Retail	38	8	3	5	54	63
88 Miscellaneous	26	2	4	11	43	49
All non-manufacturing	124	18	20	28	190	237
All industries	359	44	85	184	672	824

Notes: Pop. refers to the population of firms surviving in the period 1972–1976 and studied in earlier chapters. 3 industries, Tobacco, Shipbuilding and Leather goods, were not examined individually because of the small number of observations, but were included in 'All manufacturing'.

operations at all are excluded, the average values across industries differ less sharply. For example, in both the years, whilst Engineering and Chemicals have high average values, these do not differ much from Textiles or Paper. It is noticeable, however, that the dispersion around the mean is less for the former set of industries than for the LTI industries.

The last two columns of Table 9.2 provide the average change in overseas operations over the period 1972–1976. The average value of overseas sales went up from 23.6 per cent to 27.9 per cent for firms in the manufacturing industries, and from 22.2 per cent to 26.9 per cent for all firms in the sample. These average increases, however, hide a diversity of experience across industries. Firms in Food, Non-electrical engineering and Vehicles increased their overseas operations quite substantially. On the other hand, firms in Clothing decreased their overseas activities over this period, whilst Textiles and Electrical engineering showed only a very

156

Table 9.2 *Average proportion of sales originating in overseas subsidiaries*

Industry	no	1972 mean	1972 S.D.	1976 mean	1976 S.D.	1976–1972 mean	1976–1972 S.D.
21 Food	10	18.1	14.8	25.9	19.3	6.8	6.8
23 Drink	6	21.4	17.3	26.1	21.1	3.6	4.3
26 Chemicals	21	22.4	12.7	26.7	14.3	3.1	7.3
31 Metal manf.	13	23.8	19.8	29.3	23.3	4.3	4.1
33 Non-elec. eng.	44	29.4	16.1	35.0	18.1	5.6	6.4
36 Elec. eng.	23	22.1	25.5	22.7	17.5	0.6	21.3
38 Vehicles	14	20.5	17.9	25.9	20.4	5.4	8.7
39 Metal goods	31	23.1	13.9	27.8	15.9	4.7	5.2
41 Textiles	24	25.8	22.6	26.8	20.5	1.0	14.3
44 Clothing etc.	3	21.2	10.2	17.0	10.4	-4.2	11.0
46 Bricks etc.	22	19.4	15.4	24.0	17.4	5.6	7.9
47 Timber etc.	4	10.0	5.5	17.3	16.2	7.3	10.6
48 Paper etc.	13	25.1	18.4	29.5	18.5	4.4	5.5
49 Other manf.	10	25.3	17.9	31.9	21.3	6.6	11.8
All Manufacturing	247	23.6	17.6	27.9	18.3	4.3	10.1
50 Construction	11	16.5	13.8	27.3	14.5	10.8	14.8
70 Transport	6	12.9	8.6	16.7	11.6	3.8	8.1
81 Wholesale	16	22.6	28.0	25.6	21.7	3.0	27.1
82 Retail	16	10.9	11.9	16.8	14.5	5.7	5.3
88 Misc.	17	19.4	12.1	26.9	14.4	7.5	5.5
All industries	313	22.2	17.8	26.9	18.0	4.7	11.2

Notes: The 'mean' value is defined as follows: mean = $\frac{1}{n} \Sigma_i O_i / T_i$ where O_i and T_i denote overseas sales and total sales respectively of firm i, and n is the number of international firms in each industry.

small increase. The large deviation in this change does not suggest, however, that it is due mainly to the activities of a few firms in each of these industries, rather than being a general reflection of the experience of all firms.

Table 9.3 provides, for a small sample, an indication of the proportion of overseas sales originating in Europe (defined as the other eight members of the European Community in 1976 plus Sweden and Norway) and in the rest of the world.[3] In view of the relatively small number of firms in individual industries, we have grouped together five industries (Chemicals, Electrical and Non-electrical engineering, Vehicles and Metal goods) into the 'heavy manufacturing' sector, and for the rest consider only the aggregate of the sector. The first part of the table gives information on the division of overseas sales between Europe and the rest of the world in 1972 and 1976. For both heavy manufacturing and the other two sectors, the proportion of sales originating in Europe is rather less than that originating in the rest of the world. Although the difference is small, it is nevertheless noteworthy since, on *a priori* grounds, one might have expected it to be in the opposite direction (cf. Dunning, 1981), since European countries, both because of their geographical proximity, and because of the similarity in broad patterns of demand, would have provided a much more favourable economic environment for UK firms to set up their operations in.[4]

Table 9.3 *Percentage of sales originating in European countries and rest of the world*

Sector	1972				1976				1976-72			
	Europe		Rest		Europe		Rest		Europe		Rest	
	no	mean	S.D.	mean	S.D.	mean	S.D.	mean	S.D.	mean	S.D.	mean	S.D.
Heavy manf.	47	16.6	14.0	17.1	11.9	18.6	14.8	20.5	14.0	2.0	4.1	3.4	4.2
All manf.	87	15.1	13.4	15.0	12.2	17.5	14.4	18.4	13.9	2.4	4.6	3.4	7.7
Non-manuf.	30	9.9	9.0	10.4	10.3	12.2	9.0	16.7	13.2	2.3	5.6	6.3	9.2
All firms	117	13.8	12.6	15.3	12.6	16.2	13.4	18.0	13.7	2.4	4.3	2.7	8.5

Notes: Europe includes the eight members of the EEC (in 1976) and Sweden and
Norway. Rest includes all countries other than those included in
Europe. 1976-72 Europe mean = 1976 Europe mean - 1972 Europe mean;
similarly for Rest.

There are historical and political reasons for the dominance of UK firms in non-European economies (see Channon, 1973; Franko, 1976). Although the political links may have been weakened, these historical links, entailing large capital movements in earlier decades to some developing countries, as well as to the USA, Canada and South Africa, continue to have an influence. Furthermore, these firms would have tended to have an advantage, in organisational, technological and marketing terms, over the indigenous firms in developing countries.[5] This superiority was clearly not present for firms setting up operations in European markets. However, whilst this may have been true in the 1960s and early 1970s, more recent evidence suggests that UK MNEs are now well able to hold their own even in European markets.

9.3 Size, overseas operations and exports

This section examines two of the issues noted in the introduction to this chapter. First, we look at the relationship between overseas operations and firm size. Whilst there is an *a priori* expectation of a strong positive relationship between the two variables, the strength of this has not been examined for any large cross-section of UK firms. Second, we re-examine the relationship between the size and the export rate of firms. This issue is related to the first one: as discussed in Chapter 8, the examination of the size–export rate relationship there did not take into account the overseas activities of firms. If there is a systematic association between firm size and overseas operations, it could have a significant bearing on the earlier results.

9.3.1 *Firm size and overseas operations*

The *a priori* grounds for the expectation of a positive relationship between overseas operations and firm size are as follows. First, there are large fixed costs involved in searching, obtaining information and setting up foreign operations, which are more easily borne by large firms (see Caves, 1982, p. 71). Second, the risks involved in setting up overseas operations are considerably greater, and whilst large firms may be regarded as more risk averse than others, they have more resources at their disposal to allow them to bear those risks. Finally, large firms are more likely to have the organisation and know-how to produce successfully in foreign countries. Against this last factor one must set the possibility, however, that as the degree of overseas activity increases, there are increasing problems in managerial co-ordination (see Siddharthan and Lall, 1982), so that there may not be a linear relationship between firm size and overseas operations. Further, it may be argued that over time, with an increase in transport and communication facilities and a consequent decline in information and search costs, medium-sized or even relatively small firms may be able to increase their overseas operations considerably. More information may also make the operations seem less risky.

There is also likely to be some difference in the relationship between size and overseas activity between firms in different industries. For instance, in industries where fixed capital costs are relatively less important, or where information is readily available, the relationship may be expected to be weaker. A similar effect may obtain where production and marketing entail relatively little risk.

Following Rowthorn (1971) and Buckley and Pearce (1977), for estimation purposes the basic relationship is hypothesised to be of the form

$$M = f(S, S^2) \tag{9.1}$$

where M denotes the proportion of sales originating overseas and S denotes the size of the firm as measured by world-wide sales (£ million). The term in S^2 is included to capture the non-linear relationship (see Rowthorn, 1971).

In addition, we examine the influences arising from the main industry in which the firm operates. The estimated model thus takes the following form:

$$M = \alpha_0 + \beta_1 S + \beta_2 S^2 + \sum_{i=3}^{20} \beta_i I_i + \epsilon \tag{9.2}$$

where

M	= proportion of sales originating overseas (%)
S	= firm size
I_i	= 1 for industry i and zero otherwise
α_0	= intercept
$\beta_{i,i=1,2}$	= regression coefficients
$\beta_{i,i=3,20}$	= estimated differences from arbitrarily chosen Industry 88
ϵ	= error term

In equation (9.2) one industry is omitted (Miscellaneous), so that the estimated regression coefficients β_3–β_{20} indicate the difference in M exhibited by each industry from that of the omitted industry (cf. Buckley and Pearce, 1977). The significance of industry effects is established by testing the hypothesis that none of the industry coefficients are different from zero. This is done by omitting all the industry terms from equation (9.2) and testing the ratio of incremental variance explained by the inclusion of these variables to the unexplained variance in the full equation by a one-tailed F-test.

Variants of equation (9.2) have been estimated by previous investigators using ordinary least squares (OLS). Since the dependent variable is discontinuous – it can only be between 0 and 1 – OLS may however be not quite appropriate for this. This is so because the distribution of the error term will be truncated and so the regression coefficients will be biased and inconsistent (see, e.g. Chow, 1983). The correct procedure for this type of problem is based on the use of the Tobit model (used earlier in Chapter 7), which transforms the original variables by the use of the normal density function, and provides consistent estimates of the parameters. Since this procedure has not been used before in an analysis of this type, we estimated the equation using both OLS and Tobit and report both sets of results below.

As Table 9.4 shows, using OLS yields a significantly positive relationship between size and overseas activity for both 1972 and 1976. The relationship is, however, non-linear, indicating that as size increases the degree of overseas activity also increases, but proportionately less fast. Interestingly, even over this short time period, the magnitude of the relationship is reduced, with b_1 declining from 0.110 to 0.066 (the difference is statistically significant using the t-test). The full equation explains around 20 per cent of the variance in the dependent variable. The application of Tobit analysis yields qualitatively similar results for b_1 but the magnitude of the relationship is considerably higher. For b_2, it shows that unlike the results using OLS, the degree of non-linearity is smaller and has increased over time.

Next consider the industry effects. For 1972, five industries have regression coefficients which are significantly different from zero at the 5 per cent level. Thus Drink, Chemicals, Non-electrical engineering, Vehicles and Metal goods have a degree of multinationality of sales significantly greater than the omitted 'control' industry (Miscellaneous). For 1976 these industries plus Retail services were significant. Next, we removed the industry dummies (see bottom half of Table 9.4) and tested the assumption that none of the omitted variables is significantly different from zero by the F-test noted above. The results show that this assumption can be rejected (computed $F = 6.31$ in 1972. F at 1 per cent significance level $= 1.79$). Therefore we cannot reject the hypothesis that, for this sample of firms, industry structure has an important bearing on the overseas sales ratio.

The above regression analysis was supplemented by examining overseas activities by firms ranked in discrete size classes. There are four size classes according to sales in 1976: less than £20 million, £20–£40 million, and so on. There is also a size class for the largest – those with sales of more than £640 million. The results are given in Table 9.5. Consider Section I. In manufacturing, the 190 firms with sales of less than £20 million in 1976 had an average overseas sales ratio of 4.8 per cent. This increases to 11.4 per cent for the next size class, and so on. The differences in the four classes are statistically significant (using the Welch-Aspin Test). Interestingly, however, there is no tendency for the very largest firms – those with sales of more than £640 million – to exhibit any different overseas activity from the groups with sales greater than £160 million (the difference is greater in reality because this group also contains the largest firms). According to this evidence, there is no strong non-linear pattern.

The pattern found for manufacturing as a whole is reflected in most of the industries (Textiles being the only exception). For non-manufacturing, the differences are not generally statistically significant for the first two size classes. Nevertheless, the very largest firms have a clear tendency to have a significantly higher overseas ratio than the preceding class.

We next examined the distribution of firms excluding those which have no overseas sales (Table 9.5 Section II). The reason for the difference between this and the first section is clear. For manufacturing, less than one quarter of firms in the smallest size class have overseas operations – this proportion rises uniformly and the largest firms virtually all have some overseas sales. As far as the average values are

160

Table 9.4 *Firm size and overseas production*

Equation	Estimating procedure	Year	$\hat{\beta}_1$	$\hat{\beta}_2$	Industry dummies significant	F-values	$\overline{R}^2$
1. Including industry dummies	OLS	1972	0.110* (8.85)	-0.0006* (-6.13)	Drink, Chemicals Non-electrical engineering Vehicles, Metal goods		0.226
		1976	0.066* (8.90)	-0.0002* (-6.45)	Drink, Chemicals, Non-electrical engineering Metal goods, Retail services		0.207
	Tobit	1972	0.210 (9.23)	-0.0001 (-6.84)	as for OLS		0.199
		1976	0.126 (9.21)	-0.0004 (-7.03)	as for OLS		0.172
2. Excluding industry dummies	OLS	1972	0.104* (8.08)	-0.0006* (-5.43)		computed F (6.31)*	0.099
		1976	0.064* (8.48)	-0.002* (-5.96)		computed F (3.49)	0.105
	Tobit	1972	0.195 (8.17)	-0.0001 (-5.67)			
		1976	0.121 (8.49)	(-0.0002) (-6.19)			

Notes: t-ratios are in brackets.
* denotes significantly different from 0 at the 5 per cent level.

Table 9.5 *Firm size and overseas production (analysis by size class)*

Size in 1976 (Sales)	Manufacturing			Non-manufacturing			Chemicals			Non-electrical engineering			Electrical engineering			Textiles		
	no.	mean	S.D.	no.	mean	S.D.	no.	mean	S.D.	no.	mean	S.D.	no.	mean	S.D.	no.	mean	S.D.
I ALL FIRMS																		
≤20	190	4.8	12.4	56	2.5	8.7	8	6.4	9.4	16	14.1	24.2	13	1.8	5.0	25	4.5	10.2
≤40	86	11.4	18.4	33	3.2	9.0	6	10.8	7.6	8	26.8	6.7	5	8.2	7.1	13	5.1	11.4
≤160	117	20.7	18.5	58	11.4	17.2	8	15.9	15.0	28	27.6	19.6	7	19.1	16.5	10	29.9	23.2
>160	82	30.8	19.4	43	14.6	17.2	11	28.9	17.1	8	41.4	19.5	9	35.8	15.7	4	41.8	21.0
>640	29	31.8	20.4	9	22.1	19.0	4	25.1	27.0				5	36.9	15.7	1	26.2	-
II FIRMS WITH OVERSEAS OPERATIONS																		
≤20	44	21.7	18.7	5	27.6	12.7	4	12.8	9.8	6	37.7	26.6	3	8.1	8.9	7	16.1	14.2
≤40	36	21.0	15.9	4	26.5	3.3	2	32.5	12.6	6	35.7	11.1	4	10.3	6.2	5	13.2	15.9
≤160	90	26.9	16.7	25	26.6	17.1	5	25.4	9.6	24	32.1	17.2	7	19.1	10.5	8	37.4	19.3
>160	77	32.8	18.3	32	19.6	17.3	10	31.8	14.9	8	41.4	19.5	9	35.6	15.7	4	41.8	21.1
>640	28	32.9	19.8	8	24.9	18.3	3	33.3	26.1	-			5	37.1	15.7	1	26.2	-
All	247	27.9	18.3	66	25.3	17.4	21	26.7	14.3	44	35.0	18.1	23	22.7	17.5	24	26.8	20.5
Degree of multinationality																		
III ALL FIRMS																		
0	236	33.4	133.9	125	57.8	91.0	13	177.2	535.8	16	26.4	19.7	11	7.8	5.4	28	15.9	11.6
≤5	23	124.5	179.8	9	289.2	60.9	1	735.1	-	1	138.1	-	3	14.7	5.2	3	56.1	31.7
≤15	54	203.7	454.3	15	382.5	414.2	2	18.5	1.4	7	61.3	55.8	7	89.9	58.9	7	20.0	9.32
>15	169	270.6	488.8	41	209.0	263.4	17	428.9	975.8	36	111.6	131.0	13	513.6	584.0	14	242.9	401.8
All	482	140.0	358.4	190	127.0	212.8	33	314.2	780.6	60	83.4	109.9	34	218.7	425.5	52	79.7	226.8

Notes: For Parts I and II mean refers to overseas ratio (%) in 1976. For Part III mean refers to size of firm (£m) and the firms are ranked by the degree of multinationality measured in terms of overseas ratio (%).

concerned, there seems to be a tendency for firms with sales of less than £160 million to rely more on the domestic market (and exports) than those with larger sales. For non-manufacturing, and other industries separately, the pattern is much less clear – rather surprisingly small and medium-size companies have a slight edge over the largest. Finally Section III of the table provides an indication of the average size of the firms arranged by the degree of reliance on overseas operations. The evidence here further supports the above findings. Overall, the evidence in Table 9.5 complements that obtained in Table 9.4. A very high proportion of small firms have no overseas operations at all; when a comparison is made with those that do, a positive but by no means strong relationship between size and overseas operation is found. In particular, there is no tendency for the very largest firms to have the greatest activity overseas.

9.3.2 Exports and overseas operations

The decisions of companies, on whether to locate production overseas or to export, have been the subject of a great deal of policy interest (see e.g. Buckley and Pearce, 1977). Most of the evidence about this relates, however, to the world's giant companies. Although in terms of absolute magnitudes involved it may not seem inappropriate to focus on them, from the point of view of insight into decision making and future policy, it is interesting to examine the relationship beween these two possibilities for a wider distribution of firms. Further, in view of the results in Chapter 8 which showed a very weak negative relationship between firm size and export rate, we consider whether this relationship changes once overseas production is taken into account.

Table 9.6 provides some evidence on these two issues. Column II gives the correlation coefficient between the export rate and firm size (measured by total sales), both in 1976. For the manufacturing sector as a whole, and for all individual industries except Textiles, there is a negative relationship. However, its magnitude is very small and it is statistically insignificant (cf. Chapter 8, Table 8.1, though the sample of firms examined is somewhat different from that used in that table). In column III, the correlation is between 'adjusted' export rate (calculated as exports as a proportion of sales originating only in the domestic economy) and firm size. For both manufacturing and non-manufacturing firms, the correlation coefficient shows only a small increase (it has either a smaller negative value, or a higher positive value). This change is what would be expected from the results in the previous sub-section. However, it is not what might have been expected on *a priori* grounds. If only the very largest firms had had overseas operations, then obviously the mild negative size-export rate relationship would have shown a more marked reversal. The second part of Table 9.6 considers only firms with exports. With total sales as the denominator, there is a significant negative relationship between firm size and export rate. This is reduced for both sectors once overseas sales are taken into consideration (column III); for non-manufacturing firms there is still, however, a significant negative relationship.[6]

Finally columns IV to VI provide some evidence on the 'sourcing ratio' and its relationship with firm size. This ratio is defined as sales originating overseas divided by sales originating overseas *plus* parent company exports. It indicates the extent to which a firm meets its overseas demand by overseas production rather than by

Table 9.6 *Size, export rate and overseas activity*

Sample oF firms	I	II	III	IV	V	VI	No. of firms
I ALL FIRMS							
All manufac.	0.96*	−0.05	0.01	0.30*	0.37*	0.26*	482
All non-manufac.	0.97*	−0.04	−0.02	0.29*	0.44*	−0.01	190
21 Food	0.89*	−0.20	−0.13	0.47	0.60*	0.33*	17
26 Chemicals	0.97*	−0.09	−0.02	0.39	0.17	0.13	33
33 Non-electrical eng.	0.92*	−0.05	0.09	0.74*	0.36	0.18	60
36 Electrical eng.	0.99*	−0.06	0.08	0.30	0.53*	0.42*	34
39 Metal goods nes	0.99*	−0.03	−0.02	0.39*	0.31	0.21	49
41 Textiles	0.97*	0.09	0.21*	0.25	0.33*	0.14	52
II EXPORTING FIRMS ONLY							
All manufac.	0.96*	−0.07*	−0.01	0.32	0.36*	0.26	448
All non-manufac.	0.97*	−0.14*	−0.12*	0.35	0.46*	0.10	130

Notes: Corr. coeffs (cols I to VI) are for the correlation of firm's total
sales in 1976 with each of the variables I to IV defined as
follows:

I = Sales orginating in domestic economy;

II = Total exports/total sales;

III = Total exports/I;

IV = Total exports/total sales orginating overseas;

V = IV correlated with total sales, all firms;

VI = IV correlated with total sales, only firms with overseas
operations.

* denotes significantly different from 0 at the 5 per cent level
or higher.

exports (Dunning and Pearce, 1981, pp. 103–109). In the 'eclectic approach' noted
above we considered the ownership-specific advantages of a firm that make it internationally competitive. The second element in this approach relates to location-
specific advantages: that is, the factors which determine whether a firm uses its
ownership advantages mainly in the parent country, supplying overseas markets by
exporting, or makes use of them overseas by meeting overseas demand (or even part
of its domestic demand) from overseas production. For example, a firm may
undertake overseas production if factors of production complementary to its own
resources (such as cheap skilled labour) are more readily available abroad than at
home. Or a firm may undertake it to spread risks or to escape from higher domestic
taxation. Other relevant factors would include high transport costs, tariffs and
other trade restrictions.

Column IV shows that, for firms in manufacturing industries, the average overseas sourcing ratio was 0.30. Note, however, that it differs significantly across industries, ranging from 0.74 for Non-electrical engineering to 0.30 for Electrical engineering. What is likely to be the relationship between firm size and sourcing ratio? In view of the kind of factors noted above which would influence whether firms undertook exports or overseas production, one would expect a positive relationship. The evidence in column V suggests that if one considers all firms this is indeed the case. The larger firms do tend to have higher sourcing ratios. However, when the firms which have no overseas operations at all are excluded (column VI) there is a weaker relationship.

9.4 Overseas operations and firm characteristics and performance

The relationship between overseas operations and the characteristics and performance of domestic and international firms was examined in the following two complementary ways: first, by comparing the two sets of firms at a univariate and a multivariate level and, second, by examining the extent to which differences in the degree of multinationality may *explain* the differences in growth and profitability across firms. For the first exercise a sample of international firms was selected which had more than 15 per cent of their sales originating overseas in 1972 (181 firms; denote these by IF). To obtain the maximum discrimination between these firms and others, we compare these with the sample which had no overseas operations at all in 1972, that is the 359 domestic firms (denote these by DF). The procedure for examining the difference in characteristics of these firms was the following: for firms in each group a comparison was undertaken for some of the variables studied in earlier chapters. These included opening size, export rate and the following six variables: rate of return, profit margin, growth of net assets, growth by acquisition, growth by new fixed investment, and growth by retentions. These variables are defined in the same way as in earlier chapters, and are averaged over the period 1972–1976 in the same way; opening size is measured by net assets in 1972 (natural log) and the export rate is exports as a proportion of sales originating in the domestic economy in 1976.

The average values of the variables for the two sets of firms, and for firms in some industries, are given in Table 9.7. Consider first all firms. The difference in size is as expected. The interesting result is that for the rate of return and the profit margin: not only do the IF not have any edge over the DF but, on the contrary, the latter exhibit a significantly superior performance. With regard to the growth of assets, IF do have a slightly better performance. As for other variables, the DF have a significantly greater growth by new investment, but a lower growth by acquisition. The DF have a higher reliance on growth by retention than do the IF. This may reflect in part the ability of IF to tap foreign (as well as domestic) capital markets with greater ease than can IF (cf. Franko, 1976). Finally, note that the export rate of the IF (adjusted for overseas sales) is considerably higher than that for the DF. Thus if one considered the total reliance of the IF on overseas markets (exports and sales from overseas operations) it would be very high indeed. As the rest of Table 9.7 indicates, the pattern is in general similar for individual industries for the profitability, growth and other variables. But apart from size and export rate, the difference in the other variables between the two sets of firms is not significant.

165

Table 9.7 *Differences between domestic and international firms*

Variable	All firms			Chemicals			Non-electrical engineering			Electrical engineering			Textiles		
	X^D	X^I	$X^I - X^D$	X^D	X^I	$X^I - X^D$	X^D	X^I	$X^I - X^D$	X^D	X^I	$X^I - X^D$	X^D	X^I	$X^I - X^D$
1 Net assets(log)	6.18	8.50	2.32*	6.32	8.42	2.10*	6.81	8.05	1.24	5.2	10.3	5.1*	6.9	9.3	2.4*
2 Rate of return	21.4	19.7	-1.7*	20.4	20.1	-0.3	17.1	18.6	1.5	31.5	17.9	13.6	17.9	17.6	-0.3
3 Profit margin	10.7	10.3	-0.4*	11.1	12.2	1.1	9.9	9.6	-0.3	17.1	10.8	-6.3	9.9	10.2	0.3
4 Growth of net assets	18.3	18.7	0.4	19.1	18.8	-0.3	17.4	18.0	1.6	14.8	15.9	7.1	15.3	15.9	0.6
5 Growth by new investment	5.5	4.0	-1.0*	2.9	4.8	2.1	2.0	3.1	1.1	6.7	2.0	-4.7	2.8	3.3	0.5
6 Growth by acquisition	2.9	3.8	0.9	4.2	1.6	02.6	4.1	3.6	-0.5	8.8	2.5	-6.3	1.2	2.8	1.6
7 Growth by retentions	16.2	14.0	-2.2*	14.9	15.6	1.7	13.7	13.4	-0.3	13.0	10.8	-2.2	15.1	12.2	-2.9
8 Export rate	11.8	23.8	12.0*	13.8	27.9	13.9	19.0	36.8	16.2	21.1	17.3	-3.8	16.1	30.5	14.4*
Number	359	181		12	15		16	35		11	10		28	16	

Notes: D denotes firms with no sales originating overseas.
I denotes firms with more than 15% sales originating overseas.
* denotes significantly different from 0 at the 5 per cent level.

One qualification to this conclusion concerns the effect of firm size. It could be argued that, whilst the results do indicate the average performance of the two groups, the performance itself may be due as much to the influence of firm size as to the degree of overseas activity. To the extent that IF are larger, and large firms have lower profitability, the above result would merely be a reflection of firm size. Thus as description the results are valid as far as they go, but to obtain the effect of overseas operations we have to take size into account. This is undertaken presently; before doing that, however, it is useful to examine the degree of difference between the two sets of firms, once the interrelationships between the variables are taken into account. Whilst this is interesting in its own right, it also goes some way towards meeting the above caveat. The approach adopted here is to use 'discriminant analysis' in order to assess whether we can discriminate further between DF and IF.

The basic idea of discriminant analysis is to provide a method to 'discriminate' between the groups, in the sense of being able to tell them apart statistically. In our case no single variable may differentiate perfectly between the IF and DF – in the sense of there being no overlap between the groups.[7] But by taking several variables and combining them mathematically we may find a single dimension on which IF are clustered at one end and DF at the other. Discriminant analysis attempts to do this by forming one or more linear combinations of the discriminating variables. These 'discriminant functions' are of the form

$$D = d_1 Z_1 + d_2 Z_2 + \dots d_n Z_n \tag{9.3}$$

where D is the score on discriminant function, the d's are weighting coefficients, and the Z's are the standardised values of the n discriminating variables used in the analysis. The discriminant function is formed in such a way as to maximise the separation of the groups. Once this is done, we can measure the success (in statistical terms) with which the discriminating variables are actually discriminating when combined into the discriminant function.[8] The weighting coefficients can be interpreted much as in multiple regression analysis. In this respect, they reflect the relative contribution made by each variable to the overall discrimination achieved between the two populations. Further, one can compute the probability of allocating firms correctly to the IF or the DF group on the basis of computed discriminant functions. (If the classification were done on a random basis, half the firms would be classified accurately.)

The results of this exercise are provided in Table 9.8.[9] Significant discrimination is obtained in all cases – for all firms and for firms in the individual industries. Consider, for example, the sample of all firms. The discrimination achieved by the eight variables together, measured by D^2, is highly significant (F-statistic = 48.9). This is further reflected in the probability of correct classification, which is 82.2 per cent (last column). This pattern of significant discrimination between the groups and the high probability of correct classification is in general repeated for individual industries. Next, note the column labelled 'main discriminatory variables': it lists the variables which in the 'multivariate' context contribute most to this discrimination. Thus for all firms the most important discriminating variable was growth by retentions, followed by total growth, export rate and firm size. So, whilst in the univariate analysis there was some degree of overlap between the IF and DF, in the multivariate context there is a considerable statistical distance between the two

167

Table 9.8 *Summary of the results of the multivariate analysis*

Sample	D^2	F-statistic based on D^2	Main discriminatory variables	% correctly classified
All firms	2.46*	48.9	var 7, var 4, var 8, var 1	82.2
Chemicals	1.10*	3.51	var 8, var 1, var 5	74.1
Non-elec. eng.	0.90*	9.86	var 7, var 8, var 5, var 1	78.4
Elec. eng.	3.90*	20.41	var 1, var 5, var 4, var 3	90.5
Textiles	3.74*	6.89	var 7, var 4, var 2, var 1	84.1

Notes: * denotes significance at the 5 per cent level.
The main discriminatory variables refer to variables in Table 9.7.
Var 1 = net assets; var 2 = profitability; var 3 = profit margin;
var 4 = growth of net assets; var 5 = growth by new investment;
var 7 = growth by retentions; var 8 = export rate.

groups. It is still not the case, however, that IF have a uniformly superior performance to DF, in terms of their growth or profitability.

We next examine whether the *degree* of a firm's international operations has any systematic effect on its subsequent growth and profitability. This is in contrast to the above exercise which considered whether *on average* there was any difference between the set of domestic and the set of international firms. At the same time, this section examines the effect of firm size, industry and past performance. The *a priori* arguments concerning the impact of overseas operations on firm performance have been noted above. A suitable functional form for assessing this impact is the following:

$$L_i = f(M_i, M_i^2) \tag{9.4}$$

where L_i denotes the growth or profitability of firm i, and M_i denotes the percentage of its sales overseas. M_i^2 is included to capture non-linearities.

It is quite plausible that a firm's performance is likely to be affected by size and its main industry (see Buckley and Dunning, 1981). It is also likely to be influenced by past performance. In a cross-sectoral analysis, Whittington (1972) has shown that the past profitability of firms exercises a significantly positive effect on their future profitability. In other words, firms which have above average profitability over one time period, also tend to have above average profitability over a subsequent period. This accords with the results obtained in Chapter 3 for the growth of firms.

Both growth and profitability are computed as in earlier chapters; M_i is for 1972. The past values for growth and profitability were computed for the four-year period 1968–1971 in order to obtain the average performance over a medium-run period immediately preceding the period over which analysis is undertaken. The final estimated model was of the following form:

$$L = \alpha_0 + \beta_1 M + \beta_2 M^2 + \beta_3 S + \beta_4 S^2 + \beta_5 L_{-1} + \sum_{i=6}^{24} \beta_i I_i + \epsilon \qquad (9.5)$$

where

L = firm growth or profitability (%, average over 1972–1976)
M = overseas ratio (%, 1972)
S = firm size (sales £ million, 1972)
L_{-1} = past values of growth or profitability (%, average over 1968–1971)
I_i = 1 for industry i, 0 otherwise
α_0 = intercept
$\beta_{i,i}$ = 1 to 5: regression coefficients
$\beta_{i,i}$ = 6 to 24: estimated differences from arbitrarily chosen industry 88.

The model was first estimated using OLS for the full sample of firms. Of course, the fact that one of the independent variables, M, is discontinuous does not affect the properties of the OLS estimators. (It is only in the case where the dependent variable has a truncated distribution that OLS may be less appropriate.) Nevertheless the model was also estimated just for firms with overseas operations (firms with $M > 0$, i.e. the 313 firms included in Table 9.2). In order to isolate the effects of industry environment, in both samples estimation was undertaken with and without industry dummies.

The results of estimating equation (9.5) are given in Table 9.9. For the sample of all firms, as β_1 indicates, the degree of overseas activity has a small negative effect on firm profitability. A much more marked negative influence is exerted by firm size, with β_3 being significant in the equation with industry dummies as well as in the one without the dummies. As hypothesised, past profitability exerts a significantly positive influence. For the sample of international firms, overseas activity has a small positive effect. But here again size and past profitability exert a significant influence. For both samples, the industry environment seems to exercise a notable influence on profitability. Lastly, the goodness of fit of the equation as a whole is better for the international firms than for the sample of all firms.

As the second half of Table 9.9 shows, there is again a conspicuous lack of any strong relationship between overseas activity and firm growth. The main explanatory variable in fact appears to be firm size, which has some negative effect. The industry environment of the firms also exercises some influence on growth. It seems clear from these two sets of regression results that the proportion of firms' activity overseas exercises very little direct influence on firms' overall growth and profitability.

9.5 Summary and further considerations

This chapter has shown that the overseas production activities of a very large number of UK firms are considerable. Although there were certain industries

Table 9.9 *Overseas production and the growth and profitability of firms*

Dependent variable	Sample	Equation	$\hat{\beta}_1$	$\hat{\beta}_2$	$\hat{\beta}_3$	$\hat{\beta}_4$	$\hat{\beta}_5$	Industry dummies significant	F-values	$\overline{R}^2$
Profitability	All firms	ID	-0.10 (-0.99)	0.02 (1.47)	-0.003* (-3.57)	-0.02* (2.52)	0.32* (7.67)	Food, Chemicals Textiles, Electrical engineering		0.17
		WID	-0.11* (-1.73)	-0.02* (1.78)	-0.003* (-3.40)	0.03* (2.47)	0.35* (8.39)		computed F (4.39)*	0.12
	International firms	ID	0.06 (0.64)	0.02 (0.17)	-0.002* (-2.44)	0.007* (1.74)	0.42* (6.29)	Chemicals, Electrical, and Non-electrical engineering, Vehicles		0.23
		WID	0.07 (0.79)	-0.01 (0.09)	-0.002* (-2.36)	0.006* (1.76)	0.41* (6.68)		computed F (5.45)*	0.16
Growth	All firms	ID	0.31 (0.37)	-0.07 (-0.47)	-0.001 (-1.27)	0.0006 (0.73)	0.04* (1.69)	Food, Metal goods, Chemicals		0.07
		WID	0.37 (0.38)	-0.07 (-0.54)	-0.001* (-1.74)	0.0007 (0.80)	0.04 (1.43)		computed F (3.89)*	0.01
	International firms	ID	-0.16 (-1.20)	-0.16 (0.81)	-0.001* (-1.77)	0.0009 (0.85)	0.02 (0.54)	Chemicals, Electrical engineering, Vehicles		0.09
		WID	-0.15 (-1.17)	0.18 (0.94)	-0.002* (-1.67)	0.001 (1.15)	0.02 (0.44)		computed F (3.81)*	0.02

Notes: * denotes statistically significant at 10 per cent level. t-ratios are in brackets.
ID and WID denote equations estimated with, and without, industry dummies respectively.
All firms sample includes 672 firms. International firms include 313 firms.

which had a high proportion of firms with these activities, most industries had some. The average value of overseas sales was also quite high and had increased over time. For a smaller sample of firms it was found, however, that in the period 1972–1976 there was no significant change in the geographical distribution of this as between European countries and the rest of the world. The evidence on the questions noted at the beginning of this chapter is as follows:

(i) It was found that in a sample of all firms there was a marked positive relationship between size and the degree of overseas activity. However, once the firms which had no overseas activity at all were excluded, the relationship became much weaker.

(ii) The relationship between size and export rate was then re-examined in the light of these findings with the export rate being adjusted for overseas sales. The results showed that once this was done there was virtually no relationship between the two variables.

(iii) An investigation was undertaken into the differences in the characteristics and performance of firms with overseas operations and those without them. It was found that, in a univariate analysis the only other distinguishing variables besides firm size were export rate, and growth financed by retentions. Multivariate (discriminant) analysis showed that once a number of different variables were taken into account simultaneously, one could achieve a high degree of discrimination between the two groups. There was no tendency, however, for the growth and profitability variables to be the main discriminators.

(iv) That the degree of overseas activity may exercise an independent influence on growth and profitability across firms was then tested using regression analysis across all firms. The results showed that once the influence of size, past growth or profitability was removed there was little relationship at the individual industry level between overseas activity and firm growth or profitability.

There is some indirect support provided for the last result in a recent study by Buckley and Dunning (1981). They examine the growth in sales of 594 of the world's largest firms in the period 1972–1977, and *inter alia*, examine the 'hypothesis that the more multinational a firm's spread is, then the more likely it is to be faster growing' (p. 20). They find in fact that there is no significant independent influence exercised by the degree of overseas activity. This result holds for all firms in their sample, as well as the US firms only (314 firms) and non-US firms (280 firms). They obtain a similar result for the effect of overseas activity on firm profitability.[10]

An interesting extension of the above results relates to the comparison of the characteristics of *foreign* IF affiliates in the UK and the indigenous firms. (This is the converse of our comparison of IF from the UK and domestic firms.) The general view in this area is that these affiliates are likely to be more efficient, from both technical and allocative viewpoints, than indigenous firms (see e.g. Dunning, 1978). Some recent empirical evidence however suggests the need for a more balanced view. A study by Solomon and Ingham (1977) compared IF affiliates and indigenous companies in the mechanical engineering industry in the UK. They found that once the industrial and regional distribution of foreign IF were taken into account, there was no tendency for the affiliates to have higher profitability or growth than domestic firms. In a more extensive study by us, we examined some

800 foreign affiliates in the UK, and compared their performance with the domestic firms in the period 1971–1973 over 10 industrial sectors (Begg *et al.*, 1981). It was again found that once the industrial distribution of foreign affiliates was taken into account, there was very little difference in the performance of the two sets of firms.

Our results have a number of implications. First, they suggest some reconsideration of the widespread belief that international firms are more efficient than mainly domestic firms. They are supposed to have high capital investment, advanced technology, and innovating management resulting in high profitability, and to contribute significantly to allocative efficiency. There has been some concern in the UK, however, in the face of low growth and rising unemployment, that IF had not been undertaking sufficient new investment in the domestic economy, or that their export performance had not been fully satisfactory (Panić, 1982). The results of this study are neutral regarding the MNEs' investment in the domestic economy, but they do show that their export performance, relative to that of domestic firms, cannot be regarded as unsatisfactory. However, their role in the domestic economy goes far beyond their performance in these areas. In order to see whether they might have played some part in the growing structural disequilibrium in the UK, as has been claimed by some observers, a more detailed investigation of their conduct and performance may be appropriate (see Panić, 1982 and Holland, 1982).

In the second place, our results are suggestive in a number of ways regarding the theory of multinational corporations. They tend to support the approach which emphasises the oligopolistic rivalry amongst capitalist firms as one main motive for overseas operations (Knickerbocker, 1973). According to this approach, the nature of this rivalry is such that firms want to obtain and maintain shares in foreign markets by setting up overseas operations, even though this behaviour may not be strictly profit maximising. Rowthorn (1971), anticipating this approach, argued further that in the process of internationalisation there may be significant costs involved for the smaller and medium-sized firms who are confined to the domestic economy. Whilst this may have been true, the results suggest that in the recent period these firms have been themselves participating more and more in the international economy.

10

Summary and economic implications

This chapter provides a summary of the main results of the study, and develops some of their theoretical and policy implications. Section 10.1 summarises the basic framework and the main empirical results. Section 10.2 develops the implications of the results for economic theory. Section 10.3 considers their implications for competition and industrial policies pursued in the UK and in other industrial countries.

10.1 Summary

The basic analytical framework used in the study is the one formulated by Penrose and Marris which postulates that there is no optimal firm size but, rather, that there is an optimal growth rate in any given time period. The firm operating in imperfect product and capital markets is not identified with any particular product, or with any particular production function, but is regarded, instead, as consisting of a collection of assets – technological, organisational, managerial and marketing – which can be changed, or added to, in the course of time. Within such a framework, diversification allows the firm to circumvent demand constraints in any given market. On the supply side, the ability of the firm to undertake acquisitions also increases its potential for growth. This theoretical framework was elaborated in a number of ways in this study. Considerable attention was paid to the way the two main forms of growth – acquisitions and new investment – may interact with each other and with the financing decisions. In addition, it was suggested that the framework would be more useful if the implicit assumption of a closed economy were relaxed. By exporting, the firm can overcome demand constraints without product diversification. By producing abroad, it can overcome domestic supply constraints (in the sense of availability of factors of production), or barriers which may be placed in the way of exports.

Within this general framework, a number of aspects of each of the above inter-related activities were studied in some depth. The detailed records of over 2000 quoted firms were examined and a detailed description was provided of the characteristics of the population of firms for the period 1960–1976. The first main issue examined was the relationship between firms' size and growth, and between their growth and profitability (Chapter 3). The view that since the 1960s there had been a strong positive relationship between size and growth was shown to have little empirical support. The negative relationship obtained was, however, weak and although it was statistically significant for the aggregate of firms, it was significant for only a small number of individual industries. Next, it was found that firms with

173

above-average growth in one period tended to have above-average growth in the subsequent period. However, there was also very strong evidence of regression towards the mean. That is, firms' past deviations in growth from the average for the industry tended to disappear in the future. So above-average or below-average growth was a persistent but not a permanent feature of the individual companies within an industry. An examination of the growth–profitability relationship showed that, compared with the earlier period (1948–1960), the relationship was considerably weaker. That is, in a cross section of firms, variations in profitability explained relatively smaller variation in growth. Further, it seemed that the widely accepted assumption that profitability's effect on growth (*via* the supply of funds) for firms in all size classes is similar may not have been warranted in this period. An examination of the birth and death process of firms showed a much greater incidence of death, especially by acquisition, amongst the smaller firms and an increasing net loss in the number of independent companies in the quoted company population.

Chapter 4 examined in turn the two main forms of growth, acquisition and investment. Evidence on growth by acquisition showed it had been very important, and that, for the period 1966–1971, the average values for it exceeded those for growth by new fixed investment. A cross-sectional examination suggested, however, that there was no necessary trade-off between the two. This conclusion was maintained when the differential ability of firms to finance investment was taken into account, as well as when a possible bias in the estimation technique was removed. An investigation was then carried out into the relationship between acquisition growth and external growth – the two differing to the extent that acquired assets were also assumed to grow. External growth was considerably greater than acquisition growth, but the relative ranking of firms in different size classes was maintained. This chapter also examined the relationship between size, and investment and acquisition growth respectively. It was shown that there was no positive relationship between firm size and the propensity to grow by acquisition. This, it was argued, may have been in part a reflection of the negative relationship between size and growth. Indeed, when acquisition growth was examined as a proportion of total growth, there was some positive relationship between it and firm size. There was a mild negative relationship between firm size and investment growth.

Chapter 5 examined the related issue of the impact of acquisitions on investment, as well as on profitability. But, instead of considering acquisition expenditure *per se*, the impact of specific acquisitions was investigated. This methodology also allowed us to distinguish between the impact of horizontal and non-horizontal acquistions, and single and multiple acquisitions, as well as large and small acquisitions. The overall results showed that, whilst there was some tendency for profitability to decline following acquisition, new investment did not appear to be adversely affected. But, on average, both the decline in profitability and the improvement in investment were small. More importantly, there was a significant minority of cases where investment performance actually worsened and profitability improved. Regarding different types of merger activity, the results suggested that for horizontal mergers there may have been no improvement following acquisition – or perhaps even some decline. However, for non-horizontal mergers there was some improvement. Interestingly, single acquirers did not exhibit any better performance than multiple acquirers, but there was some indication that the relatively large acquisitions, which may have been difficult to assimilate, may have had some initial adverse impact.

The issues of financing, and the simultaneity of decision making regarding investment, acquisition and dividends, were investigated in Chapters 6 and 7. The first of these chapters examined the relationship between firm size and internal and external finance. It was found that on average high growth by external finance was not limited to the largest companies. Next, there was found to be no relationship between profitability and recourse to external finance, reflecting that the financing of acquisition, which during most of this period has been undertaken mainly by share exchange, had weakened the link between the two. It was found that in a cross-section of firms there was some negative relationship between acquisitions financed out of retentions and new investment similarly financed. There was clear evidence that the gearing ratio of the largest firms was considerably greater than that of the smaller firms but there was no difference in the retention ratio across firms in different size classes. There did not appear to be any economic 'discipline' exercised by the capital market on firms raising external finance, in the sense of a favourable effect on their subsequent profitability or growth.

Chapter 7 adopted a shorter time interval for analysis – annual observations – and examined the influence of a number of variables on investment, acquisitions and financing, as well as on dividend disbursals. All these were examined within a simultaneous equation model framework. The complete model was estimated over a number of cross sections, and each of the equations was also estimated separately to examine the influence of simultaneity bias. The results suggested a number of important determinants of these activities but the explanatory power of the equations differed considerably across years. They also indicated a degree of simultaneity between acquisitions, investment and financing. There was, however, no strong evidence of an interrelationship between dividends and investment. Models based on qualitative response, such as the Logit and Tobit models, were also employed to examine the financing and acquisition decisions, separately. These indicated a considerable improvement over the ordinary least squares method in terms of the significance of the variables.

The next two chapters examined how exports and foreign production activities may influence firm growth and performance. Chapter 8 examined the relationship between firm size and export rate, as well as that between firm growth and export growth. It emerged that there was no systematic association between firm size and export rate, but there was a strong relationship between the total growth of sales and export growth. There was also a tendency for the export rate to be negatively related to firm growth. An analysis of the relationship between export rate and export growth, and acquisitions, was then undertaken. There was no evidence of a negative relationship between acquisitions and export performance. In some cases it emerged that above-average export growth (as a proportion of sales growth) was associated with above-average acquisition activity. This relationship was not, however, statistically significant.

Chapter 9 examined firms' overseas operations, and the empirical work focused on two related issues: the differences in the characteristics of the domestic and the international firms, and the impact of overseas operations on profitability and growth. Data from companies' annual reports, supplemented by the results of a special survey, were used to classify firms according to their degree of overseas operations in two years, 1972 and 1976. These data were then combined with the data from the DI Databank to investigate the above issues. There was considerable evidence that reliance on overseas operations had been increasing over time, and an increasing number of firms had ventured abroad. It appeared that, whilst there was certainly a threshold size below which firms did not undertake overseas operations, it was rather lower than generally believed. Nevertheless, there was a strong positive relationship between firm size and degree of overseas activity. However, when only firms with overseas operations were considered, the relationship was surprisingly weak. It was certainly not the case that only the very largest firms had overseas operations. There was also no significant difference in the profitability performance of mainly domestic firms, and that of international firms – although there was a weak tendency for firms with large international operations to show somewhat higher growth.

10.2 Implications for economic theory

This section examines briefly the implications of these results for the following aspects of economic theory: the notion of the 'optimum' firm size; the motivation of management; the theory of investment; the interdependence between firms' activities; the role of stock market discipline; and lastly, the determinants of overseas production.

'Optimum' firm size. One important element in the neoclassical theory of the firm is the notion of the 'optimum' size of firm. The long-run average cost curve of the firm is supposed to be U-shaped. The justification for the rising portion of the cost curve is usually provided in terms of problems of coordination and management which arise with an increase in firm size. Superficially, at least, the above result of a mild negative relationship between size and growth may be seen to provide some support for this. It could be argued that since growth and profitability are positively correlated, the result implies a negative relationship between size and profitability. To the extent that larger firms may have greater monopoly power, this suggests that their productive efficiency may be lower compared to that of the smaller firms. We have unfortunately no indication of the precise magnitude of the larger firms' relative monopoly power. It may even be argued that with the sharp increase in import penetration and competition in firms' overseas markets, it is by no means obvious that all large firms would have significant monopoly power. In such a case the important point to note is that the larger firms are not growing by very much less than the smaller firms – in particular they do not have negative growth. Further, the average values of growth (and profitability) are only one facet of the comparative performance of these firms. The stability of this performance over time is equally important. It could be that larger firms are more risk averse and are more concerned with stability. Nevertheless, clearly the above comparison of the average values offers no support for the notion of an optimal size for a firm.

The motivation of management. The results on the size-growth relationship seem more in keeping with the newer theories of the firm which, rather than suggesting a limit on firm size, postulate a limit on its growth rate in any given time. These

176

theories regard the creation of new capacity as the main mode of expansion. (The exception is the analysis by Penrose.) The results suggest, however, that in the period under consideration the alternative mode – growth by acquisition – was almost equally prevalent. To the extent that the profitability effects of acquisition were on average negative, the results offer some support to the non-profit maximising goals accredited to management in these theories. This support, however, is not very strong and in particular does not provide a clear refutation of the long-run profit maximisation objective.[1] Furthermore, we are unable to distinguish between the goals of growth maximisation and the type of goal postulated in the behavioural theory of the firm. Both would be consistent with the evidence, and only further research can distinguish between them. If it is accepted that in general the goal may not have been profit maximisation, the finding that the small firms were as acquisition intensive as the large ones, suggests that other motivations may be common to most firms, and not just the largest ones characterised by the separation of ownership from control.

Theory of investment. Whilst the study has not been concerned with analysing rigorously the determinants of investment, nevertheless it has some relevance to the theory of investment. The crucial role of uncertainty in affecting investment has been recognised for a long time. Yet the way the firms may attempt to reduce this has been less explored. The uncertainty may relate to the future capacity in the industry, or to the ability of firms to profit from investment. It would, of course, be inappropriate to suggest that all acquisitions reduced uncertainty and thereby stimulated investment. In particular, it is notable that in the case of horizontal mergers, where monopolisation may have been an important consequence, there was on average some decline in post-merger investment. In the case of non-horizontal acquisitions, however, with the monopolisation element likely to be absent, considerations relating to uncertainty may have been more important. The uncertainty of a venture into a new industrial environment could have been reduced by this type of acquisition. It has been increasingly realised that contrary to the traditional view of firms having opportunities for investment just waiting to be exploited, it is more realistic to assume that these opportunities have to be sought, or even created. In this case, following the search theories of merger, it could again be argued that acquisitions may have played a role in providing these opportunities.

The financing of investment, and interdependent activities. This study has been concerned with a very narrow aspect of this, *viz.*, the extent to which the activities of firms are interrelated. The simultaneous relationship between acquisitions and investment suggested that, contrary to some views, these decisions are not taken in isolation from each other, nor from financing decisions. This emerged from both an analysis using total external finance and that using external finance for cash. This suggests that theoretical models which postulate investment decisions separate from financing decisions may not be entirely appropriate. There was, however, no evidence that investment and dividend decisions were interdependent. Whilst investment exerted some negative influence on dividends, the negative effect in the other direction was weak or absent altogether.

177

Stock market discipline and the theory of the firm. Stock market discipline has two aspects. The first is the takeover mechanism. Following Marris, this postulates that there would be a takeover constraint on the management of a firm which tried to pursue growth at the expense of profitability (or market valuation). We have not carried out any specific test of this, but the analysis of the death of firms by take-over over a period of eleven years (1966–1976) tended to give some support to a number of earlier studies which questioned the strength of this mechanism in recent years. There was an almost uniform decline in death due to takeover with an increase in firm size, suggesting at least that size may be a more relevant variable in determining the impact of this mechanism than other aspects of performance.

The second aspect is the discipline exercised by the capital market as an allo-cator of resources. It is a well-established argument that government policy should encourage companies to pay out higher dividends and raise long-term funds in the capital market, rather than pay out lower dividends and rely on retentions as a source of funds. The process of persuading the market to provide funds is supposed to 'discipline' firms and to cause them to invest in an efficient manner. The argu-ment has received fresh support in the face of an almost frantic search for improving the efficiency of industry, both in the UK and in the US. Our study of the relationship between external financing, and future growth and profitability, suggested that there was very little evidence for the existence of this mechanism either. This result may in part have been due to the fact that external finance was raised mainly in the process of acquisition – and acquisitions did not in the majority of cases have a favourable impact on profitability. Yet if the 'discipline' had been there, it can be plausibly argued that many firms would have experienced greater difficulty in raising external funds for acquisitions.

Oligopolistic rivalry and foreign investment. One of the well-recognised weaknesses of the modern managerial theories of the firm is that they neglect issues raised by oligopolistic rivalry between firms. It has often been remarked that since these theories were mainly formulated in a period in the 1960s when there was a secular increase in aggregate demand, they could ignore the issues raised by the interdependence of firms. Firms could pursue their growth strategies in expanding markets without being overly concerned with the response from rivals. However, in the period since the late 1960s, partly because of the noticeable decline in overall economic growth, it is recognised that interdependence has assumed important significance. There are two facets to this. First, firms wanting to expand in the domestic economy may have limited room for manoeuvre. An expansion in existing product lines will entail an increase in market share, which may entail significant outlays. Second, there may be a greater need to establish and maintain shares in foreign markets. The latter is well recognised as an element in the theory of the determinants of foreign operations. If this is a motive, one might expect (as we in fact found) that firms with high overseas involvement would not necessarily show a superior performance compared to firms which are mainly domestic. This is so since it can be argued that if the main driving force for overseas operations had been some 'ownership specific' advantage, such as superior technology or managerial talent, on average one might have seen a significantly superior overall performance. Of course, much more specific and detailed analysis would have to be done before one could accept the 'rivalry factor' as the main explanation. (Other factors may also be important, for example, firms may move outside the domestic economy in search of greater stability in their performance.) Nevertheless, the results do support the view that much greater attention should be paid to the motives of firms resulting from the competitive environment in which they operate.

10.3 Implications for public policy

The implications for public policy can be grouped under three main headings: policy regarding industrial concentration; mergers and competition policy; and industrial policy.

Policy regarding industrial concentration. The conclusion that, amongst a population of continuing firms, large firms have on average had a slightly lower growth rate than small firms in the period since 1960, raises a number of interesting points relating to the process of concentration increase in the UK. In the last few decades, the rates of increase of both industry and aggregate concentration in the UK have been amongst the highest in advanced countries.[2] With regard to aggregate concentration, Prais (1976) estimated that the share of the 100 largest firms in manufacturing net output increased from 22 per cent in 1949 to 41 per cent in 1970. Concentration increases over time can be attributed to one of the following four factors: the birth and death process of firms; the role of merger; the systematic effect of size on growth; and the law of proportionate effect (LPE). The last of these provides an indication of the role of stochastic factors: that is, factors unrelated to firm size, or any other characteristics of firms in any *systematic* way, which lead to an increase in concentration.

For the UK, a number of researchers have emphasised certain factors which are likely to have favoured the growth of large firms (that is, to have led to a positive relationship between firm size and growth). Prais has suggested that this in turn may be responsible for just under one half of the concentration increase over the period 1949–1970, the rest being accounted for by the LPE. There is general consensus that although technological factors – the technical requirement of greater plant size – may have been important, fiscal and financial factors have played a bigger role. For example, Meade (1968) suggested that one major factor favouring the growth of large companies has been the favourable tax treatment of retained earnings. Prais (1976) and Kay and King (1978) have observed that financial institutions such as pension funds and insurance companies hold a high and increasing proportion of shares in industrial and commercial companies. Since these institutions deal mainly in large blocks of shares, they have a preference for investing in large companies, which gives the latter favourable access to finance. Finally, it is worth noting that, as Curry and George (1983) emphasise, the increasing dominance of large firms may also be a response to substantial changes in the industrial environment. These changes have occurred as a result of various legal restraints such as the 1956 Restrictive Trade Practices Act, as well as of a sharp increase in the intensity of foreign competition in many industries.

Indeed merger activity itself, which according to Hannah and Kay (1981) has played a dominant role in increasing concentration, may in part be explained by the attempt of firms to adjust to a changing environment.

There are three related points emerging from this study. First, the size–growth relationship suggests that since 1960 at least the rise in concentration may have been rather more dependent on the LPE and the birth and death process than hitherto assumed. Second, there was little significant evidence to suggest that, so far as the raising of external funds was concerned, the smaller firms relied less heavily on the capital market. Of course, as far as the costs of funds are concerned, larger firms may still have had an advantage. But these two points do tend to suggest that a policy aimed at limiting the rate of concentration increase, or reducing the present levels of it, would have to be more stringent than is often realised. In particular, a policy generally advocated of encouraging faster growth in small firms by making the capital market more competitive may be insufficient. This is related to the third point that whilst acquisitions were not especially important for the largest firms, death by acquisition amongst the medium and smaller firms was much greater. Since changes in concentration depend as crucially on the birth and death process of firms as on the behaviour of surviving firms, the role of acquisitions may indeed have been an important one.

Mergers and competition policy. Following the publication of the Green Paper (1978) on Monopolies and Mergers Policy, there has been a considerable controversy in the UK on the policy which ought to be adopted towards mergers. The Green Paper came to the conclusion that there should be a neutral approach, as distinct from the current presumption in favour of mergers. A number of observers have suggested that mergers policy ought to be tightened up much more, with some suggesting a ban on all mergers, whilst others propose that the presumption should be against mergers.

The main arguments of those in favour of a stronger policy are threefold. First, the empirical evidence indicates that there are few, if any, efficiency gains from merger. Given that merger will leave economic power at best unchanged, the existing evidence on the decline in profitability following mergers suggests no gains, or a decline, in efficiency. It is worth noting, however, that in most studies the decline in profitability is observed for a majority but not by any means an overwhelming majority of mergers. Second, mergers are shown to have little disciplinary effect on other firms – in the sense of the threat of takeover forcing firms to improve their efficiency. Third, mergers have led to an excessive increase in concentration, and concentration has significantly harmful effects on productive efficiency, as well as on consumer welfare. Related to the first argument a number of writers have suggested that mergers have significant negative dynamic effects as well, for example on investment and on exports.

The results of this study regarding the effect on profitability, based on a sample of 354 mergers, are in line with the results of most other studies and may appear to be rather clear cut. Since, in general, profitability declined after merger, even under the assumption of unchanged monopoly power, this may be taken to suggest no efficiency gains, and indeed some deterioration. It is very important to emphasise, however, that the evidence is much more ambiguous than this. First, in a significant minority of cases profitability actually improved after merger. Second, even where there was a decline, the magnitude of the decline was in general small. In any case the changes in profitability have to be seen in relation to other dynamic effects, such as the effect on investment or exports. The strongest guide to monopoly policy would be given if, for example, both profitability and investment performance worsened in the vast majority of cases, and worsened considerably. The evidence does not suggest this to have been the case.

With regard to investment, in general there was no significantly adverse impact. A comprehensive investigation into the relationship between acquisition and investment, using both time series and cross-sectional analysis, revealed no general trade-off between the two activities. But it is worth noting that there was a significant difference between the horizontal and non-horizontal mergers. There appeared in general to be a noticeably greater improvement in the latter than in the former. But here again the evidence is not conclusive. For the full sample, the magnitude of the improvement was small, and in a significant minority of cases investment performance actually worsened after merger.

The implications for merger policy are also complicated by the differential effect on investment and profitability. In a number of cases, the profitability performance worsened and investment improved. Since policy is concerned with the public interest and not just shareholder interest, this outcome is not necessarily bad. One can imagine cases where profitability may have declined as a result of more competitive pricing, but investment may have improved owing, say, to a reduction in uncertainty. From the point of view of public interest this may not be regarded unfavourably. This is particularly so where post-merger profitability may be lower than pre-merger profitability, but it is still high compared to the industrial average.

From a policy perspective it is also important to notice that the analysis of the export performance of firms did not suggest any significant trade-off between it and acquisition activity. Both exports as a proportion of firm sales, and the growth in exports, showed some positive association with acquisition expenditure. Further, export performance subsequent to high acquisition activity did not seem to be affected in any adverse manner.

Lastly, the analysis of the death process of firms over more than a decade showed that there was a marked tendency for death by takeover to decline almost uniformly with firm size. Whilst the analysis was not exhaustive, it did tend to suggest that the takeover mechanism is unlikely to have been a stern disciplinarian. Nevertheless, all the results taken together certainly do not suggest that a drastic measure such as a complete ban on mergers would be appropriate. In fact, in view of the diversity of findings, the existing case-by-case approach may seem to be the best way of safeguarding the public interest.

Industrial policy. The UK, together with most other industrial countries, has pursued some form of active industrial policy since the mid 1960s. There are two aspects of the policy to which results have direct relevance. The first is related to the importance attached to firm size in industrial policy. In the UK in the late 1960s, a great deal of emphasis was placed by the Industrial Reorganisation Corporation (IRC) on the need to have larger concerns in manufacturing industries which would have sufficient resources for product development and investment and which could compete internationally. (A similar policy was pursued in France.) That the role of size continues to be regarded crucial can be judged from the discussion in the Green Paper (1978). There is no denying that the largest firms account for a very high proportion of investment and exports. Obviously, however, a more appropriate yardstick for comparing their performance would be the extent to which, as a proportion of resources at their disposal, they undertake investment and exports, and the rate at which these increase over time. Here the evidence suggests that, for both investment and exports, the larger concerns showed a performance no superior to that of other concerns. This result was particularly surprising for exports taken as a proportion of firms' sales.

It may be inappropriate, however, to conclude that since, in general, large firms do not provide these benefits, and indeed may have a number of harmful effects (for example, on consumer welfare and sovereignty), the policy of encouraging large size had been misplaced, or that existing large concerns ought to be disbanded. This is so for at least two reasons. First, although, as Prais has emphasised, in recent years the technological element has been of limited relevance in the emergence of large concerns, nevertheless in a number of major industries large size is of critical significance. In these cases, owing to indivisibilities in the production processes, and in research and development, the sort of comparison made above is of limited relevance. Second, the evidence here has not considered the interrelationships beween small and large firms. There are likely to be a number of important linkages between these firms. Large firms may, for example, be important customers and suppliers, who, because of their relatively stable behaviour and performance, may have some beneficial effects. Further, there may be a number of important spill-over effects regarding product and process innovation. Obviously, what is true of the performance of small firms where both small and large coexist, may not be true when there are no large firms. These considerations suggest that, whilst encouragement of smaller firms is likely to yield significant dividends, considerable further research has to be undertaken before one could entertain the more drastic policy measures noted above.

The second aspect of industrial policy to which the results have some relevance is the policy towards outward investment. There have been a number of attempts to introduce investment controls in the past, based mainly on their effects on the balance of payments. The more recent concern at the detrimental effects of this investment has been with the increase in manufacturing unemployment; by replacing domestic investment, foreign investment may have had an adverse effect on domestic employment opportunities, and on economic growth. (Similar concern has been voiced in the US.) Other writers have suggested that, despite these developments, the liberal policies pursued in the past should be continued. The main argument has been that firms undertaking foreign investment have certain advantages which allow them to earn higher profits overseas. It is argued that if the domestic environment improves so that these firms can obtain higher returns in the home economy, they would again invest more in that economy.

The evidence in this study tends to cast some doubt on the notion that these firms go overseas because they can earn higher returns there. Others have suggested further that even if there were a possibility that firms could earn higher returns abroad, one should not wait for the economic environment in the UK to improve so that these firms can increase investment here. For, following Myrdal's analysis of cumulative causation, it has been argued that the very fact that the companies continue to move overseas in ever-increasing numbers, and to increase their operations overseas at the expense of the UK, makes the UK environment deteriorate even further. If this argument is accepted, then there would be a case for reconsidering the relative costs and benefits of UK firms' foreign investment activities, and the policy to be adopted towards this.

Appendices

Appendix A1 The quantitative data

Reference number T^a	Variable	Years available[b]
1	Issued capital: ordinary	48–
2	Issued capital: preference	48–
3	Capital and revenue reserves	48–
4	Provisions	48–63
5	Future tax reserves	48–
7	Interest of minority share-holders in subsidiaries	48–63
8	Long-term liabilities	48–
14	Fixed assets: tangible, net of depreciation	48–
17	Stocks and work in progress	48–
22	Total net assets	48–
23	Issue of shares: ordinary	49–
24	Issue of shares: preference	49–
26	Issue of long-term loans	49–
30	Increase in current tax liabilities	49–
31	Increase in future tax reserves	49–
32	Balance of profit: depreciation provision	49–
33	Balance of profit: provision for amortisation	49–63
34	Balance of profit: other provisions	49–63
35	Balance of profit: retained in reserves	49–
36	Other receipts	49–
37	Expenditure, less receipts, on fixed assets: tangible	49–
38	Expenditure, less receipts, on fixed assets: intangible	49–
39	Expenditure, less receipts, on fixed assets: trade investments and subsidiaries	49–
40	Increase in value of stocks and work in progress	49–
41	Increase in credit given: trade and other debtors	49–
42	Expenditure *ex* provisions	49–63
43	Sundry expenditure	69–49
44	Consolidated adjustment	49

Reference number T^a	Variable	Years available[b]
45	Conversion adjustment	49–63
46	Residual adjustment	49–63
47	Change in securities	49–
48	Change in tax reserve certificates	49–
49	Change in cash	49–
55	Dividend, ordinary	49–
59	Prior year adjustments: general	49–
60	Total capital and reserves	49–
66	Total profit	
	Expenditure on acquiring subsidiaries; consideration for subsidiaries acquired ($T68$ to $T70$):	49–
	68 ordinary shares	64–
	69 preference etc. shares	64–
	70 long-term loans	64–
127	Sales	68–
128	Exports	68–

[a] The reference number T refers to the variable number in the DI Databank. The formulae given in Appendix A2 use this reference number.

[b] Data were available until 1976 unless stated otherwise.

Appendix A2 Detailed definitions of variables used in the study

A number prefixed by T represents a variable from Appendix A1

m = last year of period
p = first year of period
$o = p$ minus 1
n = number of years in the period
j = year indicator

Chapter 2

Table 2.1
Opening size = $T22_o$

Table 2.2
Total growth (net assets) =

$$\sqrt[n]{\dfrac{\sum_{j}^{m}(T23 + T24 + T31 + T35 + T36 - T43)_j + (T7 + T8)_m + (T1 + T2 + T3 + T5)_o}{T22_o}} - 1$$

Tables 2.3 to 2.10
The general definition is

$$\frac{1}{n}\sum_{j=p}^{m} Q_j$$

where

$Q_j = (T39)_j \div T22_{j-1}$	: acquisition growth
$Q_j = (T37 - T32 - T33)_j \div T22_{j-1}$	: net new investment in fixed assets
$Q_j = (T66 - T32 - T33 - T34 - T59)_j \div T22_{j-1}$	: return on fixed assets
$Q_j = (T31 + T35 + T36 - T43)_j \div T22_{j-1}$	: growth by retentions
$Q_j = [(T23 + T24 + T7 + T8)_j - (T7 + T8)_{j-1}] \div T22_{j-1}$	: growth by external finance
$Q_j = (T60 - T32 - T33 - T34 + T59)_j \div T127_j$	: profit margin
$Q_j = T128_j \div T127_j$	: export rate
$Q_j = T128_j \div T128_{j-1}$	: export growth

Chapter 3
Tables 3.1–3.3

The general definition given for Tables 2.3 to 2.10 applies to all tables unless otherwise specified.

Physical assets = $(T14 + T17)_j$
Equity assets = $(T60 - T4 - T2)_j$

Chapter 4

External growth = acquisition proportion × total growth

See text for the detailed formulations.

Chapter 5

Table 5.2

Gross investment = $T37_j$

Chapter 6

Table 6.1

Growth by equity (total) $Q_j = T23_j \div T22_{j-1}$

Growth by gearing issues (total) $Q_j = (T24 + T26)_j \div T22_{j-1}$

Acquisitions financed by retentions = total expenditure on subsidiaries — issue of shares and loans in exchange — minority interests

$$Q_j = \{T39_j - (T68 + T69 + T70)_j \\ - [(T7 + T8)_j - (T7 + T8)_{j-1}] - T26_j\} \\ \div T22_{j-1}$$

Investment financed by retentions = net investment in fixed assets + net current assets — external finance raised for cash

Net current assets $Q_j = (T38 + T40 + T41 + T42 + T43 + T44 \\ + T45 + T46 + T47 + T48 + T49 - T27 \\ - T28 - T29 - T30)_j \div T22_{j-1}$

Table 6.6

External funds raised for cash $Q_j = (T23 + T24 + T26 - T68 - T69 - T70)_j \\ \div T22_{j-1}$

Equity issues for cash $Q_j = (T23 - T68)_j \div T22_{j-1}$

Equity issues in exchange $Q_j = (T68)_j \div T22_{j-1}$

Gearing issues for cash $Q_j = (T24 + T26 - T69 - T70)_j \div T22_{j-1}$

Gearing issues in exchange $Q_j = (T69 + T70)_j \div T22_{j-1}$

Table 6.8

Gearing ratio (stock measure) $Q_j = \dfrac{(T2 + T8)_j}{(T60 + T8 - T4)_j}$

Retention ratio $Q_j = \dfrac{(T35)_j}{(T35 + T55)_j}$

Chapter 7

Table 7.2

Depreciation provision = $T32_j$

External finance = $[(T23 + T24 + T7 + T8)_j - (T7 + T8)_{j-1}]$

Dividend, ordinary = $T55_j$

Table 7.4
External finance for cash $Q_j = (T23 + T24 + T26 - T68 - T69 - T70)_j$

Chapter 8

Table 8.1
$$\text{Export rate} = \frac{T128_j}{T127_j}$$

Table 8.5
$$\text{Export growth/sales growth } Q_j = \frac{T128_j \div T128_{j-1}}{T127_j \div T127_{j-1}}$$

Chapter 9

Table 9.2
$$M = \frac{\text{'overseas sales'}}{T127_j}$$

where 'overseas sales' includes all goods produced and sold abroad by a foreign subsidiary, but excludes finished goods imported from the parent company for resale. M was obtained for 1972 and 1976.

Table 9.6
Sales originating in the domestic economy = $T127_j -$ 'overseas sales'.

Appendix A3 Supplementary results

Table A3.1 *OLS estimates of gross investment equation (using external finance for cash)*

Year	P_{t-1}	Dep	S^*	A	D	EF	$\bar{R}^2$	F
1970	0.36 (6.31)	1.21 (12.72)	0.41 (0.33)	0.07 (3.63)	−0.13 (−1.07)	0.08 (1.31)	0.31	45.7
1971	0.29 (4.71)	1.50 (16.20)	0.006 (0.58)	−0.009 (−0.79)	0.13 (0.98)	0.06 (0.93)	0.35	53.9
1972	0.62 (9.10)	1.27 (10.11)	−0.03 (−1.94)	0.11 (5.54)	−0.55 (−3.86)	0.15 (3.30)	0.31	45.7
1973	0.38 (5.93)	1.22 (9.57)	0.01 (1.79)	0.07 (3.21)	−0.24 (−0.95)	0.30 (3.79)	0.27	35.9
1974	0.27 (6.50)	1.07 (12.09)	−0.01 (−1.41)	0.15 (7.19)	−0.06 (−0.46)	0.19 (1.91)	0.36	60.3
1975	0.05 (1.14)	1.80 (23.04)	0.008 (1.22)	0.11 (1.36)	0.11 (0.58)	0.007 (0.12)	0.46	40.4
1976	0.04 (1.85)	1.91 (13.50)	0.01 (1.41)	0.09 (2.30)	0.15 (0.34)	0.001 (1.13)	0.35	45.6

Note: t-ratios are given in brackets.

Table A3.2 *OLS estimates of acquisition equation (using external finance for cash)*

Year	P_{var}	G	L	I	D	EF	$\bar{R}^2$	F
1970	0.001 (0.96)	0.13 (2.08)	−0.14 (−5.87)	0.30 (4.02)	1.29 (5.66)	−0.05 (−0.38)	0.16	18.9
1971	0.001 (0.11)	0.43 (2.44)	−0.55 (−8.80)	−0.05 (−0.26)	2.62 (3.97)	−1.49 (−3.12)	0.17	21.7
1972	0.004 (0.98)	0.01 (0.13)	−0.19 (−6.21)	0.26 (3.71)	0.97 (3.86)	0.30 (3.21)	0.15	18.4
1973	0.002 (0.91)	0.11 (1.34)	0.14 (6.62)	0.34 (5.31)	1.96 (4.72)	0.45 (3.12)	0.15	17.9
1974	0.01 (1.30)	0.003 (0.06)	0.004 (0.23)	0.50 (10.40)	0.06 (0.21)	−0.25 (−1.42)	0.29	42.6
1975	−0.001 (−1.07)	−0.003 (−0.27)	−0.02 (−2.72)	0.20 (1.16)	0.04 (0.43)	0.08 (2.71)	0.03	2.9
1976	0.03 (1.06)	0.03 (1.42)	−0.05 (−3.81)	0.34 (1.56)	0.31 (2.50)	0.50 (3.12)	0.09	4.5

Note: t-ratios are given in brackets.

Table A3.3 *OLS estimates of dividend equation (using external finance for cash)*

Year	D_{t-1}	P_t	I	A	EF	$\bar{R}^2$	F
1970	0.70 (31.80)	0.14 (14.31)	−0.02 (−2.71)	0.02 (5.06)	−0.01 (−0.81)	0.82	549.2
1971	0.73 (34.41)	0.13 (13.93)	−0.02 (−2.74)	0.003 (2.91)	−0.02 (−1.98)	0.82	571.1
1972	0.62 (19.32)	0.16 (12.02)	−0.05 (−6.01)	0.005 (1.15)	0.01 (0.82)	0.65	223.3
1973	0.43 (25.61)	0.03 (3.14)	−0.01 (−2.40)	0.12 (4.82)	−0.002 (−0.22)	0.62	183.2
1974	0.66 (34.50)	0.05 (10.01)	−0.02 (−3.68)	0.01 (3.83)	0.01 (1.15)	0.74	363.4
1975	0.79 (37.61)	0.04 (9.00)	0.001 (0.39)	0.03 (3.34)	0.03 (5.60)	0.76	399.1
1976	0.61 (36.34)	0.05 (11.19)	−0.03 (−1.17)	0.01 (1.31)	0.02 (1.27)	0.61	186.3

Note: t-ratios are given in brackets.

Table A3.4 *OLS estimates of external finance equation (using external finance for cash)*

Year	G	P	I	A	D	$\bar{R}^2$	F
1970	0.04 (2.20)	−0.05 (1.19)	0.07 (2.72)	−0.08 (−0.70)	0.13 (1.36)	0.07	7.5
1971	0.08 (4.61)	−0.002 (−0.52)	0.02 (1.17)	−0.01 (−3.44)	0.03 (0.53)	0.06	6.3
1972	0.02 (0.62)	−0.003 (−0.19)	0.013 (4.20)	0.04 (2.03)	0.19 (1.75)	0.08	9.3
1973	0.02 (0.78)	−0.05 (−8.71)	0.05 (3.21)	0.02 (2.36)	−0.16 (−1.41)	0.23	31.1
1974	−0.01 (−0.93)	−0.03 (−1.51)	0.03 (1.99)	−0.02 (−1.82)	0.10 (1.25)	0.01	1.5
1975	0.04 (2.52)	−0.002 (−0.20)	0.04 (1.95)	0.12 (2.33)	0.59 (5.05)	0.06	7.1
1976	0.02 (1.41)	−0.01 (−1.71)	0.03 (1.81)	0.05 (1.71)	0.14 (1.41)	0.08	9.4

Note: t-ratios are given in brackets.

Table A3.5 *3SLS estimates of gross investment equation (using external finance for cash)*

Year	P_{t-1}	Dep	S^*	A	D	EF
1970	0.33	1.02	−0.001	0.25	−0.22	−1.17
	(5.91)	(10.61)	(−0.54)	(9.90)	(−1.61)	(−5.05)
1971	0.41	1.19	−0.14	0.26	0.08	1.73
	(4.03)	(9.32)	(−3.52)	(4.72)	(0.43)	(5.31)
1972	0.31	0.86	−0.01	−0.13	−0.08	1.50
	(3.51)	(1.94)	(−1.53)	(−2.21)	(−0.47)	(4.61)
1973	0.36	1.00	0.01	0.16	−0.51	0.24
	(6.32)	(8.71)	(1.98)	(5.51)	(−1.58)	(1.46)
1974	0.21	1.23	−0.002	0.08	0.35	−0.17
	(4.84)	(9.74)	(−0.25)	(1.34)	(1.66)	(−0.61)
1975	−0.002	1.86	0.005	0.23	0.56	−0.12
	(−0.04)	(22.41)	(0.71)	(1.86)	(2.15)	(−0.96)
1976	0.03	1.03	0.01	0.34	−0.31	0.35
	(1.67)	(1.71)	(2.12)	(2.35)	(−0.52)	(1.82)

Note: t-ratios are given in brackets.

Table A3.6 *3SLS estimates of acquisition equation (using external finance for cash)*

Year	P_{var}	G	L	I	D	EF
1970	−0.001	−0.13	−0.01	0.96	0.58	5.13
	(−1.41)	(−1.31)	(−0.52)	(4.14)	(1.32)	(8.51)
1971	−0.002	0.73	−0.09	2.12	−0.27	−17.74
	(−0.40)	(2.95)	(−1.99)	(4.05)	(−0.22)	(−16.23)
1972	−0.004	0.16	−0.005	−1.71	−0.18	6.19
	(−0.53)	(1.29)	(−0.45)	(−5.75)	(−0.21)	(27.21)
1973	0.03	0.10	0.001	0.38	2.43	5.01
	(7.54)	(0.76)	(0.06)	(2.21)	(3.01)	(12.00)
1974	0.002	0.02	−0.003	−0.96	−1.23	4.79
	(4.86)	(0.33)	(−0.31)	(−7.94)	(−2.89)	(15.26)
1975	−0.001	−0.03	−0.02	−0.13	−0.30	0.35
	(−0.83)	(−2.13)	(−0.45)	(−0.41)	(−2.91)	(21.51)
1976	0.02	0.06	0.03	0.45	0.25	0.31
	(3.61)	(3.12)	(0.64)	(2.42)	(1.44)	(4.13)

Note: t-ratios are given in brackets.

Table A3.7 *3SLS estimates of dividend equation (using external finance for cash)*

Year	D_{t-1}	P_t	I	A	EF
1970	0.71	0.13	−0.04	0.04	−0.10
	(30.20)	(11.82)	(−2.94)	(7.54)	(−2.51)
1971	0.72	0.13	0.02	−0.01	−0.42
	(28.53)	(11.30)	(1.33)	(−7.81)	(−11.50)
1972	0.59	0.16	−0.14	−0.05	0.45
	(14.61)	(7.44)	(−4.92)	(−5.23)	(6.61)
1973	0.43	0.03	−0.04	0.20	0.01
	(24.20)	(2.96)	(−3.93)	(5.91)	(0.26)
1974	0.66	0.05	−0.02	0.02	0.01
	(34.11)	(7.69)	(−1.67)	(2.03)	(0.41)
1975	0.79	0.04	0.01	0.05	0.05
	(31.51)	(8.12)	(1.48)	(0.81)	(3.46)
1976	0.74	0.12	−0.06	0.03	0.35
	(31.63)	(4.11)	(−1.34)	(7.24)	(2.95)

Note: t-ratios are given in brackets.

Table A3.8 *3SLS estimates of external finance equation (for cash)*

Year	G	P	I	A	D
1970	0.02	−0.03	−0.12	0.16	−0.03
	(1.40)	(−1.13)	(−3.17)	(18.31)	(−0.42)
1971	0.03	−0.001	0.12	−0.05	−0.04
	(2.31)	(−0.51)	(4.03)	(−21.23)	(−0.60)
1972	−0.03	0.001	0.28	0.16	0.03
	(−1.30)	(0.57)	(5.96)	(30.71)	(0.22)
1973	0.0002	−0.01	−0.01	0.16	−0.37
	(0.01)	(−9.62)	(−0.22)	(17.63)	(−2.52)
1974	−0.003	−0.003	−0.17	0.17	0.26
	(−0.21)	(−0.17)	(−4.85)	(8.74)	(2.58)
1975	0.08	0.002	0.03	3.31	0.99
	(1.96)	(0.85)	(0.44)	(17.31)	(2.94)
1976	0.04	−0.02	0.04	−0.03	0.11
	(2.10)	(−2.69)	(3.18)	(−1.62)	(1.65)

Note: t-ratios are given in brackets.

Table A3.9 *Tobit and Logit analysis: external finance equation*

	Tobit analysis					Logit analysis				
	G	P	I	A	D	G	P	I	A	D
1970	0.10 (2.20)	-0.02 (-0.10)	0.01 (0.26)	0.16 (0.69)	-0.09 (-6.30)	1.53 (1.98)	-0.54 (-0.30)	3.65 (3.65)	-0.44 (-0.84)	4.03 (0.99)
1971	0.20 (4.56)	-0.19 (-1.71)	-0.01 (-0.68)	0.39 (1.69)	-0.09 (-6.33)	2.48 (3.11)	-2.23 (-1.19)	2.78 (2.95)	-0.34 (-1.05)	4.70 (1.19)
1972	0.12 (1.37)	-0.01 (-0.04)	0.09 (2.34)	0.54 (1.64)	-0.20 (-7.16)	1.20 (1.60)	-1.90 (-1.30)	1.44 (1.70)	0.58 (1.54)	6.50 (2.07)
1973	0.12 (2.32)	-0.08 (-0.94)	0.06 (2.92)	0.19 (0.65)	-0.09 (-4.91)	2.61 (3.31)	-0.48 (-0.37)	0.92 (1.40)	0.88 (1.93)	4.47 (1.04)
1974	0.11 (1.43)	-0.09 (-1.98)	0.10 (2.45)	0.09 (1.06)	-0.06 (-1.45)	0.90 (1.14)	-2.51 (-2.20)	1.14 (1.20)	-0.26 (-0.53)	12.91 (2.62)
1975	0.13 (2.45)	-0.31 (-0.85)	0.06 (1.74)	0.21 (1.11)	-0.03 (-1.45)	1.55 (2.14)	1.52 (1.61)	1.76 (2.08)	1.28 (0.69)	14.24 (2.88)
1976	0.18 (1.92)	-0.07 (-1.63)	0.03 (2.13)	0.17 (1.84)	-0.32 (-1.31)	1.34 (2.19)	-1.43 (-1.41)	2.63 (1.87)	-1.59 (-0.67)	2.33 (4.70)

Note: t-ratios are given in brackets.

Table A3.10 *Investment and acquisitions: summary of empirical results*

Chapter	Method of analysis	Sample/time period	Result
4	OLS regression	Average values 1960-1965, 1966-1971 and 1972-1977	Significantly positive relationship between the variables
5	Difference in the pre-merger and post-merger values	354 mergers over the period 1967-1974	On average a positive effect of mergers on investment
6	Correlation	Average values 1966-1971 and 1972-1976. Acquisitions and investment financed by retentions	Significantly negative relationship
7	OLS and 3SLS regression	Annual cross-sections, 1970-1976	On average a positive relationship

Table A3.11 *Firm size and export performance*

	Export rate mean	S.D.	Pearson correlation coefficient(a)	No. of firms
1968-71				
Manufacturing	12.49	12.75	-0.03	740
Non-manufacturing	3.36	9.78	-0.11*	281
All industries	9.95	12.68	-0.08*	1021
1972-76				
Manufacturing	13.28	12.03	-0.02	587
Non-manufacturing	3.19	6.87	-0.15	237
All industries	10.66	12.66	-0.01	824

Notes: (a) The correlation refers to the correlation between opening size (measured by sales), and subsequent export rate.
* indicates significantly different from 0 at 5 per cent level.
Export rate is the annual average of firm's exports/sales ratio, averaged across the sample.

Notes

Notes to Chapter 1

1   See for example Layard and Walters (1978). The constraint on selling outputs and buying inputs is of course absent in the perfect competition framework.

2   Marshall's (1890) 'trees-in-the-wood' analogy points in the same direction, though in this case an eventual limitation on growth is postulated.

3   In fact, as is well recognised, in the multi-period context with uncertainty, profit maximisation is not even well-defined.

4   This is the approach adopted in explaining the investment behaviour of the firm. See, for example, Junankar (1973) and Nickell (1978).

5   See Downie (1958). (Penrose's paper on the growth of firms had been published in 1955, but the theory was more fully set forth in the 1959 publication.) It is worth noting that Robinson's 1953 study on the structure of competitive industry foreshadowed many of the important aspects of the newer theories of growth. Earlier still, of course, Marshall and Marx had quite a lot to say about the growth of firms (see, for example, Gray, 1980, Chs 11 and 13).

6   If the acquired assets are managed more efficiently, or if acquisition leads to economies of scale in production, there would be some benefits from acquisitions too (see Chapter 4).

7   For the impact of organisational structure on different forms of growth, see Alberts and Segall (1966). Also see Hart *et al.* (1973) for the argument that managerial problems may worsen following acquisition.

8   See Lynch (1971). Of course, high acquisition activity is not a necessary condition for a high P/E ratio. The stock market may form highly favourable expectations of the future profits of a firm which had not engaged in any previous take-over activity. Such a firm would then be in a good position to expand externally if it so wished.

9   I am grateful to Dr G. Meeks and the Esmée Fairbairn Trust for allowing me access to the Databank. For details of the Databank see Meeks (1977).

Notes to Chapter 2

1   The accounting rate of return as used here is only an approximation to the rate of return used in economic theory (which is based on discounting). It is likely to be a less misleading indicator of the true *ex post* return, the longer the period over which it is measured and the larger the number of observations (see Whittington, 1980, p. 338). For a theoretical discussion on the relationship between the accountant's rate of return and the internal rate of return, see Kay (1976).

2   Only since the end of the period under study have firms been required to publish inflation-adjusted figures.

3   This reflects the financial developments in this period, whereby companies switched to short-term debt – which is not included in this measure (see

Flemming *et al.*, 1976). The link between stock (inventory) appreciation and the reliance on retentions is important for this development. Other things being equal (real rate of return and rate of growth), more rapid increase in prices of stocks leads to a higher conventional profitability measure and to higher growth by retentions.

4　Analysis was also undertaken for firms in individual industries. The results have had to be excluded for reasons of space. They are available from the author.

5　Export growth is defined as the arithmetic average of the proportionate change in exports (that is, exports in year $t + 1$/exports in year t, averaged over the five-year period, 1972–1976).

Notes to Chapter 3

1　The most recent ones are Eatwell (1971), Samuels and Chesher (1972), Singh and Whittington (1975), Smyth *et al.* (1975), Meeks and Whittington (1975b), Meeks and Whittington (1976), and Chesher (1979).

2　It is worth noting that the operation of (i) does not imply that the industrial concentration cannot be increasing. Even if the growth of firms is independent of firm size, if there is a dispersion in growth rates, concentration would increase over time (see Kalecki, 1945 and Prais, 1976). Further, it depends on the particular way in which firms enter or leave the population (see, for example, Ijiri and Simon, 1977).

3　Cf. Singh and Whittington, 1975. This equation can be derived from equation 3.1 by multiplying the error term by an arbitrary constant α_1 and taking logarithms, assuming $\beta = 1$.

4　This argument is based on that used by Whittington (1980) in his examination of the relationship between firm size and profitability.

5　A similar argument applies to the persistency of profitability across firms (see Whittington, 1971).

6　Growth was measured in terms of net assets, physical assets and equity assets. The results obtained were similar using these three measures; only those using net assets are reported here.

7　In econometric terms, the issue is that of identification, where a number of structures generate the same reduced form. It is most familiar in estimation of supply and demand models (see, for example, Wallis, 1973, pp. 47–54. For the identification of the supply-growth curve see Singh and Whittington, 1968, footnote 2 Chapter 7, and their reply to Fisher, 1969).

8　Two other models were tested: (a) $g_{i,t} = \alpha + \beta \log p_{i,t} + \epsilon_{i,t}$; this tests the hypothesis that growth-rate increases by a constant amount as profitability increases by a given proportion; (b) $\log g_{i,t} = \alpha + \beta \log p_{i,t} + \epsilon_{i,t}$; this tests the hypothesis that a given proportionate change in profitability leads to a given proportionate change in the growth rate. Testing of these two models required the exclusion of firms with negative values of growth and profitability, involving about 6 per cent of firms. In most cases, equation 3.4 provided the best fit, and results for that only are reported in the text.

Notes to Chapter 4

1　Skewness is defined as follows: $E((X_i - X)/s)/n$ where X_i denotes the variable, X the mean, s standard deviation and n the number of observations. The measure is zero when the distribution is bell-shaped. A positive value indicates that the observations are clustered more to the left of the mean with most of the extreme values to the right.

2　See the discussion above, and Mueller (1969) for the expectations regarding this. See also Ijiri and Simon (1977) pp. 192–195, where the authors discuss the application of the law of proportionate effect to growth by acquisition.

3   Equation 4.1 was also estimated using an additional term of the form $(\log S)^2$. The results were similar to those reported.

4   To the extent that non-acquiring firms are likely to be pursuing different goals or facing different constraints or to have different opportunities compared to the rest of the population, the above may be justified. The issue of whether or not to include firms undertaking no acquisition is similar to that when considering, for example, the relationship between firm size and export rate, or between firm size and the propensity to undertake direct investment abroad. These questions are elaborated in Chapters 8 and 9.

5   The difference in variance of firms in different groups was significant in several cases: e.g., comparing firms with assets greater than £16m and the rest, the null hypothesis of no difference in variance was rejected for all three time periods, for both variables. The computed F-values for acquisition were 3.60, 2.65 and 2.35 for the three periods respectively. For this reason the Welch-Aspin test, which allows for differences in variance, was used.

6   The classic study is by Berle and Means (1932) for the US. For the UK see Sargent Florence (1961). The prevailing view was challenged by Nyman and Silberston (1978) for the UK. However, Cosh (1978) suggests that there is still a strong positive relationship between firm size and degree of management control.

7   See Meeks (1977, p. 26) for a discussion of the identification problem relating to the profitability-acquisition relationship. In a cross section it is reasonable to assume that it is the profitability to acquisition relationship which is identified. In Chapter 5 we adopt a different methodology to study the acquisition to profitability relationship.

8   Kalecki distinguished between 'embodied' and 'disembodied' technical change, the former taking place only when a new vintage of capital stock came into service, but the latter occurring in all vintages.

9   Dasgupta and Stiglitz (1980) argue that oligopolistic rivalry between large firms may encourage technical innovation, which may lead to investment. Acquisition of one firm by another need not necessarily result in a decrease in such rivalry (Hughes, 1978). Acquisition by a medium-sized firm of another of similar size may lead to an increase in such rivalry.

10   To emphasise, in a cross section we cannot reasonably ensure that *all*, or even most, of the factors which account for differences in the ability and willingness to grow are taken into account. Hence the cross-sectional framework has to be supplemented.

11   It is worth noting that the effect of profitability in Table 4.4 is very similar to that in Table 4.5, indicating that multicollinearity is not a serious problem in this case.

12   Another explanation could be that the population is different. However, there is no reason why the exclusion of firms which ceased to exist after the first period should have resulted in any systematic difference in the degree of association between the two forms of growth.

13   In some cases the magnitude of the bias would be small. Suppose a firm makes one major acquisition at the beginning of the period, and as a result of the above effect there is a spurious positive relationship. For subsequent years, however, there would be no such effect so that, if there were an underlying negative relationship, the average positive effect would tend to be reduced or reversed. Further, the effect is likely to be stronger the earlier in the companies' financial year the acquisition is made. If it is made towards the end of the year, there would be little or no effect even in that year.

14   Analytically, this is the simplest assumption to adopt. If one assumes that

across firms acquisitions are distributed evenly throughout the year, the procedure becomes complex, without increasing explanatory power. This procedure was first employed by Aaronovitch and Sawyer (1975b).

Notes to Chapter 5

1 In an oligopolistic environment, firms may be expected to recognise their mutual interdependence, so that even without a collusive agreement, uncertainty regarding the output and price of an industry's product will be small. See Chamberlain (1933) pp. 46–47. However, as is well established, when cost functions and/or market shares vary between firms within such an industry, conflicts arise which unless resolved through collusive agreements, would give rise to just such an uncertainty. If these agreements are not possible, because of legal or economic factors, acquisition would provide one possible means for its reduction.

2 This statistical approach inevitably excludes a great deal of qualitative information which can be obtained only by interviews or questionnaires. But it does allow us to cover most of the mergers (satisfying certain conditions discussed presently) which occurred in the UK in this period. (See Reddaway (1972) for its appropriateness.) The method should be regarded as complementary to the case studies approach (see, for example, Cowling *et al.*, 1980). We focused on the most recent period for which data were available. Mergers are studied over an eight-year period to capture the effect of variations in the underlying economic conditions.

3 Since the analysis is extensive – covering from one to eight post-merger years, and covering merger activity in eight years – any remaining bias due to inflation is likely to become apparent in a comparison of the performance for the post-merger years – especially since inflation was by no means constant in the post-merger period of 1968–1976. An analysis was also undertaken of the change in the firms' investment to asset ratio, normalised by the corresponding industry's investment to asset ratio. The results of this exercise were similar to those reported in the text.

4 The results, using this sample, should perhaps be seen as descriptions of the specific population of larger British quoted firms which merged in the late sixties to mid seventies. Nevertheless it is reasonable to presume that the results may also apply to subsequent mergers among similar firms.

  Industry investment totals were obtained from the Databank. Companies reclassified out of an industry were included in their old industry – to obtain as constant a population as possible. In order to take into account investment of companies removed from the DI population because they failed to meet the size criterion, industry investment figures were augmented by a factor reflecting the proportionate investment of these companies in their industry's investment in the year before their exclusion. Note also that these investment figures include firms' total investment: i.e. domestic as well as foreign direct investment. Companies with a high proportion of their activities overseas are, however, excluded from the DI Databank, and from our sample.

5 One main condition which a merger had to satisfy to be included in our sample was that both the acquirer and the victim had at least five years' data available prior to the merger year, so that a reference figure of investment could be computed, and data were available for at least two post-merger years for comparison.

6 For some analysis using net investment, see Kumar (1981).

7 A comparison of the total actual expenditure on investment (unadjusted by industry investment) revealed a considerable increase in the post-merger years compared to the pre-merger reference period. This increase was statistically significant for several of these years. In view of the substantial

inflation during the period, this cannot by itself be taken as evidence that merger does not hamper investment.

8   This test is constructed as follows: for each pair of merging firms, denote the difference (post-merger–pre-merger performance) being positive as a 'success'. Let n be the number of pairs of firms. Then if the null hypothesis (that there is no change in firms' performance) is true, the number of successes is a binomial variable, say x, corresponding to independent trials for an experiment for which the probability of success $p = 1/2$.

The binomial distribution can be approximated by a normal distribution, the approximation being accurate even for small n. The test of the null hypothesis $p = p_0$ ($p_0 = 1/2$ in this case) is then based on the statistic

$$t = \frac{|x - np_0|}{\sqrt{np_0(1 - p_0)}}.$$

Since the binomial distribution is discrete, to set up a correspondence between the set of binomial ordinates and the areas under the normal curve, the standard correction was applied. (That is decrease the absolute value of $x - np_0$ by $1/2$.)

For individual industries a similar test was applied.

9   A company making an acquisition within its industry and also outside it in the *same* year or the year following it has been excluded to avoid problems in interpreting the results. This reduced the sample of mergers from 354 to 273.

10   The definition of non-horizontal merger is problematical. The procedure adopted here has been a rather crude one – of using DI's allocation of firms to industries (at the 2 digit SIC level) and to call non-horizontal the acquisition of a firm in one industry by an acquirer in another.

11   Lev and Mandelker (1972) used a similar matched-pair technique to study the growth rate of merging firms in the United States. They found in fact that the average annual growth rate (measured by sales and operating income, and assets) of their sample of merging firms was less than that of the control group of firms in the post-merger period. However, the differences were generally insignificant. More importantly, there is likely to have been some bias in their results due to imperfect matching and aggregation across industries and different time periods. (These problems are acknowledged see p. 89 and p. 102.) For example, the growth of merging firms in one two-digit industry was compared with the growth of non-merging firms in a different industry.

12   Note that by using this methodology there is no ambiguity regarding the direction of causality; it is the effect of acquisition on profitability which is identified (cf. Chapter 4).

13   Unlike Meeks, we have averaged the difference between pre-merger and post-merger profitability across years. There are three other differences: (i) We considered mergers in a later time period, *viz.* 1967–1974; (ii) we examined the impact of acquisitions even after the first merger – thus all multiple acquirers were included. (Note that Meeks does not exclude multiple acquirers altogether; only after a first merger is the record of multiple acquirers terminated.) (iii) The pre-merger reference period in our study is five years, whereas in Meeks's study it is three years.

Notes to Chapter 6

1   Stiglitz (1974) has shown that once the possibility of bankruptcy is admitted, even within the neoclassical framework, the source of financing becomes relevant.

2   If, in addition, it is assumed that firms aim to maximise growth of sales,

the neoclassical approach is further weakened. This is because it is likely that there would be projects which firms would be willing to finance out of retentions, even though they have a negative net present value (see Wood, 1975, p. 8).

3   The rate at which variability in returns declines with an increase in firm size can be calculated using the law of large numbers. Suppose that the large firm is equivalent to a group of *independent* small units all of equal size and having similar characteristics. The variability of return would be expected to fall inversely with the square-root of the number of units in the group. Usually there will be some association in the returns of units belonging to a single firm, so that the variability of a group does not decline as rapidly as given by the above rule (Prais 1976, pp. 92–99).

4   For a survey of the main trends in the sources and uses of funds (from 1952 to 1976) for UK industrial companies (based on National Income Blue Book) see Thomas, 1978, pp. 304–335. For an earlier investigation which impinges on some of the issues raised here, see Meeks and Whittington, 1976.

5   The argument would be that in capital intensive industries barriers to entry would be high. These would allow firms to set product prices which would generate a volume of internal funds sufficient to finance a high proportion of investment (cf. Eichner 1976, pp. 71–74). On barriers to entry, see Bain, 1956 and Demsetz, 1982. Also, see George, 1971, pp. 107–113, for a succinct discussion on the relationship between pricing policies and growth.

6   Only the results for the aggregate of industries are presented. In keeping with the analysis of growth by gearing issues, the gearing ratio is defined as the ratio of long-term liabilities to firms' net worth. The retention ratio is defined as the balance of profits retained as a proportion of retained profits and ordinary dividends. The variables are defined precisely in Appendix A1.

7   There is a considerable literature on the level and determinants of corporate gearing in the UK. See, for example, Coates and Wooley (1974) and Fox (1975) on this and also on the wide choice of measures available for it. The average for the period 1966–1971 is slightly lower than that obtained by Coates and Wooley for the same period (see their Table 1). However, this study's sample of companies is different from theirs, as is the method of averaging across firms (as elsewhere in this study Table 6.8 is based on an unweighted average, whereas they use a weighted one). Note that the average for this period hides the fact that from 1968–1970 there was a small increase in the gearing ratio.

8   The conclusion here is similar in its implications to that for the discipline exerted by the stock market *via* the takeover mechanism (see Singh, 1971, 1975).

9   An additional factor would be that profitability as used is an imperfect proxy for the economist's measure of the rate of return for assessing the efficiency of investment (cf. Meeks and Whittington, 1976, Section 5).

Notes to Chapter 7

1   This formulation assumes that the decisions relating to production and marketing are taken before the above set of decisions (i.e. in equations 7.1–7.5). The view is that investment affects sales and firm income only with a lag, so that current investment affects mainly future output, and that current output (and hence current income) is not affected by current investment. Whilst this may not be strictly valid, it is sufficiently accurate to serve as a good simplification. In any case in the literature profits and sales have been traditionally considered to be predetermined in cross-sectional analysis of investment.

Note that the investment and financing decisions are postulated as being co-determined. For a discussion of an alternative view which regards firms' decision making as sequential see Bain *et al.* (1975). In this approach, investment decisions are taken first, and the issue of financing is tackled subsequently.

2   To test these hypotheses about the determinants of acquisition, one procedure has been to compare the pre-merger characteristics of merging firms with data for a control group of firms, composed of either a matched pair of non-merging firms, or with industry averages (see Mueller (ed.) 1980, pp. 49–52, and Chapter 5 above). There have been few attempts to model acquisition expenditure in general (not just the determinants for particular mergers). Further, there has been a paucity of investigation into the interaction of acquisitions with other decision variables.

3   The pioneering work in this area is by Lintner (1956). See also Fama (1974) and Bhattacharya (1979). The importance of prospective dividend policy in conveying information (and influencing share valuation) in addition to prospective earnings, has not been sufficiently emphasised. Sargent Florence (1961) noted, for example, that Keynes pointed out the precariousness of the market valuation of the yield of an investment when based on the convention that the existing state of affairs will continue into the future. Keynes noted several factors which accentuate this precariousness. These however did not include the uncertainties of dividend policies (see Keynes, 1936, pp. 153–158).

4   The corporate tax system by changing the relative tax costs of dividends and retentions is also likely to influence the distribution of earnings (see King, 1977, ch. 4). This influence is, however, likely to be more important in a time series investigation, than in the cross-sectional exercise attempted here. It may, however, affect comparisons between years. See also Whittington (1974).

5   In effect, by deflating acquisition by K_{t-1}, we simply convert the variable into growth by acquisition. In view of the possibility of a spurious positive relationship between investment and acquisition growth across firms (see Chapter 4), investment expenditures were deflated by K_{t-1} *plus* half the expenditure on acquisitions in the given year, the latter variable being used as a proxy for assets of the acquired firms. Although this is a rather crude procedure, it would nevertheless reduce the bias. Note also that by deflating by K_{t-1}, the size of firm in the acquisition ceases to be an independent variable.

6   The normalisation assumes that the variance of the error term in each equation is proportional to the square of opening net assets. Whilst this may not correspond exactly to the behaviour of the error term, it is not an unrealistic assumption (see Kumar, 1984c).

7   The 3SLS method was preferred to the maximum likelihood procedure (ML) because it is simpler. ML involves the assumption of the normality of residuals and requires the formulation and evaluation of the likelihood functions for the random variables of all the equations. It may be argued that a partial information method, such as the 2SLS, would be more appropriate since it is less sensitive to specification errors. The model was estimated for some years using this method but, since the variance–covariance matrix of the error term was non-diagonal, 3SLS was more appropriate. This is to be expected since the variables are measured annually, and over this period decisions concerning any one variable would affect, and be affected by, other variables, leading to covariance between the equations.

8   The average acquisition expenditures (as a proportion of opening net assets) were as follows for the years 1970–1976 respectively: 4.2%, 6.4%, 6.9%, 5.7%, 2.4%, 0.8% and 1.5%.

9   The interest rate variable was dropped after the initial estimation since it was always insignificant, and in a number of cases had the wrong sign.

10   As regards the goodness-of-fit of the investment equation as a whole, unlike OLS, there is no formal criterion for estimating the overall contribution of right-hand side variables in explaining the variability in the left-hand side variable, in *any particular* equation. For the system of equations as a whole there is the system $\bar{R}^2$ – measuring the joint variability in endogenous variables explained by the system. This was very high – between 0.67 and 0.79 – for the model as a whole for all seven cross sections.

11   It should be emphasised that there is only a limited collinearity between external finance for new funds and total external finance, the simple correlation between the two variables being around 0.27.

Notes to Chapter 8

1   See, for example, Newbould, 1970, p. 35 and Cowling *et al.*, 1980, pp. 148–158. A similar emphasis emerges in the acquisitions investigated by the Monopolies and Mergers Commission.

2   The restriction to manufacturing firms is justified since their export involvement is considerably greater than that of the non-manufacturing, non-financial firms included in the DI population. (For some analysis of non-manufacturing firms see Chapter 9.) 1968 was the first year for which data on exports were widely available, and the 9-year period (1968–1976) was chosen to provide continuous records for the firms. Note that the sample includes all firms, and not just those undertaking exports.

3   The same argument applies to the case of a diversified firm some of whose products may not be exportable.

4   This exercise was also repeated for three industrial sectors separately (Chemicals, Non-electrical engineering, and Textiles), with results similar to those noted above.

5   We also examined the performance of those firms which undertook extensive acquisition expenditure in the period 1965–1976, and a negligible amount in the ensuing period, and compared it with firms which had negligible acquisition expenditure for the whole of the period 1965–1976. The results of this investigation, in general, were in keeping with those reported in the text.

Notes to Chapter 9

1   It is worth noting that the earlier studies by Hymer and Rowthorn (1970) and Rowthorn (1971) examine the relationship between the size and growth of multinationals from different countries, but not the influence of multinationality as such on growth.

2   More technology-intensive industries are those which spent at least 2 per cent of their net output on research and development in 1974; less technology-intensive industries spent a lower percentage (cf. Dunning, 1979).

3   Note that since we have obtained the information only where it was given, the sample cannot be regarded as truly representative. The average reliance on overseas sales is considerably greater than in Table 9.2, but there is no reason to suppose that there is any systematic bias, and an examination of the industry and size distribution of firms confirmed this.

4   Note that this argument is appropriate for the sample of firms examined in this chapter. Obviously, if the activities of the firms are resource-based, such as in mineral mining and petroleum extraction, the source of these resources would be the determining factor (cf. the propensity of US firms to establish a high proportion of their operations in Canada, as noted in the study by Horst, 1972).

5   Even in the developing economies, it might be argued that the presence of other European firms, and so the oligopolistic rivalry overseas, would have required UK firms to have an edge over these European firms. However, the challenge from other European firms was small during the 1950s and 1960s (see Franko, 1976).

6   As noted in Chapter 8, similar results have been obtained for export rates for other countries such as Belgium, France and Japan. However it seems that no adjustment for overseas activities has been attempted for companies in these countries.

7   For a description of this technique see Van de Geer (1971) or Kendall and Stuart (1976).

8   The statistical significance of the function is examined by using an F-test based on the Mahalanobis generalised distance statistic.

9   The results given are those which simultaneously used all the variables considered in the univariate analysis. Several other combinations of variables were tested, but since the function with all the variables yielded the best fit (in terms of the F-statistic) only this is reported.

10   As noted earlier, Siddharthan and Lall (1982) find in fact that overseas activity exercises a uniformly negative effect on growth in their sample of US firms. But they say: 'we are inclined to ascribe our findings to the nature of the period studied' (p. 10). Note that they find, in their sample of large firms, that there was little relationship between size and overseas activity, the simple correlation being -0.142.

Notes to Chapter 10

1   It is worth repeating that in a dynamic context – if the firm undertakes acquisition, say to reduce uncertainty – the objective of management could still be long-run profit maximisation.

2   There is considerable evidence that since the mid 1970s concentration in the UK has been rising very slowly, or even declining (see Kumar, 1984b, Hughes and Kumar, 1984). However, this phenomenon seems to have occurred in other advanced countries, too, and it is not clear that the UK's relative position has changed.

Bibliography

Aaronovitch, S. and Sawyer, M. (1975a). *Big Business*, London, Macmillan.

Aaronovitch, S. and Sawyer, M. (1975b). Mergers, growth and concentration, *Oxford Economic Papers*, March.

Alberts, W. and Segall, J. (1966). *The Corporate Merger*, Chicago, Chicago University Press.

Alchian, A. (1957). Uncertainty, evolution and economic theory, *Journal of Political Economy*, Vol. 58.

Amemiya, T. (1981). Qualitative response models: a survey, *Journal of Economic Literature*, December.

Anderson, G. (1981). 'The external financing decisions of the industrial and commercial sector', Discussion Paper 8112, University of Southampton.

Auquier, A. (1980). Size of firms, export behaviour, and the structure of French industry, *Journal of Industrial Economics*, December.

Auquier, A. and Caves, R. (1979). Monopolistic export industries, trade and optimal competition policy, *Economic Journal*, September.

Bain, A., Day, C. and Wearing, A. (1975). *Company Financing in the United Kingdom*, Oxford, Martin Robertson.

Bain, J. S. (1956). *Barriers to New Competition: Their Character and Consequences in Manufacturing Industries*, Cambridge, Mass., Harvard University Press.

Baran, P. and Sweezy, P. (1966). *Monopoly Capital*, New York, Penguin.

Barker, T. (1977). International trade and economic growth: an alternative to the neo-classical approach, *Cambridge Journal of Economics*, June.

Bhattacharya, S. (1979). Imperfect information, dividend policy and the bird in the hand policy, *Bell Journal of Economics*, Spring.

Baumol, W. J. (1965). *The Stock Market and Economic Efficiency*, New York, Fordham University Press.

Baumol, W. J., Reim, P., Malkliel, B. and Quandt, R. (1970). Earnings retention, new capital and the growth of the firm, *Review of Economics and Statistics*, November.

Begg, I., Hughes, A., Kumar, M. S. and Singh, A. (1981). 'The performance of domestic and foreign subsidiaries in the UK', paper presented at the 'International Conference on the impact of large firms on the European Economy', Brussels.

Berle, A. and Means, G. (1932). *The Modern Corporation and Private Property*, New York, Macmillan.

Blume, M. E. (1980). The financial markets, in Caves and Krause (eds.) (1980).

Buckley, P. J. and Dunning, J. H. (1978). The influence of firm size, industry, nationality and degree of multinationality on the growth and profitability of the world's largest firms, 1962–1972, *Weltwirtschaftliches Archives*, Vol. 2.

Buckley, P. J. and Dunning, J. H. (1981). 'The growth and profitability of the world's largest firms', paper presented at the 'International conference on the impact of large firms on the European Economy', Brussels.

Buckley, P. and Pearce, R. (1977). 'Overseas Production and Exporting by the World's largest enterprises', University of Reading Discussion Paper no. 37.

Business Monitor (1980). *M3 Company finance*, London, HMSO.

Business Monitor (various issues). *M7 Acquisitions and mergers of industrial companies*, London, HMSO.

Cable, J. (1977). A search theory of diversifying merger, *Recherches Economiques de Louvain*, September.

Caves, R. E. (1974). The causes of direct investment: foreign firms' shares in Canadian and UK manufacturing industries, *Review of Economics and Statistics*, Vol. 56, no. 3, August.

Caves, R. E. (1979). Industrial structure and international trade, *Journal of Industrial Economics*, December.

Caves, R. E. (1982). *Multinational Enterprise and Economic Analysis*, Cambridge, CUP.

Caves, R. E. and Krause, L. B. (eds.) (1980). *Britain's Economic Performance*, Washington, D.C., The Brookings Institution.

Chamberlain, J. (1933). *The Theory of Monopolistic Competition*, Cambridge, Mass., Harvard University Press.

Channon, D. F. (1973). *The Strategy and Structure of British Enterprise*, London, Macmillan.

Chesher, A. (1979). Testing the law of proportionate effect, *Journal of Industrial Economics*, June.

Chung, K. and Weston, J. (1981). 'Investment opportunities, synergies and conglomerate mergers', paper presented at the Conference on Large Firms in Brussels, June.

Coates, J. and Wooley, P. (1974). Corporate gearing in the EEC, *Journal of Accounting and Business Finance*, May.

Cooper, R., Hartley, K. and Harvey, C. (1970). *Export Performance and Pressure of Demand*, London, Allen and Unwin.

Cosh, A. (1978). 'Executive incomes and shareholdings, business motivation, and company performance – a study of UK companies, 1969–73', unpublished Ph.D dissertation, University of Cambridge.

Cosh, A. and Hughes, A. (1982). 'Ownership characteristics and company performance', Faculty of Economics, Cambridge.

Cosh, A., Hughes, A., Kumar, M. S. and Singh, A. (1983). 'Financial institutions and industrial performance', mimeo, DAE, Cambridge.

Cosh, A., Hughes, A. and Singh, A. (1980). The causes and effects of takeovers in the United Kingdom, in Mueller (ed.) (1980).

Coutts, K., Godley, W. and Nordhaus, W. (1978). *Industrial Pricing in the United Kingdom*, Cambridge, CUP.

Cowling, K. (ed.) (1972). *Market Structure and Corporate Behaviour*, London, Gray Mills.

Cowling, K., Stoneman, P., Cubbin, J., Cable, S., Hall, G., Domberger, S., and Dutton, S. (1980). *Mergers and Economic Performance*, CUP.

Chow, G. (1983). *Economitrics*, New York, McGraw-Hill.

CSO (1979). *Economic Trends*, London, HMSO.

Curry, B. and George, K. D. (1983). Industrial concentration: a survey, *Journal of Industrial Economics*, March.

Cyert, R. and March, J. (1963). *A Behavioural Theory of the Firm*, New York, Prentice-Hall.

Daniel, W. (1976). Wage determination in industry, *Political and Economic Planning*, June.

Dasgupta, P. and Stiglitz, J. (1980). Industrial structure and the nature of innovative activity, *Economic Journal*, June.

Davenport, M. (1971). Leverage and the cost of capital, *Economica*, May.

Demsetz, H. (1982). Barriers to entry, *American Economic Review*, March.

Department of Industry (1979). *Survey of Institutions' Holdings*, reported in Wilson (1980).

Department of Industry (1984). *Overseas Transactions*, London, HMSO.

Department of Industry (various issues). *Trade and Industry*, London, HMSO.

Devine, P. J., Lee, N., Jones, R. M. and Tyson, W. J. (1979). *An Introduction to Industrial Economics*, 3rd edn, London, George Allen and Unwin.

Dhrymes, P. and Kurz, M. (1967). Investment, dividend and external finance behaviour of firms, in R. Ferber (ed.) (1967).

Downie, J. (1958). *The Competitive Process*, London, Duckworth.

Dunning, J. H. (1978). 'Recent developments in research on multinational enterprises: an economist's viewpoint', University of Reading Discussion Paper no. 42.

Dunning, J. H. (1979). The UK's international direct investment position in the mid-1970s, *Lloyds Bank Review*, April.

Dunning, J. H. (1981). *International Production and the Multinational Enterprise*, London, George Allen and Unwin.

Dunning, J. H. and Pearce, R. D. (1981). *The World's Largest Industrial Enterprises*, London, Gower.

Dyas, G. P. and Thanheiser, H. T. (1976). *The Emerging European Enterprise*, London, Macmillan.

Eatwell, J. (1971). Growth, profitability and size: the empirical evidence. Appendix A, in Marris and Wood (1971).

Eichner, A. (1976). *The Megacorp and Oligopoly*, New York, CUP.

Eisner, R. (1978). *Factors in Business Investment*, Boston, Mass., Ballinger.

Fama, E. (1974). The empirical relationship between the dividend and investment decisions of firms, *American Economic Review*, June.

Feldstein, M. and Green, J. (1983). Why do companies pay dividends?, *American Economic Review*, March.

Ferber, R. (ed.) (1967). *Determinants of Investment Behaviour*, New York, Columbia University Press.

Firth, M. (1979). The profitability of takeovers and mergers, *Economic Journal*, June.

Fisher, G. R. (1969). Review of Singh and Whittington (1968), *Economic Journal*, June.

Flemming, J. S., Price, L. D. and Byers, S. A. (1976). The cost of capital, finance and investments, *Bank of England Quarterly Bulletin*, June.

Fox, R. (1975). Leverage in UK companies 1967–1973, *Business Ratios*, May.

Franko, L. (1976). *The European Multinationals*, London, Harper and Row.

Friedman, M. (1953). *Essays in Positive Economics*, Chicago, University of Chicago Press.

Galbraith, J. K. (1972). *The New Industrial State*, New York, Penguin.

George, K. D. (1971). *Industrial Organisation*, London, Allen and Unwin.

George, K. D. (1972a). The changing structure of competitive industry, *Economic Journal* (supp.), March.

George, K. D. (1972b). The large firm in modern society, *Journal of Industrial Economics*, April.

George, K. D. and Joll, C. (eds) (1975). *Competition Policy in the UK and EEC*, Cambridge, CUP.

George, K. D. and Joll, C. (1981). *Industrial Organisation*, London, Allen and Unwin.

George, K. D. and Ward, T. S. (1975). *The Structure of Industry in the EEC: an International Comparison*, Cambridge, CUP.

Glejser, H. (1969). A new test for heteroscedasticity, *Journal of American Statistical Association*, March.

Glejser, H., Jacquemin, A. and Petit, J. (1980). Exports in an imperfect competition framework, *Quarterly Journal of Economics*, May.

206

Gort, M. (1969). An economic disturbance theory of mergers, *Quarterly Journal of Economics*, November.

Goudie, A. and Meeks, G. (1982). Diversification by merger, *Economica*, November.

Grant, R. (1977). The determinants of the inter-industry pattern of diversification by UK manufacturing enterprises, *Bulletin of Economic Research*, November.

Gray, A. (1980). *The Development of Economic Doctrine: An Introductory Survey* (2nd edition), London, Longman.

Green Paper (1978). See Monopolies and Mergers Commission.

Hague, D. C., Oakeshott, W. C. F. and Strain, A. A. (1974). *Devaluation and Pricing Decisions*, London, Allen and Unwin.

Hannah, L. and Kay, J. (1977). *Concentration in Modern Industry*, London, Macmillan.

Hannah, L. and Kay, J. (1981). The contribution of mergers to concentration growth: a reply to Professor Hart, *Journal of Industrial Economics*, March.

Hart, P. (1962). The size and growth of firms, *Economica*, February.

Hart, P. and Clarke, R. (1980). *Concentration in British Industry 1935–1975*, Cambridge, CUP.

Hart, P. E., Utton, M. and Walshe, G. (1973). *Mergers and Concentration in British Industry*, Cambridge, CUP.

Hey, J. D. (1979). *Uncertainty in Microeconomics*, Oxford, Martin Robertson.

Hindley, B. (1973). Take-overs: 'victims and victors', in Institute of Economic Affairs, Readings 10, *Mergers, Take-overs and the Structure of Industry*, London, IEA.

Hirsch, S. (1976). An international trade and investment theory of the firm, *Oxford Economic Papers*, July.

Holland, S. (1982). *Industrial Planning*, London, Allen and Unwin.

Holmes, P. H. (1978). *Industrial Pricing Behaviour and Devaluation*, London, Macmillan.

Hood, N. and Young, S. (1979). *The Economics of Multinational Enterprise*, London, Longman.

Horst, T. (1972). Firm and industry determinants of the decision to invest abroad, *Review of Economics and Statistics*, August.

Hughes, A. (1976). Company concentration, size of plant and merger activity, in M. Panić (ed.), *The UK and West German Manufacturing Industry, 1954–72*, London, HMSO.

Hughes, A. (1978). Competition policy and economic performance in the UK, in *Competition Policy*, London, NEDO.

Hughes, A., Mueller, D. and Singh, A. (1980). Competition policy in the 1980s: the implications of the international merger wave, in Mueller, D. C. (ed.) (1980).

Hughes, A. and Kumar, M. S. (1983). 'Concentration in the British Economy', a study prepared for the Office of Fair Trading, UK.

Hughes, A. and Kumar, M. S. (1984). Recent trends in aggregate concentration in the UK economy, *Cambridge Journal of Economics*, September.

Hymer, S. (1970). *The International Operations of National Firms*, Cambridge, Mass., Harvard University Press.

Hymer, S. and Rowthorn, R. (1970). MNCs and international oligopoly: the non-American challenge, in Kindleberger, C. D. (ed.), *The International Corporation*, MIT Press.

Ijiri, Y. and Simon, H. (1977). *Skew Distributions and the Sizes of Business Units*, Amsterdam, North-Holland.

Junankar, P. (1973). *Investment: Theories and Evidence*, London, Allen and Unwin.

Kaldor, N. (1957). A model of economic growth, *Economic Journal*, December.

Kaldor, N. (1972). The irrelevance of equilibrium economics, *Economic Journal*, December.

Kaldor, N. (1981). 'Industry: the public sector', speech in the House of Lords, 4 February.

Kalecki, M. (1945). On the Gibrat Distribution, *Econometrica*, April.

Kalecki, M. (1971). *Selected Essays on the Dynamics of the Capitalist Economy*, Cambridge, CUP.

Kamien, M. I. and Schwartz, N. L. (1972). Market structure, rivals' response and the firm's rate of product improvement, *Journal of Industrial Economics*, April.

Kay, J. (1976). Accountants, too, could be happy in a golden age: the accountants rate of profit and the internal rate of return, *Oxford Economic Papers*, November.

Kay, J. A. and King, M. (1978). *The British Tax System*, Oxford, OUP.

Kendall, M. and Stuart, A. (1976). *The Advanced theory of statistics*, Volume 3, (3rd edition), High Wycombe, Bucks., Charles Griffin and Co. Ltd.

Keynes, J. M. (1936). *The General Theory of Employment, Interest and Money*. London, Macmillan, 5th edition (1966).

Kindleberger, C. P. (1969). *American Business Abroad: Six Lectures on Direct Investment*, New Haven, Conn., Yale University Press.

King, M. (1977). *Public Policy and the Corporation*, Cambridge, CUP.

Knickerbocker, F. (1973). *Oligopolistic Reaction and the Multinational Enterprise*, Cambridge, Mass., Harvard University Press.

Kuehn, D. A. (1975). *Takeovers and the Theory of the Firm*, London, Macmillan.

Kumar, M. S. (1980). 'The Profitability of Mergers in the UK', mimeo, DAE, Cambridge.

Kumar, M. S. (1981). Do mergers reduce corporate investment?, *Cambridge Journal of Economics*, June.

Kumar, M. S. (1982). 'Growth, Acquisition, Investment and Foreign Markets', Ph.D. dissertation, University of Cambridge.

Kumar, M. S. (1983). 'Equity holdings by financial institutions: an international comparison', mimeo, DAE, Cambridge.

Kumar, M. S. (1984a). Comparative analysis of UK domestic and international firms, *Journal of Economic Studies*, December.

Kumar, M. S. (1984b). International trade and industrial concentration, *Oxford Economic Papers*, (forthcoming).

Kumar, M. S. (1984c). Size, growth and acquisition activity, *Journal of Industrial Economics*, (forthcoming).

Layard, R. G. and Walters, A. A. (1978). *Micro Economic Theory*, New York, McGraw-Hill.

Lee, T. A. (1974). Accounting for and disclosure of business combinations, *Journal of Business Finance and Accounting*, Spring.

Leibenstein, H. (1966). Allocative Efficiency vs. X-efficiency, *American Economic Review*, June.

Lev, B. and Mandelker, G. (1972). The micro-economic consequences of corporate mergers, *Journal of Business*, January.

Levine, P. and Aaronovitch, S. (1981). The financial characteristics of firms and theories of merger activity, *Journal of Industrial Economics*, December.

Lintner, J. (1956). Distribution of incomes of corporations among dividends, retained earnings, and taxes, *American Economic Review*, May.

Loasby, B. J. (1971). Hypothesis and paradigm in the theory of the firm, *Economic Journal*, December.

Lynch, H. H. (1971). *Financial Performance of Conglomerates*, Boston, Harvard University Press.

McClelland, W. (1972). The IRC 1966/71: an experimental period, *Three Banks Review*, June.

McFetridge, D. C. (1978). The efficiency implications of earnings retentions, *Review of Economics and Statistics*, May.

Maddala, G. S. (1977). *Econometrics*, New York, McGraw-Hill.

Marris, R. (1964). *The Economic Theory of Managerial Capitalism*, London, Macmillan.

Marris, R. (1967). Profitability and growth in the individual firm, *Business Ratios*, Spring.

Marris, R. (1979). *The Theory and Future of the Corporate Economy and Society*, Amsterdam, North-Holland.

Marris, R. and Wood, A. (eds) (1971). *The Corporate Economy*, London, Macmillan.

Marshall, A. (1980). *Economics of Industry* (3rd edn), London, Macmillan (1964).

Meade, J. E. (1968). Is the new industrial state inevitable. *Economic Journal*, June.

Meeks, G. (1974). Profit illusion, *Bulletin of Oxford University Institute of Economics and Statistics*, November.

Meeks, G. (1977). *Disappointing Marriage: A Study of Gains from Merger*, Cambridge, CUP.

Meeks, G. and Whittington, G. (1975a). Directors' Pay, Growth and Profitability, *Journal of Industrial Economics*, September.

Meeks, G. and Whittington, G. (1975b). Giant companies in the United Kingdom 1948–69, *Economic Journal*, December.

Meeks, G. and Whittington, G. (1976). The Financing of Quoted Companies in the United Kingdom, Background Paper no. 1, *Royal Commission on the Distribution of Income and Wealth*, London, HMSO.

Merret, A. and Sykes, A. (1965). *The Finance and Analysis of Capital Projects*, London, Longman.

Meyer, J. and Kuh, E. (1957). *The Investment Decision*, Cambridge, Mass., Harvard University Press.

Millward, N. and McQueeney, J. (1981). *Company Take-overs, Management Organization and Industrial Relations*, Department of Employment Paper no. 16, London, HMSO.

Modigliani, F. and Miller, M. H. (1958). The cost of capital, corporation finance and the theory of investment, *American Economic Review*, June.

Monopolies Commission (1970). *A Survey of Mergers 1958–1968*, London, HMSO.

Monopolies and Mergers Commission (1978). *Review of Monopolies and Mergers Policy: A Consultative Document*, London, HMSO.

Mueller, D. C. (1967). The firm decision process: an econometric investigation, *Quarterly Journal of Economics*, February.

Mueller, D. C. (1969). A theory of conglomerate mergers, *Quarterly Journal of Economics*, August.

Mueller, D. C. (1972). A life cycle theory of the firm, *Journal of Industrial Economics*, July.

Mueller, D. C. (1977). The effects of conglomerate mergers: a survey of empirical evidence, *Journal of Banking and Finance*, December.

Mueller, D. C. (ed.) (1980). *The Determinants and Effects of Mergers*, Cambridge, Mass., Oelgeschlager, Gunn and Hain.

Newbould, G. (1970). *Management and Merger Activity*, Liverpool, Gateshead Ltd.

Newbould, A. and Luffman, A. (1978). *Successful Business Policies*, London, Gower Press.

Nickell, S. (1978). *The Investment Decision of Firms*, Welwyn Garden City, CUP/ Nisbet.

Nyman, S. and Silberston, A. (1978). The ownership and control of industry, *Oxford Economic Papers*, March.

O'Brien, D. P. (1978). Mergers: time to turn the tide, *Lloyds Bank Review*.

Panić, M. (1982). International direct investment in conditions of structural disequilibrium, in Black, J. and Dunning, J. H. (eds.), *International Capital Movements*, London, Macmillan.

Panić, M. and Joyce, P. (1980). UK manufacturing industry: international integration and trade performance, *Bank of England Quarterly Bulletin*, March.

Parker, J. (1978). *The Economics of Innovation*, (2nd edition) London, Longman.

Penrose, E. T. (1959). *The Theory of the Growth of the Firm*, Oxford, Blackwell.
Pepper, G., Thomas, R. and Wood, G. (1978). Evidence to Wilson Committee, *Evidence on Financing, Vol. 7.*
Pigou, A. C. (1924). *The Economics of Welfare*, London, Macmillan.
Prais, S. J. (1976). *The Evolution of Giant Firms in Britain.* Cambridge, CUP.
Rapp, W. (1976). Firm size and Japan's export structure, in H. Patrick (ed.), *Japanese Industrialization and its Social Consequences*, Berkeley, University of California Press.
Reddaway, W. B. (1968). *Effects of UK Direct Investment Overseas. Final Report*, Cambridge, CUP.
Reddaway, W. B. (1972). An analysis of take-overs, *Lloyds Bank Review*, April.
Reid, S. (1968). *Mergers, Managers and the Economy*, New York, McGraw-Hill.
Richardson, G. (1961). *Information and Investment*, Oxford, OUP.
Robinson, E. A. G. (1953). *The Structure of Competitive Industry*, Cambridge, CUP.
Rowthorn, R. (1971). *International Big Business 1957–1967*, Cambridge, CUP.
Salter, W. E. G. (1966). *Productivity and Technical Change*, Cambridge, CUP.
Samuels, J. M. (1965). Size and growth of firms, *Review of Economic Studies*, April.
Samuels, J. M. and Chesher, A. D. (1972). Growth, survival and size of companies 1960–69, in Cowling (ed.) (1972).
Sargent Florence, P. (1961). *Ownership, Control and Success of Large Companies*, London, Sweet and Maxwell.
Saunders, C. (1978). 'Engineering in Britain, West Germany and France: some statistical comparisons', Sussex European Papers No. 3.
Scherer, F. M. (1980). *Industrial Market Structure and Economic Performance*, 2nd Edition, Chicago, Rand McNally.
Shorey, J. (1975). The size of the work unit and strike incidence, *Journal of Industrial Economics*, March.
Siddharthan, N. and Lall, S. (1982). The Recent Growth of the largest US Multi-nationals, *Oxford Bulletin of Economics and Statistics*, February.
Simon, H. (1955). On a class of skew distribution functions, *Biometrika*, December.
Simon, H. (1963). Problems of methodology: discussion, *American Economic Review: Papers and Proceedings*, Vol. 53, no. 2, May.
Singh, A. (1971). *Take-overs, Their Relevance to the Stock Market and the Theory of the Firm*, London, CUP.
Singh, A. (1975). Take-overs, economic natural selection and the theory of the firm, *Economic Journal*, September.
Singh, A. and Whittington, G. (1968). *Growth, Profitability and Valuation*, Cambridge, CUP.
Singh, A. and Whittington, G. (1975). The size and growth of firms, *Review of Economic Studies*, January.
Smith, C. T. B. *et al.* (1978). *Strikes in Britain*, Department of Employment Manpower Paper no. 13, London, HMSO.
Smyth, D., Boyes, W. and Peseau, D. (1975). *Size, Growth, Profits and Executive Compensation in Large Corporations*, London, Macmillan.
Solomon, R. and Ingham, K. (1977). Discriminating between MNC subsidiaries and indigenous companies, *Oxford Bulletin of Economics and Statistics*, May.
Solow, R. (1971). Some implications of alternative criteria for the firm, in Marris and Wood (1971).
Steiner, P. O. (1975). *Mergers: Motives, Effects, Control*, Ann Arbor, Michigan University Press.
Stiglitz, J. (1974). On the irrelevance of corporate financial policy, *American Economic Review*, December.
Stopford, J. M., Dunning, J. H., and Kofferberich, T. (1981). *The World Directory*

of Multinationals, London, Macmillan.

Thomas, W. A. (1978). *The finance of British Industry*, London, Methuen.

Utton, M. (1972). Mergers and growth of large firms, *Oxford Bulletin of Economics and Statistics*, May.

Utton, M. A. (1971). The effects of mergers on concentration in UK manufacturing industry 1954–65, *Journal of Industrial Economics*, November.

Utton, M. A. (1979). *Diversification and Competition*, CUP.

Utton, M. A. (1982). *The Political Economy of Big Business*, Oxford, Martin Robertson.

Van de Geer, J. P. (1971). *Introduction to Multivariate Analysis for the Social Sciences*, San Francisco, W. H. Freeman.

Vaupel, J. W. (1971). Characteristics and motivation of the US corporations which manufacture abroad, quoted in Dunning, J. H. (1973). The determinants of international production, *Oxford Economic Papers*, November.

Vernon, R. (1971). *Sovereignty at Bay: The Multinational Spread of US Enterprises*, New York, Basic Books.

Vernon, R. (1977). *Storm over the Multinationals: The Real Issues*, London, Macmillan.

Wallis, K. (1973). *Topics in Applied Econometrics*, London, Gray-Mills.

Weston, J. F. (1957). *The role of mergers in the growth of large firms*, Berkeley, University of California Press.

Whittington, G. W. (1971). *The Prediction of Profitability*, Cambridge, CUP.

Whittington, G. (1972). The profitability of retained earnings, *Review of Economics and Statistics*, Vol. LIV, no. 2, May.

Whittington, G. (1974). *Company Taxation and Dividends*, London, Institute for Fiscal Studies, Lecture Series Number 1.

Whittington, G. (1980). The profitability and size of United Kingdom companies 1960–74, *Journal of Industrial Economics*, December.

Williamson, O. E. (1964). *Economics of Discretionary Behaviour: Managerial Objectives in a Theory of the Firm*, Englewood Cliffs, N.J., Prentice Hall.

Williamson, O. E. (1975). *Markets and Hierarchies: Analysis and Anti-trust Implications*, New York, Free Press.

Wilson, H. (1980). *Report of the Committee to Review the Functioning of Financial Institutions*, London, HMSO.

Winters, A. (1981). *An econometric model of the export sector*, Cambridge, CUP.

Wood, A. (1975). *A Theory of Profits*, Cambridge, CUP.